Opening
Acts

In loving memory of Dr. Wallace Bacon,
Professor Emeritus of Interpretation/Performance Studies,
Northwestern University

Opening Acts

Performance in/as Communication and Cultural Studies

Judith Hamera, *Editor*

California State University, Los Angeles

SAGE Publications
Thousand Oaks ▪ London ▪ New Delhi

For information:

 Sage Publications, Inc.
2455 Teller Road
Thousand Oaks, California 91320
E-mail: order@sagepub.com

SAGE Publications Ltd.
1 Oliver's Yard
55 City Road
London EC1Y 1SP
United Kingdom

Sage Publications India Pvt. Ltd.
B-42, Panchsheel Enclave
Post Box 4109
New Delhi 110 017 India

Printed in the United States of America

Library of Congress Cataloging-in-Publication Data

Opening acts : performance in/as communication and cultural studies /
Judith Hamera, editor.
    p. cm.
Includes bibliographical references and index.
ISBN 1-4129-0557-5 (cloth)—ISBN 1-4129-0558-3 (pbk.)
    1. Communication—Social aspects. 2. Culture. 3. Dialectic. I. Hamera,
Judith.
HM1013.O64 2006
302.2'01—dc22   2005002567

This book is printed on acid-free paper.

05   06   07   08   09   10   9   8   7   6   5   4   3   2   1

Senior Acquisitions Editor:	Todd R. Armstrong
Editorial Assistant:	Deya Saoud
Production Editor:	Kristen Gibson
Copy Editor:	Elisabeth Magnus
Typesetter:	C&M Digitals (P) Ltd.
Cover Designer:	Janet Foulger

Contents

Acknowledgments

This volume was a labor of love, inspired by the rich and incisive scholarship of its contributors; I am grateful to all of them.

Special thanks to Todd Armstrong, Senior Acquisitions Editor, Deya Saoud, Editorial Assistant, and Elisabeth Magnus, Copy Editor, at SAGE Publications. I appreciate their complete professionalism, diligence, care, and deep good humor throughout this process more than I can say.

I owe Carl Selkin, Dean of the College of Arts and Letters at California State University, Los Angeles, a great debt of gratitude for his unceasing and unstinting support, and for a vision of the humanities encompassing the best that performance, in all its forms, has to offer. Thanks, too, to Josh Fleming for his assistance with manuscript preparation.

Sincere thanks and much love to Alfred Bendixen for good food, good humor, good company, and good advice. As E. B. White wrote, "It's not often that someone comes along who is a true friend and a good writer." Alfred is both.

Dwight Conquergood, beloved teacher, scholar, mentor, and dear friend, passed away as this book was going into production. His influence on performance studies, and particularly on the intersections of performance, communication, and cultural studies, was enormous and profound. As you will see from the Introduction, *Opening Acts* would not have been possible without his rigor, clarity, bravery, and precision in charting the multiple and evolving dimensions of performance studies.

This book is dedicated to the memory of Dr. Wallace Bacon, Professor Emeritus of Interpretation/Performance Studies at Northwestern University. His work inspired many of the scholars included here. In very real ways, institutionally, intellectually, and inspirationally, his concept of performance as offering "a sense of the other" was the beginning of our discipline.

We are particularly grateful to the following reviewers, whose comments and suggestions were invaluable.

Elizabeth Bell
University of South Florida

J. Gary Knowles
Ontario Institute for Studies
in Education of The University
of Toronto

Christie Logan
California State University,
Northridge

Carrie Sandahl
Florida State University School
of Theatre

Rebecca Schneider
Brown University

Kelly S. Taylor
University of North Texas

Joost Van Loon
Nottingham Trent University

Handel Kashope Wright
University of Tennessee

Introduction

Opening *Opening Acts*

Judith Hamera

$\mathbf{P}$lato hated performers. Consider his dialogue *Ion* (1998). Here, the hapless rhapsode of the title, a solo artist who interprets the works of great poets like Homer for large audiences, provides a pliant patsy for the relentless Socrates. By the end of the dialogue, Ion seems to shrivel in the withering heat of Socrates' critique: The rhapsode is artless, irrational, a virtual disease vector of irrationality, and three removes from the Truth. Some might suggest that this doesn't bode well for the future of performance as a critical tool. Others, citing Socrates' massive rhetorical overkill, might argue that anything making Plato this nervous must have something going for it.

The Purposes of *Opening Acts*

When I served as the editor (1997–2000) of *Text and Performance Quarterly*, the journal of the (U.S.) National Communication Association, I regularly received manuscripts from scholars in communication, cultural studies, and the humanities; these manuscripts were flush with respect and enthusiasm for performance and its value as a critical tool, for the ways performance opens up cultures, actions, and identities as complex sets of processes, rather than isolating them as things. These were interesting papers filled with thoughtful arguments about compelling sites. Yet there was often something missing. Many of these authors—well intentioned all—seemed unaware of the long and distinguished history of performance-based scholarship or were not familiar with the rich, generative work of current performance studies scholars.

Because performance offers capacitating, useful critical strategies for bridging communication, cultural studies, and contemporary critical theory, it seems perpetually "born yesterday." It wasn't. Acknowledging this rich history, and the important work of current performance studies scholars, is much more than the bibliographic equivalent of the obligatory thank-you note to the relatives for a gift, whether that gift is actually appreciated or not. A more nuanced understanding of performance leads to more rigorous, mindful, and principled analyses and applications. It generates a deep understanding of the epistemological underpinnings, the conceptual challenges, the methodological pragmatics, and the representational politics open to researchers across the human sciences, and particularly in communication and cultural studies. It means exchanging the exuberant "innocence" of "discovering" performance and claiming it for oneself alone for a rich and diverse intellectual neighborhood of hardworking, precise, and playful interlocutors, whose creative scholarly turns inspire defter, richer ones in those who engage them.

Opening Acts has three purposes:

1. To outline conceptual foundations and commitments of, and key contributors to, performance-based research;

2. To link developments in performance theory and methods to those in critical communication and cultural studies; and

3. To provide models of performance as a theoretical, methodological, and representational practice, written by scholars in communication, performance, and theater studies.

Though it offers historical grounding for key aspects of performance-based research, *Opening Acts* is not a history. Likewise, it is not a primer of performance studies. Rather, this book offers a critical palette, an organizing support mechanism for the full range of pigments and possibilities that constitute the critic's toolkit.

Performance is central to contemporary views of culture as enacted, rhetorical, contested, and embodied. It functions as an organizing trope for examining a wide range of social practices. Recently, it has gained currency in linguistic and rhetorical formulations of the performative. Yet to grant performance and the performative credence as analytical tools is one thing; to employ them deftly in service of rigorous, interdisciplinary, situated cultural criticism is another. *Opening Acts* takes this employment as its task, demonstrating the generative utility of performance in cultural and communication studies.

Meanwhile, Back at the Amphitheater . . .

In *Ion,* Socrates sees performance as simultaneously too much and not enough. Its stock in trade is excessive affect: too much emotion.

Socrates: You [Ion] are chanting, say, the story of Odysseus as he leaped up to the dais, unmasked himself to suitors, and poured the arrows out before his feet. . . . When you chant these things, are you in your senses? Or are you carried out of yourself, and does not your soul in an ecstasy conceive herself to be engaged in the actions you relate . . . ?

Ion: How vivid, Socrates, you make your proof for me! I will tell you frankly that whenever I recite a tale of pity, my eyes are filled with tears, and when it is one of horror or dismay, my hair stands on end with fear, and my heart goes leaping.

Socrates: Well now, Ion, what are we to say of a man like that? (p. 33)

Socrates' second concern is sociopolitical: This upwelling of affect is contagious. It has too much influence.

Socrates: Now then, are you aware that you produce the same effects in most of the spectators too? (p. 33)

Yet, at the same time, performance is not enough. It is not systematic enough; it is "just like Proteus," a shape-shifter that "twists and turns this way and that" (p. 37). It is not disciplined enough; it refuses to know its place and limit itself to conventional, discrete categories of knowledge. Finally, and most damning for Plato, it is not True enough; it is a blurry, degraded copy of reality, which is itself a copy of the ideal. These arguments are foundational turns in the antitheatrical bias that challenges performance-based scholars to this day.

And yet, note the overarching irony in Plato's case against Ion: It is itself a play script, set in motion, dramatized. One critic (Richter, 1998) characterizes it as "spectacle" (p. 19). Plato himself plays a role, ventriloquizing his teacher Socrates. It seems that the performing spirit of shape-shifter Proteus has insinuated itself into the Procrustean champion of eternal truth.

In *Ion* and in Book 10 of his *Republic,* Plato articulates a theory of representation ("mimesis") that upholds a series of binarisms. These, in turn, undergird classical Western epistemology: true/false, presence/absence, culture/nature, male/female, reality/imitation. The first term in each binarism is privileged. Contemporary performance-based scholars owe a debt to critical theorists, and particularly to Jacques Derrida, who revealed the intimate interdependence of these seemingly opposing terms: Each is unthinkable without the other. Moreover, Derrida (1978) exposed the play always already circulating in language, the lifeblood of the social bond. Simply by doing what it does, language "Prote-izes" us all, even Plato. The collapse of these epistemological binaries, and the play intrinsic to language, cleared the methodological and analytical paths for performance-based scholarship. Dwight Conquergood (1995) succinctly summarizes the consequences of these Copernican moves: "Performance privileges threshold-crossing, shape-shifting, and boundary-violating figures, such as shamans, tricksters, and jokers, who value the carnivalesque over the canonical, the transformative over the normative, the mobile in the monumental" (p. 138). Further, in the Derridean spirit of collapsing binaries, *Opening Acts* examines the carnivalesque *in* the canonical (Edwards, Chapter 7), the transformative *in* the normative (Hawes, Chapter 1), and the mobile *in* the monumental (Bowman, Chapter 4).

Conquergood (1995) goes on to describe some of the theoretical developments that contribute to contemporary performance studies scholarship:

> Victor Turner, inspired by his performance ethnography collaborations with Richard Schechner, coined the epigrammatic view of "performance as making, not faking" (1982: 93). His constructional theory foregrounded the culture-creating capacities of performance and functioned as a challenge and counterpoint to the "antitheatrical prejudice" that, since Plato, has aligned performance with fakery and falsehood (Barish 1981). After his sustained work on social drama, cultural performance, liminality, and, of course, definition of humankind as *homo performans,* it would be hard for anyone to hold a "mere sham and show" view of performance. Turner shifted thinking about performance from mimesis to poiesis. (p. 138)

The result of this emphasis on performance as making is an interdisciplinary blend of methods and vocabularies with an underlying "commitment to praxis, to multiple ways of knowing that engage embodied experience with critical reflection . . . a caravan: a heterogenous ensemble of ideas and methods on the move" (pp. 139–140).

Keywords: *Performance, Performativity, Culture, Critical*

Raymond Williams (1983) used the notion of "keywords" to chart the shifting social, historical, and political values that adhere to language, and particularly to terms central to critical cultural analysis. A complete summary of these values for the four relevant keywords here is beyond the scope of *Opening Acts*. What I attempt to do here is describe how these keywords work operationally; to this end, I outline the commonly held presumptions that accompany circulation of these terms through performance, communication, and cultural studies, including the essays in this book.

As Conquergood (1995) states, *performance is a term on the move*. He observes, "Any attempt to define and stabilize performance will be bound up in disagreement and this disagreement is itself part of its meaning" (p. 137). As previously noted, Victor Turner (1982) characterizes performance as "making, not faking" (p. 93). Richard Schechner (1985) defines it as "restored" or "twice-behaved behavior" (pp. 35–36). Richard Bauman (1986) understands

> performance as a mode of communication, a way of speaking, the essence of which resides in the assumption of responsibility to an audience for a display of communicative skill, highlighting the way in which communication is carried out, above and beyond its referential content. (p. 3)

Thus "performance may be understood as the enactment of the poetic function" (p. 3). Diana Taylor (2003) extends these definitions beyond communication:

> On another level, performance also constitutes the methodological lens that enables scholars to analyze events *as* performance. Civic obedience, resistance, citizenship, gender, ethnicity, and sexual identity, for example, are rehearsed and performed daily in the public sphere. To understand these *as* performance suggests that performance also functions as an epistemology. Embodied practice, along with and bound up with other cultural practices, offers a way of knowing. The bracketing for these performances comes from outside, from the methodological lens that organizes them into an analyzable "whole." (p. 3)

Marvin Carlson (1996) summarizes the diverse intellectual trajectories that contribute their definitions of performance. Shannon Jackson (2004) describes how these intellectual trajectories have congealed in specific institutional histories.

What operational understanding of performance can critical communication and cultural studies scholars take away from these diverse definitions? At what points do they cohere to create useful analytical possibilities?

Performance is both an event and a heuristic tool that illuminates the presentational and representational elements of culture. Its inherent "eventness" ("in motion") makes it especially effective for engaging and describing the embodied processes that produce and consume culture. As event or as heuristic, performance makes things and does things, in addition to describing how they are made or done.

This emphasis on doing, on process, accounts for the gerunds in all the titles in this book: opening, engaging, animating, interrogating, synthesizing, and embracing.

Performativity is a particular linguistic method of making and doing. The term finds its roots in J. L. Austin's (1975) *How to Do Things With Words.* A "performative" is a type of utterance that does something; its effect coincides with its use. Frequently used examples of performatives are "I now pronounce you husband and wife" and "You're under arrest." (My students have remarked on how often these two examples seem to be "coupled.") Judith Butler (1993) extends the possibilities of performativity beyond the simply linguistic. For Butler, performativity is a way to explore the enunciation and apparent stability of identity categories, particularly sexuality and gender. Briefly put, a performative is both an agent of and a product of the social and political surround in which it circulates. Its effects are reinforced through repetition. Gender and sexuality were the identity categories initially theorized as performatives; they were engaged as "made" and not "natural" or inevitable, and therefore as available for intervention and un- or remaking. Butler and other critical scholars have also extended the notion of the performative to include race, class, and other dimensions of identity (see Johnson, 2003). Thus performativity is a specific means of material and symbolic social production that centers on the repetition and apparent stability of a particular kind of embodied utterance.

Culture is one of Williams's most complex and important keywords. In *The Sociology of Culture* (1995), he characterizes two general working definitions that he labels "(a) idealist" and "(b) materialist" and defines these as follows:

> (a) an emphasis on the "*informing spirit*" of a whole way of life, which is manifest over the whole range of social activities but is most evident in "specifically cultural" activities—a language, styles of art, kinds of intellectual work; and (b) an emphasis on "*a whole social order*" within which a specifiable culture, in styles of art and kinds of intellectual work, is seen as the direct or indirect product of an order primarily constituted by other social activities. (pp. 11–12)

Contemporary critical analysis, however, works both within and across these approaches. According to Williams, this orientation

> has many elements in common with (b), in its emphasis on the whole social order, but it differs from it in its insistence that "cultural practice" and "cultural production" (its most recognizable terms) are not simply derived from an otherwise constituted social order but are themselves major elements in its

constitution. It then shares some elements with (a), in its emphasis on cultural practices as (though now among others) *constitutive*. But instead of the "informing spirit" which was held to constitute all other activities, it sees culture as the *signifying system* though which necessarily (though among other means) a social order is communicated, reproduced, experienced and explored. (pp. 12–13; italics added)

A performance-based critique shares these presumptions and, in addition, teases out some specific elements it also regards as central to an operational definition of culture. These are:

- Culture is a system in process—as Conquergood (1991) says, "a *verb* instead of a noun" (p. 190).
- Culture is embodied. It is set in motion, put into play, resisted, and embraced by material bodies rooted in specific histories and social exigencies.
- It is heterogeneous and contested, not unitary and monolithic.
- Cultural processes can be observed in, and across, everyday practices and popular and officially sanctioned productions. Indeed, these domains routinely interanimate and interpenetrate one another.

Critical, like *culture,* has both a vernacular and an academic operational definition. The vernacular definition emerges in a colleague's account of describing his work, a book about Henry James, to his mother. "Oh," she said. "You've written a biography of Henry James." "No, Mother," he replied, "I've written a critical study of Henry James's work." "Oh, now, dear," she sighed. "Why couldn't you just write something nice?"

In academic analysis, *critical,* like *culture* and *performance,* crosses multiple theoretical and methodological domains. D. Soyini Madison (2005) notes that the critical social theory used by performance-based researchers "evolves from a tradition of 'intellectual rebellion' that includes radical ideas challenging regimes of power that changed the world" (p. 13). She then goes on to describe some specific operational objectives that characterize critical research:

to articulate and identify hidden forces and ambiguities that operate beneath appearances; to guide judgments and evaluations emanating from our discontent; to direct our attention to the critical expressions within different interpretive communities relative to their unique symbol systems, customs, and codes; to demystify the ubiquity and magnitude of power; to provide insight and inspire acts of justice; and to name and analyze what is intuitively felt. (p. 13)

The complex workings of power, and social positions that accrue to bodies based on multiple dimensions of difference, are central to critical performance-based scholarship.

How to Use *Opening Acts*

Now that you understand the basic keywords and presumptions of performance-based scholarship, you can use the essays in *Opening Acts* in four general ways.

1. You can turn focused attention to those essays that analyze sites you are particularly interested in: conversation, tourism, or the history of public speaking in America, to name only three. The contributors assembled here offer bracing, creative readings of their sites; their detailed critiques are a genuine highlight of this collection. I would encourage you to read beyond the specifics, though, even as you engage them, for these authors' arguments have relevance beyond the sites that inspire them.

2. Read these essays as methodological exemplars. Notice how they define performance and how they integrate their definitions into their theoretical and field work, close analysis, or historical scholarship. Notice how they handle the issues of power and difference so central to critical scholarship.

3. Read these essays as intellectual conversations with theorists in and outside performance, communication, and cultural studies. Reference lists are catalogs of interlocutors. Who do these authors speak into, with or against? Finally,

4. Read these essays as performances, as acts of poiesis, as crafted turns in ongoing research projects that can challenge and inspire you. Note how contributors situate themselves in their own work. Attend to the kinds of textual, political choices they make when representing their sites. Consider the reasons why some contributors engage in or discuss actual performances.

Opening Acts contains eight essays organized into five sections: "Engaging the Everyday"; "Animating Locations"; "Interrogating Histories"; "Synthesizing Scholarship"; and "Embracing Performances." This structure is more of an enabling organizational fiction than an accurate reflection of divisions in performance-based research, as you will see when you read the essays. Each section begins with a short introduction outlining the major vocabularies, presumptions, and commitments that performance-based scholarship brings to bear on the relevant area of inquiry. The essays that make up each section are also briefly introduced.

Section 1, "Engaging the Everyday," is foundational. All sites and events examined in *Opening Acts* are, or were, daily ones rooted in the micropractices of specific life-worlds. Here, in discussions of performance in/as everyday life, the critical commitments of a performance approach emerge with special clarity. That is why this section's introduction is the longest. Each subsequent section builds on the presumptions set forth in "Engaging the Everyday," reinforces them, and adds unique inflections to them. In "Animating Locations," this involves special attention to the performative productions and consumption of space and place. "Interrogating Histories" examines specific representations of/in the past and goes further to examine how histories themselves are produced and consumed.

Borders bleed and boundaries blur one into another in critical performance-based analyses. "Synthesizing Scholarship" makes this point explicitly by examining the intersections of text, performance, place, and history. Finally, "Embracing Performances" concludes with a playful, lyrical, soulful reflection on the theoretical allegiances, the deep history, and the social and affective force of performance.

Performance studies as a discipline and as a critical, methodological practice is not a monolith. Diverse choruses of voices representing a range of intellectual commitments, methodological choices, and institutional histories are the strengths of this approach to scholarship. *Opening Acts* presents some particularly productive and representative turns in this larger conversation, not all of them; it is not meant to be comprehensive or definitive.

Conquergood (2002) has called for performance-based approaches to help scholars imagine new critical possibilities for communication and cultural studies. These possibilities can "revitalize the connections between artistic accomplishment, analysis, and articulations with communities; between practical knowledge (knowing how), propositional knowledge (knowing that), and political savvy (knowing who, when and where)" (p. 153). The contributors to *Opening Acts* show us the ways.

References

Austin, J. L. (1975). *How to do things with words*. Cambridge, MA: Harvard University Press.

Bauman, R. (1986). *Story, performance, and event: Contextual studies in oral narrative*. Cambridge, UK: Cambridge University Press.

Butler, J. (1993). *Bodies that matter: On the discursive limits of sex*. New York: Routledge.

Carlson, M. (1996). *Performance: A critical introduction*. London: Routledge.

Conquergood, D. (1991). Rethinking ethnography. *Communication Monographs, 58*(2), 179–194.

Conquergood, D. (1995). Of caravans and carnivals: Performance studies in motion. *TDR: The Drama Review, 39*(4), 137–141.

Conquergood, D. (2002). Performance studies: Interventions and radical research. *TDR: The Drama Review, 46*(2), 145–156.

Derrida, J. (1978). *Writing and difference.* (A. Bass, Trans.). Chicago: University of Chicago Press.

Jackson, S. (2004). *Professing performance: Theatre in the academy from philology to performativity.* Cambridge, UK: Cambridge University Press.

Johnson, E. P. (2003). *Appropriating blackness: Performance and the politics of authenticity.* Durham, NC: Duke University Press.

Madison, D. S. (2005). *Critical ethnography.* Thousand Oaks, CA: Sage.

Plato. (1998). *Ion.* In D. H. Richter (Ed.), *The critical tradition: Classical texts and contemporary trends* (pp. 29–37). Boston: Bedford.

Richter, D. H. (1998). Introduction to Plato. In D. H. Richter (Ed.), *The critical tradition* (pp. 17–20). Boston: Bedford.

Schechner, R. (1985). *Between theatre and anthropology.* Philadelphia: University of Pennsylvania Press.

Taylor, D. (2003). *The archive and the repertoire: Performing cultural memory in the Americas.* Durham, NC: Duke University Press.

Turner, V. (1982). *From ritual to theatre.* New York: PAJ.

Williams, R. (1983). *Keywords: A vocabulary of culture and society.* New York: Oxford University Press.

Williams, R. (1995). *The sociology of culture.* Chicago: University of Chicago Press.

I

Engaging the Everyday

Introduction

Judith Hamera

Everyday life is everywhere and nowhere: the cellular mechanics of identity and culture so ubiquitous as to be invisible. All too often, it enters scholarship as sets of demographic snapshots—what a segment of the population eats, buys, or sees at the movies—or in petri dishes, where autonomous individuals address one another seemingly unencumbered by the complex specificities of geography, history, and the rhetorical-political fields they both produce and reply to. Or everyday life is simply "synecdochized" into compelling anecdotes for rhetorical texture.

What gets left out when the intricacies of the everyday are reduced in these ways? The presumptions and vocabulary of performance studies offer four responses and remedies.

1. *Reductive conceptions of everyday life ignore basic communication and cultural infrastructure: bodies in/and dialogue.* Here we can take our cue from Michel de Certeau's (1984) *The Practice of Everyday Life* (Volume 1). In the dedication, "To a common hero, an ubiquitous character," de Certeau observes:

> We witness the advent of the number. It comes along with democracy, the large city, administrations, cybernetics. It is a flexible and continuous mass, woven tight like a fabric with neither rips nor darned patches, a multitude of quantified heroes who lose names and faces as they become the ciphered river of the streets, a mobile language of computations and rationalities that belong to no one. (p. v)

But, as one anonymous hero, "#6" of the BBC television series *The Prisoner*, protested, "I am not a number!" More specifically, for Certeau, these ubiquitous characters are "the murmuring voice[s] of societies" (p. v). As we shall see in the essays throughout this volume, the very fabric of space time they enter, speak into, walk around, and change is dotted with rips and darned patches: residues of hands at work. A performance studies approach engages this banal and beautiful work of culture, and the names, voices, and hands that accomplish it, from what Dwight Conquergood (2002) characterizes as "the ground level" of daily practice, in the embodied "thick of things" (p. 146). This way of knowing is itself "grounded in active, intimate, hands-on participation and personal connection: 'knowing how' and 'knowing who'" versus a more distanced approach emphasizing "'knowing that' and 'knowing about'" (p. 146).

Certeau's everyday heroes "come before text" (p. v). Conquergood (2002) reminds us, "Only middle-class academics could blithely assume that all the world is a text because reading and writing are central to their everyday lives and occupational security" (p. 147). He is especially critical of anthropologist Clifford Geertz's now classic characterization of cultural analysis: "The culture of a people is an ensemble of texts, themselves ensembles, which the anthropologist strains to read over the shoulders of those to whom they properly belong" (quoted in Conquergood, 2002, p. 149). Conquergood argues, "Geertz figures culture as a stiff, awkward reading room" (p. 150). He calls instead for a methodology rooted in Ngũgĩ wa Thiong'o's notion of "orature," not a simple reversal of the orality-literacy binarism but rather a reminder of "how these channels of communication constantly overlap, penetrate, and mutually produce one another" (p. 151) in daily life.

Michael Bakhtin (1981) offers a complementary view, one based on reconceiving disembodied textual voices as material, social ones. Bakhtin's notion of dialogism emphasizes the embodied, contestory nature of the utterance, the communicative prima materia of everyday life. Interlocutors, each from their unique corporeal, sociocultural addresses, forge conversational turns that live "in between": between one another, between what can and cannot be said, between individual meanings and collectively sanctioned structures, between centripetal forces of cultural cohesion and centrifugal forces of cultural stratification. He writes:

The processes of centralization and decentralization, of unification and disunification, intersect in the utterance; the utterance not only answers the requirements of its own language as an individualized body of a speech act, but it answers the requirements of heteroglossia as well. . . . Every utterance participates in the "unitary language" [in its centripetal forces and tendencies] and at the same time partakes of social and historical heteroglossia [the centrifugal, stratifying forces] . . . The authentic environment of an utterance, the environment in which it lives and takes shape, is dialogized heteroglossia, anonymous and social as language, but simultaneously concrete, filled with specific content as an individual utterance (p. 272).

Note the resonances between Bakhtin's dialogism and Certeau's characterization of everyday life: Both are simultaneously concrete, personal, anonymous and collective. Moreover, both are enmeshed in embodied, processual dynamics of response-ability, literally the possibilities and pragmatics of response. For Certeau's anonymous heroes, these involve the daily "*savoir faire* of simultaneously undecidable and inevitable coexistence" (Mayol, 1998, p. 15). For Bakhtin,

> The listener and his [sic] response are regularly taken into account when it comes to everyday dialogic and rhetoric, but every other sort of discourse as well is oriented toward an understanding that is "responsive"—although this understanding is not particularized in an independent act and is not compositionally marked. Responsive understanding is a fundamental force, one that participates in the formulation of discourse, and it is moreover an *active* understanding. (pp. 280–281)

Here, the possibility of response is built into dialogue, even when the actual circumstances might involve "two people taking turns broadcasting at each other" (Peters, 1999, p. 262). However, not everyone is, in fact, free to respond, or to do so in the same key as his or her interlocutors. Dialogism is not social equivalence. Performance approaches' emphasis on embodiment in engaging everyday life means attending to the lived realities of multiple dimensions of difference that affect response-abilities. This leads to the second response/remedy.

2. *Reductive conceptions of everyday practices ignore the social, historical, and political realities that enable or constrain communication.* These realities organize the range of communicative and cultural possibilities available to interlocutors. These realities have both rhetorical and material consequences; indeed they determine how, where, why, and for whom the rhetorical becomes the material in everyday life.

Two examples of differential positioning and response-ability in everyday practices are illustrative. The first involves a recent revision to the Nielsen ratings data-collection protocols. The company changed its methods of monitoring the daily viewing habits of its sample households from logs kept by viewers to "Local People Meters" (LPMs), data collection devices for specially equipped televisions. A number of organizations protested the change on the grounds that shows featuring underrepresented groups would be undercounted in the resulting ratings for a variety of reasons, including the relatively limited numbers of their constituents represented in "Nielsen families" (see "Don't Count Us Out," 2004; Hernandez & Elliott, 2004). Nielsen responded that these concerns were unfounded because the new methods would ensure a higher degree of accuracy. But, for the concerned citizens who protested, "accuracy" translated into the potential to further marginalize certain shows on the grounds of statistics that were skewed from the outset to favor an already privileged "majority"; moreover, any intrinsic social good that might accrue to a particular show would take a distant second place after that show's ratings profile.

The second example comes from Patrick Chamoiseau's (1997) ethnonovel *Solibo Magnificent*. Ostensibly a murder mystery, at least for some of its protagonists, the novel is a work of orature, a complex and compelling example of the inventiveness of everyday practices set in Fort-de-France, Martinique. At this point in the novel, the police have been called to the body of master storyteller Solibo, still surrounded in death by his audience, who seem, to the officials, like a ragtag group of ne'er-do-well suspects. Chief Inspector, Evariste Pilon, and his Chief Sergeant, Bouafesse, commence the interrogation:

> "We'll have to find out this man's civil status. Mr. Longue-Bête, what is your age, profession, and permanent address?"
>
> "Huh?"
>
> "The Inspector asks you what hurricane you were born after, what you do for the béké, and [in] what side of town you sleep at night," Bouaffesse specifies.
>
> "I was born right before Admiral Robert, I fish with Kokomerlo on Rive-Droite, and I stay at Texaco by the fountain. . . ."
>
> "Tell us what transpired."
>
> "Huh?"
>
> "What happened to Solibo?" Bouafesse transmits.
>
> "*Pawol la bay an gôjet,* the word slit his throat." (pp. 95–96)

In very real ways, the interlocutors in these examples are speaking across each other. The conceptual frames that organize their responses come from the material consequences that accrue to differentially positioned bodies and vastly different social, historical, and political realities. For organizations of media consumers, suspicion of Nielsen's practices arises from decades of national and grassroots struggles over the politics and practices of representation: Who determines (in)visibility, how, where, and why? In Chamoiseau's novel, the linguistic and conceptual categories of privileged "civil status" have no meaning for Solibo's audience; as Rose-Myriam Réjouis (1997) notes, "[T]his is not a translation between two languages but really a translation of discourse, of ways of telling" (p. 180).

Conquergood (2002) reminds us:

> Oppressed people everywhere must watch their backs, cover their tracks, suck up their feelings, and veil their meanings. The state of emergency under which many people live demands that we pay attention to messages that are coded and encrypted; to indirect, nonverbal, and extralinguistic modes of communication where subversive meanings and utopian yearnings can be sheltered and shielded from surveillance. (p. 148)

Performance-based analyses are especially alert to the historical, political, and material circumstances that organize embodied experiences of everyday life. Moreover, they are attentive to the multisensory nature of diverse subjects' communicative possibilities.

In *Telling Bodies, Performing Birth* (1999), Della Pollock examines birth stories located "everywhere and nowhere," like the everyday life of which they are a part. Throughout the book, she examines the gendering, racing, and classing practices and effects of discourses about birth in ways that exemplify a performance-based concern for the complex political and corporeal matrices that frame experience. Consider her discussion of pain in childbirth:

> If I have learned anything about pain from listening to women tell birth stories, it is that pain is ordinary. Not in the sense of universal or so elemental as to collapse different kinds, interpretations, experiences of pain into one ultimate experience and so either to enable its easy dismissal . . . or to promote a unitary identification of "woman" with pain that replicates the masculine/feminine, culture/nature split that has so often been used against particular women . . . Rather, I think of pain now as ordinary in Mary Russo's sense of feminism as an "ordinary" practice, as "heterogenous, strange, polychromatic, ragged, conflictual, incomplete, in motion, and at risk" . . . Performed beyond the boundaries of anatomical discourse and its capacity to annihilate pain as meaning by dissecting and isolating it to segmented body parts or reflexes (in effect, by the rule of "divide and conquer"), pain exceeds medical/masculine distinctions in a surplus confabulation that is dense with the possibility of renewing body-meaning in diverse modes of practicing—rehearsing, reviewing, doing—pain. (pp. 170–71)

Another example of performance-based scholarship's attention to the multisensory particulars that accrue to differently positioned bodies comes from an analysis of literal theaters. In "Filthy—Nay—Pestilential" (1998), Tracy C. Davis examines the class-inflected deployment of public health discourse in British theater regulation and maintenance. Davis writes:

> Concerns for audiences long predated concern for theaters' employees, and though the standards specified for workers were out of synch with other industrial sectors, the movement to instill and (eventually) enforce standards for the audience's health is resonant with some of Britain's largest public works schemes. . . . Though the complaints reveal much about the commercial sector's halting acceptance of sanitary standards, they also show much about the social history of odor, linking behaviors of private hygiene in this quintessential public space to anxieties related to the ascendant class system. . . . [W]ith the very real concerns about disease transmission and the necessity to convince the prosperous patrons that theaters could accommodate them inside safely from the urban stench, a concern about social segregation became conflated with a health issue up to 1868, and . . . a resulting element in the West End was the creation of greater class specificity in theaters so that miasmatic contamination from the lower classes was simply not a problem. (p. 166, 173)

Davis's examination of the routine social "circumstances of the theater relative to the culture that it served, contained, and embodied" (p. 162) reminds us of another important aspect of the performance paradigm: the intimate connection between the work of cultural production and that of cultural consumption as these are undertaken by embodied subjects in everyday life. This leads us to our third response to what gets lost in generalized or reductive accounts of that life, and to performance studies' third remedy.

3. *Reductive accounts of everyday practices separate the processes of producing culture from those of consuming it.* Michel de Certeau (1984) is particularly eloquent about the complex interrelationships between cultural production and consumption in his essay positing "reading as poaching." He writes in terms that recall Conquergood's concern with textual privilege and Chamoiseau's Chief Inspector's request for clarification of "civil status":

> What is then the origin of the Great Wall of China that circumscribes a "proper" in the text, isolates its semantic autonomy from everything else, and makes it the secret order of "a work"? Who builds this barrier constituting the text as a sort of island no reader can ever reach? This fiction condemns consumers to subjection because they are always going to be guilty of infidelity or ignorance when confronted by the mute "riches" of the treasury thus set

aside. . . . By its very nature available to a plural reading, the text becomes a cultural weapon, a private hunting preserve, the pretext for a law that legitimizes as "literal" the interpretation sanctioned by *socially* authorized professionals. (p. 171)

But Certeau challenges this view of official authoritarian production of literal meaning versus passive, subjugated consumption. He does so by reframing reading as poiesis in affective terms—quite a contrast to mechanistic encoding/decoding models of human communication and media consumption:

The reader produces gardens that miniaturize and collate a world, like a Robinson Crusoe discovering an island, but he [sic], too is "possessed" by his own fooling and jesting that introduces plurality and difference into the written system of a society and a text. He [sic] is thus a novelist. (p. 173)

An important corollary implicit in Certeau's (and Conquergood's and Chamoiseau's) critique concerns the freighted binary of public versus private, where each term is a differentially privileged site of production and consumption. One of my students explained the everyday dynamics of value in this binarism very well. Men, she said, are professional "chefs" because they get reviewed by critics and people go out and pay to eat their food, while women are everyday "cooks," unsung and unseen at home, working there for free. Value accrues disproportionately to the socially sanctioned public producers. Performance-based approaches are alert to the interanimating facets of production and consumption that hide in the light of everyday practices, removed from, even resistant to, "officially sanctioned" public discourses. Two examples are illustrative.

For Plato (2001), rhetoric was "cookery" (p. 98). For Certeau's collaborator Luce Giard (1998), cooking is not only rhetorical, it is world making:

[T]he everyday work in kitchens remains a way of unifying matter and memory, life and tenderness, the present moment and the abolished past, invention and necessity, imagination and tradition—tastes, smells, colors, flavors, shapes, consistencies, actions, gestures, movements, people and things, heat, savorings, spices, and condiments. Good cooks are never idle or sad—they work at fashioning the world, at giving birth to the joy of the ephemeral. . . . Women's gestures and women's voices that make the earth livable. (p. 222)

Kristin Langellier and Eric Petersen (2004) offer family storytelling as another everyday practice that (re)produces its subjects even as it is consumed by them.

Performing family stories creates an imagined community to celebrate identity and values. . . . Approaching family storytelling as small group culture resists the idealization or romanticization of a "natural" family to examine how communication practices produce family. . . . Family storytelling is a survival strategy of small groups in which they articulate who they are to themselves, for themselves, and for the next generations, engaging memory and anticipation as embodied and material practices of human communication. (p. 35)

Langellier and Petersen diligently trace the intertwined dynamics of production and consumption in everyday storytelling across multiple contexts, and they remind us of one important fact: Research in critical communication and cultural studies is itself a practice of everyday life, not a function of a sterile lab or a gilded ivory tower. They write, "Storytelling changes things—but by the time we realize it we are already enmeshed in a world of stories" (p. vii). I (Hamera, 2002) put this another way: We don't just perform or study or teach bodies. We do so *in* bodies (p. 121). This leads to a performance approach's fourth response to research endeavors that reduce or decontextualize everyday life, and to the fourth remedy.

4. *Reductive, decontextualized approaches to everyday life eliminate the researcher, who is an integral part of the communicative and cultural context of that life.* Anthropologists have been particularly attentive to this misleading separation of the knower from the known. Consider the work of the late Barbara Myerhoff, student of Victor Turner and an especially engaged observer of the complex, situated performances that are produced and consumed in everyday routines, including those of research. Her immensely popular ethnography, *Number Our Days* (1978), begins, not with a distanced site survey, but with her interrogation by her informants—her audition, if you will.

"So what do you want with us here?" asked Basha.

"Well, I want to understand your life, find out what it's like to be older and Jewish, what makes Jews different from other older people, if anything. I'm an anthropologist and we usually study people's cultures and societies. I think I would like to learn about this culture."

"And what will you do for us?" she asked me.

"I could teach a class in something people here are interested in—how older people live in other places, perhaps."

"Are you qualified to do this?" Basha shot me a suspicious glance. (p. 14, 15)

As Dwight Conquergood has demonstrated, examinations of researcher positionality in everyday communication practices are more than rigorous exercises in self-reflexivity, more, even, than researcher reciprocity, though these are vitally important. A researcher's immersion in the everyday communicative and cultural worlds of others makes moral demands that transcend any academic goals. In his "Health Theatre in a Hmong Refugee Camp: Performance, Communication, and Culture" (Conquergood, 1988), he describes his collaboration with camp residents, using his knowledge of performance pragmatics to assist them in addressing urgent public health needs. This kind of principled intervention moves beyond simply identifying where the researcher stands in relation to a research endeavor; it is morally and politically engaged research that acknowledges a shared world, a shared repertoire of skills, and shared exigencies even as it recognizes irreducible facts of difference. In this work, performance-based scholars and Certeau's everyday heroes address their challenges and opportunities creatively in complex acts of poesis remarkable precisely because these are simultaneously routine and profound.

In the first essay of this section, "Becoming Other-Wise," Leonard Hawes lays out a template for examining the micropractices of communication in everyday life. He further offers performance as a method for revealing emotional and political dynamics of everyday communication that typically hide in plain sight. This essay also explores the multiple resonances between communication, critical cultural theory, and performance as they come together in everyday practice. Bryant Alexander's essay, "Telling Twisted Tales," examines the multiple variables involved in the daily practices of pedagogy and research, especially those that arise from competing claims to "ownership" of a specific site. In so doing, we see how research is itself a practice of everyday life, intimately linked to the most local endeavors, and to the range of performances of identity that make that life, and these local endeavors, go.

References

Bakhtin, M. M. (1981). *The dialogic imagination* (C. Emerson & M. Holquist, Trans.). Austin: University of Texas Press.

Certeau, M. de. (1984). *The practice of everyday life* (Vol. 1; S. Rendall, Trans.). Berkeley: University of California Press.

Chamoiseau, P. (1997). *Solibo magnificent* (R. M. Réjouis & V. Vinkurov, Trans.). New York: Vintage.

Conquergood, D. (1988). Health theatre in a Hmong refugee camp: Performance, communication, and culture. *TDR: The Drama Review 32*(3), 172–208.

Conquergood, D. (2002). Performance studies: Interventions and radical research. *TDR: The Drama Review, 46*(2), 145–156.

Davis, T. C. (1998). Filthy—nay—pestilential: Sanitation and Victorian theaters. In D. Pollock (Ed.), *Exceptional spaces: Essays in performance and history* (pp. 161–186). Chapel Hill: University of North Carolina Press.

Don't count us out. Retrieved October 25, 2004, from www.dontcountusout.com/about/.

Giard, L. (1998). The rules of art. In M. de Certeau, L. Giard, & P. Mayol (Eds.), *The practice of everyday life: Vol. 2. Living and cooking* (T. J. Tomasik, Trans.; pp. 215–222). Minneapolis: University of Minnesota Press.

Hamera, J. (2002). Performance studies, pedagogy, and bodies in/as the classroom. In N. Stucky & C. Wimmer (Eds.), *Teaching performance studies* (pp. 121–130). Carbondale: Southern Illinois University Press.

Hernandez, R., & Elliott, S. (2004, March 31). Planned Nielsen changes criticized. [Electronic version]. *New York Times.* Retrieved October 25, 2004, from http://www.nytimes.com/2004/033/31/business/media/31adco.html?e.

Langellier, K. M., & Petersen, E. E. (2004). *Storytelling in daily life: Performing narrative.* Philadelphia: Temple University Press.

Mayol, P. (1998). Propriety. In M. de Certeau, L. Giard, & P. Mayol (Eds.), *The practice of everyday life: Vol. 2. Living and cooking* (T. J. Tomasik, Trans.; pp. 15–34). Minneapolis: University of Minnesota Press.

Myerhoff, B. (1978). *Number our days.* New York: Simon & Schuster

Peters, J. D. (1999). *Speaking into the air: A history of the idea of communication.* Chicago: University of Chicago Press.

Plato (2001). *Gorgias.* In P. Bizzell & B. Herzberg (Eds.), *The rhetorical tradition: Readings from classical times to the present.* Boston: Bedford.

Pollock, D. (1999). *Telling bodies, performing birth.* New York: Columbia University Press.

Réjouis, R. M. (1997). Afterword: Sublime tumble. In P. Chamoiseau, *Solibo magnificent,* by P. Chamoiseau. (R. M. Réjouis & V. Vinkurov, Trans.; pp. 175–184). New York: Vintage.

1

Becoming Other-Wise

Conversational Performance and the Politics of Experience

Leonard Clyde Hawes

Cultural studies is predicated on the assumption that, in addition to being configured *macro*scopically, deployed strategically, and driven economically—if not determined in the last instance—sociocultural phenomena are also managed *micro*scopically, performed tactically, and realized politically. A crucial project for cultural studies, conversational studies, and critical theory is to theorize, track, and critique conversations as courses of action, lines of flight, paths of resistance, and openings for transformation. Conversations foreclose as well as disclose ways of escaping from and relocating to different subject positions; at the same time they redraw ideological boundaries. Theorizing conversations in such a fashion renders dominant practices and their transparent codes as audible fictions that put into practice novel as well as mundane modes of resistance and surrender. Paying genealogical attention to discursive formations and their discontinuities and ruptures is one way this critical-experiential-political work proceeds. This essay develops a theoretical rationale for thinking through the microphysics of power in terms of the micropractices of conversation.

Conversations as Micropractical Flows and Microphysical Traces

Conversations, as assemblages of strategic and tactical micropractices, are dialogical as well as dialectical—intimately political. Certainly conversation can, and does, take on a disputational organization. Left as dialectical formats, however, conversations are often hollow. Here is Bakhtin's (1986) characterization of dialectics and dialogics: "Take a dialogue and remove the voices . . . remove the intonations . . . carve out abstract concepts and judgments from living words and responses, cram everything into one abstract consciousness—and that's how you get dialectics" (p. 147).

Dialectically organized conversations, then, are contradictory and oppositional; dialogically organized conversations can be, and often are, contradictory and oppositional as well as heteroglossic and unfinalizable. They are digital, synchronic translations of analogic, diachronic desire. Julia Kristeva (1984, pp. 21–106) might formulate this feature of conversation as the practices of producing symbolic language from semiotic desire. For Kristeva, subjects-becoming—*thetic subjects*—leave a chaotic, fluid, turbulent, and oceanic domain of the *semiotic chora*—that which comes before language—and enter into the domain of the symbolic, of language, logic, order, patriarchy, and hierarchy. The tensions between the semiotic and the symbolic never ultimately resolve themselves. Instead, a thetic subject, as Kristeva insists, is a subject in process/on trial. Individuals are not fixed, unitary subjects; they are, rather, multiple, fluid, in process, and nonlinear (Martin, 1988, pp. 117–214). Translating the semiotic into the symbolic, that which cannot be said and is beyond language, is the desire that produces that which must be said and cannot go without saying (Tyler, 1987, pp. 103–145). In this sense, *conversational micropractices discursivize practical consciousness*, as Giddens (1979, pp. 9–48) theorizes it. These micropractices are practical insofar as they say and do what must be said and done.

It would be a mistake to theorize conversation as a totality, as some coherent, bounded, unitary phenomenon. One of my critical tasks is to deconstruct conversation into its multiple voices and diverse micropractices, some of which install and position individuals into discursive formations as conversed and conversing subjects, and some of which cut off individuals from discursive possibilities. The installation of an individual, as a conscious subject, into the regime of language is, in large measure, the marking of identity and difference, of presence and absence, of sound and silence, of self and other. In the realm of language, an individual is alternatingly, and often simultaneously, subject *and* object. Subject/object divisions and oscillations are coded in conversational formats and performed by means of exchanges—taking and giving turns (Sacks, Schegloff, & Jefferson, 1974, pp. 696–735). The boundaries of division and the movements of oscillation are learned in a (m)other's arms, in touching, voicing, listening, and nurturing—or their absences—and are produced and reproduced in contextually sensitive formats that articulate subjects adept at performing in accord with the logics of sociocultural exchange systems (Miles, 1991). Such discursive micropractices interpellate individuals—as interlocutors—into the speaking voices of performing bodies. Installed into these discursive universes, an individual is positioned, as interlocutor, to address *self* and one or more *others*. So positioned, interlocutive subjects are in positions to give and take turns and to engage in the practices of division and oscillation that constitute the circuitries of common sense and the conventional wisdom of everyday life.

I am referring here to a matter of scale; *practices* are notable and observable to common sense, whereas *micropractices* are observable only to more finely attuned ears and eyes. It is by means of their apparent invisibility that power is exercised; who would think of conversational practices and micropractices as suffused with power? Isn't the real world one of actions and pronouncements? Actions speak louder than words, don't they? Conversations and the fantastic arrays of realities they perform are material manifestations of consciousness. As such, conversations are overlooked/overheard and not attended to, not only because they are so densely pervasive, but also because they are assumed to be inconsequential, the small change of everyday life. This is precisely where their effectivity lies; they formulate and speak us; they are conventional formats and mundane performances. They produce us and, in so doing, leave us with seemingly unmistakable impressions that we are originating authors of our ideas and thoughts.

Conversational micropractices situate, identify, produce and trace these interlocutive subjectivities. When speaking ceases, conversed subjectivity dissolves into silence; no visible traces are left behind unless recorded. As a microtechnology of subject(ive) experience located within voices' bodies, conversations are indexical referencing devices. To lose one's place is to lose one's identity; keeping track of one's identity has material and spiritual consequences in the seemingly mundane daily affairs of living. This is a theme that many feminisms have made historically and continue to make in a variety of ways in ongoing contestations with dominant and dominating patriarchal authorities. When one is not speaking, it is vitally important to listen or other-wise to attend well enough to follow along. Knowing one's place as an interlocutive subject—staying in it and keeping track of it—has undeniably real political and personal consequences.

In their performances, conversations are nonlinear phenomena; they resemble rhizomes much more than hierarchies (Deleuze & Guattari, 1988, pp. 3–25; Deleuze & Parnet, 1987, pp. 30–35).

> That's it, a rhizome. Embryos, trees, develop according to their genetic performation or their structural reorganizations. But the weed overflows by virtue of being restrained. It grows between. It is the path itself. The English and Americans, who are the least "author-like" of writers, have two particularly sharp directions which connect: that of the road and of the path, that of the grass and of the rhizome.... Henry Miller: "Grass only exists between the great non-cultivated spaces. It fills in the voids. *It grows between—among other things.*" The flower is beautiful, the cabbage is useful, the poppy makes you crazy. But the grass is overflowing, it is a lesson in morality. The walk as act, as politics, as experimentation, as life: "I spread myself out like a fox BETWEEN the people that I know the best" says Virginia Woolf in her walk among the taxis. (p. 30)

Like rhizomes, conversations grow from the middle, given that there are no beginnings and endings other than those imposed from the outside. Granted, conversational micropractices are ideologically formatted and hegemonically circumscribed; nevertheless, conversations wander down blind alleys, slam into dead ends, topple off sheer cliffs, get turned around, become asphyxiated, repeat aimlessly, and suddenly break off. They circle around and fold back onto themselves; they retrieve and recreate, recall and adumbrate in ways that elude the assumptive foundations of formal logics and dialectics.

Much of the theoretical and cultural significance of conversational micropractices lies in their performative locations along the seams of speech/language. On the one hand, conversations partake of both speech and language; on the other, they have little to do with either. Insofar as language is that which its (collusional) members assume they know in common—that which goes without saying—language is a practical consciousness, an implicitly held common sense. Speech, on the other hand, is a discursive consciousness—an individuated, explicit performative sense—insofar as it is that which must be said because it cannot be assumed to pass in silence. Speech can be thought through as the discursive appropriation of, and at the same moment the discursive formulation of, practical consciousness, in what Mikhail Bakhtin (1986, pp. 133–157) calls a dialogue of *utterances.*

Michel de Certeau (1984) locates distinctions between speech and language in the problematics of enunciation, which he characterizes in terms of its four properties. First, language takes place by means of speaking; speech realizes language by actualizing portions of it as potential and possibility. Second, speaking appropriates language in the very act of speaking it. Third, speech presupposes a particular *relational contract* with an "other"—real or fictive. And fourth, speech instantiates a *present* as the time for an "I" to speak (p. 33). In these ways, conversational micropractices produce and reproduce sociocultural structures and formations by means of binding time to space. They are more or less transparent mediational practices of and for structuration. The question I set for myself in this essay is: How do these conversational micropractices—so seemingly innocuous and innocent of power—produce and consume ideologies of everyday living?

Conversation is a term designating a large but finite assemblage of discourse micropractices that produce and reproduce cultures and their social formations. How is this performed conversationally? Both ethnomethodology generally and conversation analysis particularly have invested heavily in the finely grained descriptions of the indexicality and reflexivity of everyday life (Garfinkel, 1967; Heritage, 1984; Turner, 1974). There are growing research literatures that describe arrays of interactional sociolinguistic and ethnomethodological devices and procedures instrumental in the co-production of conversation. Sociolinguistic variation, ethnomethodological conversational analysis, extended standard theory, and ethnography of communication share several theoretical and methodological assumptions (Schiffrin, 1994). However, situating any of this work in the intimately political worlds of the conversants themselves is still relatively rare. Conversational moves, devices, and properties (e.g., greetings, repetitions, questions and answers, accounts, correction invitations, address terms, stories, paraphrasing, quoting, pronouns, gossiping, visiting, politeness, hosting, telephone talking, among others) are seldom explored as modes of consciousness, structures of feeling, or shapes of experience; nor are they often fitted into the dominant, residual, and emergent features of their sociocultural traditions, institutions, and formations. Anita Pomerantz (1989) makes a clear distinction between two different frameworks for analyzing conversation as she reviews a collection of conversation analytic studies: the Sequence framework and the Interactants' World framework. They are two different ways of writing conversation analytic work. The former can be thought of in more structuralist terms, whereas the latter makes more sense as phenomenology. The former positions itself outside the phenomenon and describes its structural features and properties. The latter positions itself within a phenomenon and works to describe it from an interactant's subject position. I want to take a different course and follow several lines of cultural studies, performance theory, and conversational studies to foreground some pivotal differences distinguishing these traditions.

Everyday conversations are identified, reified, described, and analyzed, but rarely are they abstracted back into the material and spiritual relations of the political economics of the daily lives of their interlocutors. One is left with little sense of how these conversational micropractices produce and reproduce the structural and poststructural conditions of the experience of late-modern life. V. N. Volosinov's (1973) theoretical and critical work in the philosophy of language, Mikhail Bakhtin's (1981, 1984, 1986) work in speech genres, poetics, and dialogics, and Michel Foucault's (1979, 1986, 1988, 2001) and Julia Kristeva's (1975, 1984) theorizations of the revolutionary potentials of poetic language serve as a theoretical and dialogical context for conducting a socioculturally oriented examination and critique of conversation, work that goes beyond analytics and dialectics to dialogics.

Rules, Rituals, and Performances as Art and Practice

In *Philosophical Investigations,* Wittgenstein (1963) encapsulates many of the current dilemmas confronting theories of discourse that invoke rules to explain communicative practices:

> What do I call "the rule" by which he proceeds?—the hypothesis that satisfactorily describes his use of words, which we observe; or the rule which he looks up when he uses signs; or the one which he gives us in reply when we ask what his rule is?—But what if observation does not enable us to see any clear rule, and the question brings none to light?—for he did indeed give me a definition when I asked him what he understood by "N," but he was prepared to withdraw and alter it. So how am I to determine the rule according to which he is playing? He does not know it himself.—Or, to ask a better question: What meaning is the expression "the rule by which he proceeds" supposed to have left to it here? (pp. 38–39)

For Pierre Bourdieu (1977, 1990), the theoretical status of a rule is the presupposed solution to these very difficulties, the difficulties posed by an inadequate theory of practice. Insofar as there is no adequate theory of practice, there is a compensating emphasis on rules and codes as devices for explaining practices as accomplished social facts, as products of, rather than processes of, production. Rules are the structural keys to the engines of social praxis; the difficulty is that rules themselves are products of discursive knowledge. Rules are discursive inventions whose value lies in their retrospective accounts of social practices. Insofar as our understanding of practice is incomplete, rules are rationalistic devices that supposedly account for practical outcomes. Yet to have a code of rules as a model for performative practice is to fall far short of saying much at all about the everyday practical circumstances of the production and consumption of conversation.

To account for everyday conversational practices in terms of conversational rules—whatever the relation between rule and practice is taken to be—is to hold to the position that practice is a product of rules, which has the consequence of privileging synchronic competence over diachronic performance. Discourse, as systems of rules and codes of relations, is thereby in the master position. It is for speech to be obedient to those discursive rules, consequently reproducing and more deeply inculcating the epistemic bias and its unresolvable paradoxes, chief among them being that to explain conversational performance in terms of codes and rules is to undermine the very possibility of ever theoretically accounting for everyday conversation. This condition is a direct consequence of a discourse whose voice takes a position of observer and one that conceptualizes everyday conversational practices as representational objects of observation. Conversation comes to be theorized from a position of outside observer rather than from an interlocutive position.

Practicality, Temporality, and Spatiality: Common Sense and Conventional Wisdom

Given that conversation is a turn-taking system, I want to open this section with the problematic of subjectivity and how to locate subject positions and agency in such systems. Pierre Bourdieu's (1977, pp. 30–71; 1990, pp. 1–141) concern with the individual operations of exchange systems (of whatever kinds—land, cattle, women, challenges, gifts, utterances)—locates the practicing subject within the moment of a practice's production rather than outside practice and time. He aims at a science of the dialectical relations between theoretical and practical knowledges that include, for him, scientific as well as everyday practices. Instead of positioning the practicing subject outside everyday temporality, he locates it as close to the seam of space/time as possible—the better to construct the generative principles of practices.

Time is the medium through which spatio-structural contradictions are worked through/out, and analytic concerns shift to practices of and for making time take place. For Bourdieu, these practices are strategies; for Certeau, they are tactics. Both refer to temporal practices that materialize in space but are not inscribed in space "once and for all time." Intervals between durations of actions constitute the temporal embodiments and amplifications of contradictions that are resolved more or less precisely by these unfolding discursive tempos. Variable intervals of time between actions accommodate the acceptable arrays of contradictions to be taken account of practically, to be appropriated and worked through time, and that materialize as practices. Bourdieu (1977) writes:

To restore to practice its practical truth, we must . . . reintroduce time into the theoretical representation of practice which, being temporally structured, is intrinsically defined by its *tempo*. The generative, organizing scheme which gives . . . improvised speech its argument, and attains conscious expression in order to work itself out, is an often imprecise but systematic principle of selection and realization, tending through steadily directed corrections, to eliminate accidents when they can be put to use, and to conserve even fortuitous successes. (p. 4)

As these broadly deployed micropractices of selection and realization—of bricolage and performance, of temporal practices for producing and reproducing the tempos of everyday life—conversations resolve appropriate contradictions and discrepant understandings and suppress the materialization of others. As multiply mediated, conversations can be likened to the play of a spontaneous semiology that orchestrates regulated improvisation of practices whose regions of performance lie somewhere between the seemingly open set of mundane practices of everyday life and the more constrained practices of custom, ceremony, and ritual: between individual style and social custom (Turner, 1969, 1974, 1982, 1987).

It is important to note that, for Bourdieu, such improvisational performances only *appear* to be free and easy. The object of Gregory Bateson's (1936; 1972, pp. 159–239) theorizing of play, for example, is this very domain of the metacommunication of the practical knowledge of micropractices that enable subjects to act on the differences between *for play/for real.* In fact, an apparently improvisational process has its play regulated by a more or less definite set of precepts, aphorisms, formulas, and codes. Improvisation is not random, unprecedented free activity but rather innovative play both *of* and *on* conventional(ized) forms. Conversations consist of those micropractices carried along by, and, on occasion, carried away with and carried beyond, practical knowledges, which are the practical resources of and for the performance of conversational discourse.

Consider Bourdieu's (1990) notion of the material installation of *habitus* (which Bourdieu always italicizes). *Habitus*—or *opus operatum* (i.e., a product of practice)—consists in the structures constitutive of a particular environment, whereas *disposition*—*modus operandi* (i.e., modes of practice)—is both the distinctive mark of *habitus* and a way or style of being. The domestic organization of the house, the social organization of the agrarian calendar, and the sexual organization of labor, for example, are homologues constituting the *habitus*: "*Disposition* expressed first *the result of an organizing action,* with a meaning close to that of a structure; it also designates a *way of being,* a *habitual state* (especially of the body) and a *predisposition, tendency, propensity,* or *inclination*" (p. 214).

Consider the practices of children's performances of games, which occur in all societies to structurally exercise children's practical mastery of the dispositions necessary for them to participate in an assortment of exchange systems (Sawyer, 1997). Here—in the riddle, the challenge, the duel, the put-on, the tease, the dare, the con—children learn the logics of challenge/riposte, the modus operandi of a protean *habitus*.

Before newborn *Homo sapiens* enter the *habitus* of eventual sociocultural formations, they are readied, more or less, in the *habitus* of family. An infant enters a family system as a sociocultural signifier with its status and oppositionality already largely fixed. Already, it has been overdetermined, largely without explicit deliberation, how a newborn is to be raised and tended, by whom, for how long, in what places, at what times, and in relation to whom. An infant immediately, and not usually as a result of conscious intention, becomes an emerging and developing embodiment of *habitus*, the material locus of dispositions and their principles of regulated improvisation:

> [I]t is in the dialectical relationship between the body and a space structured according to the mythico-ritual oppositions that one finds the form of the structural apprenticeship which leads to the embodying of the structure of the world—the appropriating by the world of a body thus enabled to appropriate the world. (Bourdieu, 1977, p. 89)

The domestic organization of the house, or whatever the structure of domestic space in which an infant finds itself, is both engendered and sexualized, both spatialized and temporalized, and politicized through and through. "The house, an *opus operatum*, lends itself to a deciphering which does not forget that the 'book' from which the children learn their version of the world is read with the body, in and through the movements and displacements which make the space within which they are enacted as much as they are made by it" (Bourdieu, 1977, p. 90).

To summarize his argument, and thereby to compress it drastically, Bourdieu contends that social space in general, and its primordially minimalist gesture—the house—in particular, is organized according to an ensemble of homologous relations—fire:water :: cooked:raw :: high:low :: light:shade :: night:day :: male:female :: inside:outside, and so forth. The primal *habitus* of house marks the infant with these homologous signs, and the child becomes the embodied dispositions reproducing the structured relations into which it was born. A socioculturally embodied subject reproduces practices that are products of a modus operandi over which the subject has little discursive consciousness. The modus operandi often has an objective intention or logic that both is larger than and outruns a subject's partial consciousness.

Contradictions are inevitable among homologous relations organizing the social cosmology and the bodily cosmogony.

One of the suggestive implications of this line of theorizing is that corporeality, as sociocultural embodiment, as the object of the seemingly trivial and inconsequential practices of dress, demeanor, bearing, manners, and style, is the materiality of memory. The body is the text of signs written by experience and recorded as marks of character, and a mnemonic medium in which are inscribed the principles of the content of culture:

> The principles embodied in this way are placed beyond the grasp of consciousness and hence cannot be touched by voluntary, deliberate transformation, cannot even be made explicit; nothing seems more ineffable, more incommunicable, more inimitable, and, therefore, more precious than the values given body, *made* body by the transubstantiation achieved by the hidden persuasion of an implicit pedagogy, capable of instilling a whole cosmology, an ethic, a metaphysic, a political philosophy, through injunctions as insignificant as "stand up straight" or "don't hold your knife in your left hand." (Bourdieu, 1977, p. 94)

The Political Economics of Conversational Turn Taking

A *turn* is self-reflexive; it materializes as itself only in relation to another turn. And such a self-reflexive relationship is the basis of ideological transparency. An alternative formulation of conversation is a mimetic form. The Greek term *mimesis* captures the existential validity of transparency (Taussig, 1993). *Mimesis* translates as self-imitation or self-present-in-motion. Here is Alasdair MacIntyre's (1981) conception of it:

> In conversations we do not only elaborate thoughts, arguments, theories, poems, dramas; we gesture, we draw, we paint, we sing. In so doing we give structure to our thought; we interpret a reality that was already partially constituted by the interpretation of the agents engaged in the transaction and our interpretation is more or less adequate, approaches or fails to approach truth more nearly. What was the free play of conversational transaction becomes structure mimesis and mimesis always claims truth. (p. 43)

Given *turn* as a constitutive feature of conversation, and given the self-reflexiveness of a turn, that which is constituted in and through the taking of turns is itself self-reflexive. Conversation imitates itself by inscribing itself in the movement of a turn's *taking place*. To take a turn is to orient and attend to a sociocultural life-world by inscribing space/time in and through the acoustic/kinesthetic movements of conversing. A turn and its space, time, and movement are co-extensive. A conversational move is to take a turn, and the micropractices of taking turns inscribe worlds of subjects, objects, and their interpenetrated relations of power. Turns are values and as such are sought, avoided, given, and taken, and the ways in which turn taking distributes its participating members can be thought through in political-economic terms. As with any political economy, the organization of turn taking reproduces the very distributional structures of that which it organizes. I am referring here to a kind of "circular organization" that theoretical biologists and cognitive scientists call *autopoiesis* (Varela, 1979), a term coined to refer to the dynamics of autonomy proper to living systems, systems that reproduce themselves.

Conversational micropractices are the structures of sharing and community, as well as of hoarding and alienation; turns are distributive. Much of sociocultural dynamics is structured in and around the taking of turns, and producing turns ranges from the metonymic to the metaphoric. Everyday life is punctuated *turningly,* and crucially, much of the time those punctuational systems are transparent arrangements for assessing who has what rights and obligations in the seemingly ordinary schemes of things. To illustrate: *Common goods* is a fundamentally different mode of distribution than is *individual portioning.* The analogy is to buffet dining as opposed to à la carte dining. For a buffet, the choices are all present and available, whereas for à la carte someone presupposes the right to determine for you how much you get and how often you get it. The more fascist the dining, the more the regime presumes the right to serve the portions. The more anarchic the dining, the more the individual diners presume the right to serve themselves.

The analogy is apposite for conversation. In a family system, turns are distributed somewhere along a common goods/à la carte continuum. The diversity of a subject's styles of taking turns is either maximized or minimized, empowered or suppressed. Passivity is the ultimate income of fascism; chaos is the ultimate outcome of anarchism. Somewhere along these lines, family systems articulate their conventional practices in the material forms of rights and obligations, pursuant to turns, in competition for dominance and control (of the system). Structures and codes of turn distribution become conventionalized as common sense. A subject's identity, in large measure, is a conventionalized assemblage of discursive micropractices, tactics for giving and getting, taking and surrendering turns. A turn, given this line of thinking, is an opening, a possibility. But what is done with turns is integrally related to how and when turns materialize and how turns are embodied and fleshed out. Individuals are installed in discourse as conversed and conversing subjects of distributed conversations. Coming to discourse as a conversed and conversing subject, then, is coming to pragmatic, ethical, aesthetic, political, erotic, and spiritual consciousness at one and the same time.

And so there is in the very production and consumption of conversational micropractices a morality whose ideology appropriates space/time and informs the power relations of production and consumption. The hegemonic effectivity of conversational micropractices is actualized in the production and consumption of quotidian common sense and common places. The temporality of this everyday life is produced as if experience were sequential and linear rather than archeological and nonlinear, if not chaotic. Time is commodified and is capable of being scheduled, regulated, organized, routinized, measured, and controlled (Foucault, 1979, pp. 170–194). Nevertheless, even in moments of scheduled ordinariness, there is palpable, undeniable fear and terror on the faces of their embodied bearers; everyday practices, at such times, seem to be losing their common sense in the misfires and tragicomic ruptures of everyday life (Koelb, 1990, pp. 189–215).

Conversational micropractices articulate conventional wisdom with circumstantially punctuated experience. The properties of conversational micropractices most responsible for the production and reproduction of this ordinariness and mundanity are its transparent methods of *cutting out* and *turning over*—of both *in*forming and *per*forming—sociocultural forms of life. In his critique of Foucault's microphysics of power and of Bourdieu's notion of *habitus*, Certeau argues that each theoretical discourse *cuts out* a particular phenomenon from its context and inverts it or *turns it over*. In Foucault's case, "it" is the microphysical practices of surveillance and discipline, and in Bourdieu's case, "it" is the domestic practices of *habitus*. The discourse takes one of its features out of its (con)text and turns it into a principle that explains (almost) everything. Turn taking is a universalizing practice for locally and micropractically producing, allocating, and regulating power and desire. Such formats regulate patterns of dominance and submission by enforcing codes of rights and obligations. So, a turn takes what it finds—and what it finds are living relations to the real conditions of existence, interpellated subjects as interlocutors, subjects cut out as speakers and conversed as authorities—and it fashions an utterance, which necessarily rearranges those everyday material conditions.

Once the analogic relations of practical consciousness are digitalized by way of their transfiguration into the discursive practices of conversation, different gaps and absences become apparent; speech digitalizes the analog of semiosis. But speech cannot exhaust language, conversation cannot exhaust discourse, any more than a digital recording can exhaust an analog signal. The continuity of practical consciousness becomes the discontinuity of discursive practice. The turning and reversing of conversation break up analogic experience into digital, circumstantial experience, the codes and formats of which are the performative structures of conversation. What must be said and done to fill in the gaps and ruptures between formats of changing circumstances, and what stitches together the seams of temporary coherence into transparent common sense, changes with each utterance, necessitating another turn to address and redress the newly produced gaps. *Utterance*, here, is the name for the ways and means—the styles—of turning; it is the name for the practices of making time take place in the conjunctures and fissures of everyday circumstances.

Taking a turn by producing an utterance is at one and the same moment radical assertion and repressive conformity. It asserts change and difference in the same movement as it punctuates reality in formats of tradition and convention. The conversational micropractices of making time take place are simultaneously fascistic and anarchistic. They are fascistic insofar as individuals are obligated to be subjects of conventional turns as emblems of membership and good faith. And they are anarchistic insofar as turns can be taken to violate convention and foundationally transform both practical and discursive consciousness. Barthes (1977) puts it this way: "Language, as performance of the language system (*langage*), is neither reactionary nor progressive. It is quite simply fascist; for fascism is not the prohibition of saying things, it is the *obligation* to say them" (p. 14).

As ways of inscribing time in place, utterances are both presences and absences, both assertions and repressions. As such, turns are moves in relations of power. Coded rituals and ceremonies take on the appearances of relationships and communities. From this vantage, rules of politeness can be read as the specification of rules for what must be articulated so that face-threatening circumstances are either avoided altogether or blunted and camouflaged simultaneously. Unstated in Brown and Levinson's (1978, pp. 56–289) catalog of conversational relations, for example, is the hegemonic power lying dormant, but always at the ready, to ensure that only the appropriate is articulated with practice. To violate the rules of politeness is to risk embarrassment and shame, certainly, but also madness and death at the extreme hegemonic edges.

Power relations, then, materialize in the most microscopic of sociocultural practices realized in the process of collective living, articulating differences that become, upon their materialization, signs of values, commodities marking status differences and thereby power relations. To live in the everyday world of late-modern capitalism is to live in a world of constantly shifting alliances among signs. Conversational micropractices are ways of modifying one's positionality among signs of power, means of shifting alliances, methods of accommodating individuated benefits and of taking care of practical affairs.

The Embodiment of Memory and Practical Consciousness

To take part in the turn-taking political economy of conversation is to trust in some kind of covenant of sociality. And that trust presupposes memory and imagination; they both remember and represent. Illuminating the outlines of memory and imagination, conversation's taking place in turns reaffirms the covenant (tense) of the present. As an infant enters the symbolic realm, the analogic world of the semiotic begins to break up, to digitalize, into discontinuous experience. The gaps marking off these discontinuities are the spaces in practical consciousness that summon (interpellate) the voices of discursive consciousness. Such spaces are the locations for turns to take place, for discursive consciousness to be performed in and through the formats of conversational micropractices, and for those formats to interpellate their interlocutors onto the landscapes of practical affairs.

Circumstances play on the bodies of subjects who may, in turn, respond to these material and spiritual conditions by giving voice to them. Immanent circumstances give voice to the wisdom and folly of memory, which is not simply some recording, storage, and retrieval apparatus. Rather, memory is played by the presences and absences of circumstances. Material and spiritual circumstances play the bodies of memory's subjects as the embodiments of practical consciousness (Cohen, 1994; Csordas, 1994). Circumstances disclose the ruptures that summon conversation to make time take place and to transform circumstance into experience. In the same moment as they bridge circumstantial gaps in practical consciousness, conversational micropractices produce ruptures, as circumstances, again to be transformed into the formatted experience of conversing subjects. Memory's voices are repeated as conversational micropractices that interpellate interlocutors as the embodiments of experience.

I want to suggest that conversational micropractices are performed memory, and responsible for reproducing the infrastructures of sociocultural formations. Memory is neither a general nor an abstract idea. A master, for example, is a subject surrendered to experience, someone whose experience produces micropractices demonstrating principles of economy. Experienced micropractices obtain maximum effect from minimum effort. A master makes it look easy. An experienced pianist, for example, is one whose discursive practices evidence practical consciousness; she knows her way around the keyboard (Sudnow, 1978, 1979). Memory is embodied in the temporality of its micropractices, in the discursive formats of practical consciousness. It is the micropractical body that knows, and the experience of such embodied knowledge takes place in time. The same can be said to be true of conversational interlocutors. As an interlocutor, an "I" speaks what an "I" thinks, and it thinks what it knows; and an "I" knows its own experience as memory that is formatted in the very conversational micropractices it speaks. An "I" is unable to converse out of or beyond what it knows—acknowledging for the moment the multiple ways of knowing. An "I" speaks prior experience as thoughts, and an "I" experiences those structures of feeling as the continuity of an "I's" own identity. Memory, materialized as conversational micropractices, reproduces itself in the spaces of time as continuity and identity. Improvisation consists of performing aesthetically pleasing variations on the structures themselves, already known to memory. What is outside memory is no-thing and non-sense—Kristeva's *semiotic chora*; it is unthinkable and unspeakable (Tyler, 1987, pp. 103–145).

Insofar as memory is embodied in the temporality of practice, and a turn is the material embodiment of memory in circumstance, micropractices carry memory into the spaces in which an "I" finds subject positions for living its everyday life. Memory temporarily animates those spaces, promising to weave them together into moments of coherence. It is in this manner that continuity and tradition are reproduced. Current circumstances play memory and call up micropractices whose formats reproduce sociocultural formations in time.

Certeau reminds us that memory has no prefabricated, ready-made, or totalizing organizational structure but rather is mobilized relative to what happens. Memory plays on and is played by circumstances that produce experience in places that belong to the other. The places memory irrupts into, and occupies temporarily, are gaps in the boundaries of the codes of practical consciousness. They digitalize language, and memory irrupts into and plays on these indexical spaces that beckon conversational practices to bridge the gaps. These gaps and fissures that a turn produces are the places of the other. Speaking breaks out experience that produces other gaps and spaces; the process is infinitely self-recursive. These practices of memory are responsible for organizing the occasions of everyday modes of action, for transforming ways of thinking into styles of doing, for evidencing experience in practice, and for discursivizing practical consciousness.

Micropractical Production and Reproduction of the Ideology of Everyday Life

The configurations of cultural contradictions and paradoxes are suppressed and camouflaged on the micropractical level of conversation. The seemingly obvious, mundane, routine, normalizing practices and knowledges of everyday life constitute the ontological and epistemological infrastructures of common sense. And common sense is hegemony's material manifestation at the micropractical level. The critical study of conversation and the critical study of hegemony at this point become one and the same enterprise. The silences of what cannot be spoken mark the boundaries of conversation. Conversational micropractices, in other words, perform and reproduce ideological codes that normalize the contradictions contained within hegemonic boundaries, usually without calling them into question. Any given embodied subject, as interlocutor, however, is in process.

Volosinov (1973) argues that the notion of a qualitative difference between "inner" and the "outer" is invalid. The structure of experience is as social as the structure of ideology. An utterance is a two-sided act; it is directed simultaneously toward the addresser and toward the addressee. The two sides constitute the two poles of a continuum along which experience can be apprehended and structured ideologically. The "I-experience," at its extreme, loses its ideological structuredness and with it its apprehensibility. It approaches the physiological reaction of animality in losing its verbal delineation. At the other extreme is what Volosinov calls the "we-experience," characterized by a high degree of differentiation, the mark of a change/expansion of consciousness. The more differentiated the collective in which an individual orients herself, the more vivid and complex her consciousness.

For Bakhtin's (1986) essay "The Problem of Speech Genres," the editors write:

> Ideology should not be confused with the politically oriented English word. Ideology as it is used here is essentially any system of ideas. But ideology is semiotic in the sense that it involves the concrete exchange of signs in society and history. Every word/discourse betrays the ideology of its speaker; every speaker is thus a ideologue and every utterance an ideologeme. (p. 101)

Native language learning is an infant's gradual immersion into conversational communication. Volosinov argues that experience and its outward objectifications are articulated in embodied signs. Again, experience does not exist independent, somehow, of its embodiment as signs. It is not a matter of experience organizing utterances; rather, the reverse is the case. Utterances organize experience. And it is the immediate social situation and its broader sociocultural milieus that determine, from within themselves, the structure of each utterance. Utterances then form and orient to experiences of the speaker's partial consciousness.

Conversation, in short, is inherently ideological. It is into and against this ideological world that speaking subjects come to partial consciousness. Realized utterances, as gesture and speech, influence experience by tying inner life together and sharpening differentiations. Volosinov uses the term *behavioral ideology* to delineate our unsystematized speech, which endows every act, and therefore our every conscious state, with meaning. For Volosinov, "Language acquires life and historically evolves precisely here [in its concrete connection with a situation] in concrete verbal communication, and not in the abstract linguistic systems of language forms, nor in the individual psyche of speakers" (p. 95). Consequently, "Marxist philosophy of language should and must stand squarely on the utterance as the real phenomenon of language—speech as the socioideological structure" (p. 97).

Let me now turn to the sociological side of discourse and the matter of ideology. Complementing the conception of consciousness as dialogical is Thompson's (1984) conception of ideology as the thought of the other, the thought of someone other than oneself, thought that serves to sustain relations and structures of domination:

> To characterize a view as "ideological" is already to criticize it, for ideology is not a neutral term. Hence, the study of ideology is a controversial, conflict-laden activity. It is an activity which plunges the analyst into a realm of claim and counter-claim, of allegation, accusation and riposte. (p. 14)

To characterize conversation as ideological is to grant it its own agency and autonomy. Conversation is no more neutral than is ideology. Utterances of the ongoing stream of conversation are, by their very existence, ideological, and when conversation is dialogical and more truly heteroglossic, it summons a response. An utterance stands as a summons or challenge to precedent; it summons a response from another interlocutor giving voice to partial consciousness. Behavioral ideology entails the speaking of experience into autonomous self-consciousness, and such self-consciousness rests on a foundation of opposition, difference, contradiction, claim, and counterclaim. In these ways, Thompson and Volosinov concur on the relations between conversation and ideology:

> To explore the interrelations between language and ideology is to turn away from the analysis of well-formed sentences or systems of signs, focusing instead on the ways in which expressions serve as a means of action and interaction, a medium through which history is produced and society reproduced. The theory of ideology invites us to see that language is not simply a structure which can be employed for communication or entertainment but a sociohistorical phenomenon which is embroiled in human conflict. (Thompson, 1984, p. 2)

Recall that for Bourdieu, dispositions are learned—without being explicitly modeled, taught, or instructed—in and through daily participation in the practices of everyday life. They are the material embodiments of everyday practices. As everyday discursive practices, conversation articulates the experience of subjects' consciousness with the meanings of sociohistorical conditions. And it is the articulation of meaning with experience, and thereby the closing off of meaning, that constitutes the ideological nature of dialogical conversation. Insofar as ideology consists of the ways and means by which meaning and signification serve to sustain relations and structures of domination, conversing articulates meaning with experience, which produces consciousness as embodied subjects at the same time that it produces history and reproduces sociocultural formations. Dialogical conversation is a double articulation; it mediates consciousness and ideology.

Reflexivity, Indexicality, and Implicativity

The focus of my work in conversational studies has been critically ontological, which is to say that it records and then deconstructs, reconstructs, and reperforms everyday conversations. Rather than traveling to other places to investigate other ways of life lived by exotic others, these studies are autoethnographic—self-reflexive, self-indexical, and self-implicative interrogations of the conversational politics of everyday experience. To reflect, index, and implicate one's subjectivity (i.e., experience) and one's self (i.e., identity) in the choices (i.e., agency) that one calls one's "life" is to begin considering what Nietzsche referred to as the doctrine of eternal return: the constant affirmation of the intensities and forces of becoming—of life as flow, as difference. One steps back from actual perception to the singularity of those perceptions, creating a gap that enables reflexivity, indexicality, and implicativity. The ethics of eternal return affirms life by moving beyond present perceptions to an imagined eternal whole of difference (Colebrook, 2002, p. 176). To affirm becoming-life is to make a self-reflexive turn, to locate one's self (i.e., identity) and subjectivity (i.e., experience) indexically, and to ask about the ethical rather than the moral implications of one's life choices (i.e., agency) is to make a self-implicative turn. Questions of self-implication, which are ethical questions, do not necessarily entail questions of incrimination, insinuation, accusation, and confession, which are moralistic questions. Self-implication, in a methodological sense, is a reflexive and indexical process of taking on (i.e., assuming) the implications of eternal return.

A subject begins to understand that its identity consists in multiple selves that collaborate and collude in co-producing the conditions of its circumstances. As a subject changes its practices and lines of actions, its conversational dynamics, of necessity, change as well. Deleuze and Guattari argue that macropolitical forces and generalities consist in micropolitical parts and singularities, the implication being that changes on the macropolitical plane of activity can be brought about only by changes on the micropolitical plane of power. Conversation, in this frame, is a powerful microdiscursive medium for resistance as well as transformation/transportation (Schechner, 1985, pp. 117–150). Mikhail Bakhtin (1986, pp. 60–102) calls the process coming to partial consciousness; Deleuze and Guattari (1988, pp. 252–294) call it "becoming."

For the past 15 years I have been collecting, analyzing, and critiquing recorded two-person family conversations—more than 250 of them thus far. *author's research* During those years I conducted a seminar in conversation, dialogue, conflict, and culture. Each seminar participant tape-records and transcribes a conversation with someone with whom they have an intensely affective relationship that is currently deadlocked. Not surprisingly, participants most often select their interlocutor from what they consider to be their family—a parent, sibling, spouse, relative, or mate. The project is described at the seminar's outset, and its several stages are laid out along a 15-week time line. Participants select their interlocutors and ask for and if necessary negotiate their interlocutors' agreements not only to have a conversation but to tape-record it. Neither I nor the other seminar participants listen to each other's tape-recorded conversations; the interlocutor, who does not attend the seminar, is so informed and, assuming he or she agrees, signs the consent forms. The transcribed version of the conversation is then rehearsed and reperformed in the seminar.

These conversations often, but not always, take place in experiential spaces of considerable anxiety. Many participants are anticipating an imminent conversation they have been avoiding, displacing, dissociating, or otherwise distancing themselves from for as long as 30 or 40 years. Now they are stepping into an unknown present from a dreaded past that has been stratified in imaginary time. And the often dreaded and yet wildly anticipated conversation is about to be recorded, territorialized no longer in a compartmentalized past but rather deterritorialized and dispersed in space and time, available to be relistened to and witnessed. It is an experience of being thrown into the immanence of desiring production, of the intensities and excesses of abundant connections, of being flush in the moment. Within a matter of minutes into their conversations, if that long, they are no longer conscious of the tape recorder's presence. Many indicate that the conversation carries them along once they are thrown into it. Some are not temporally aware again until they hear the "click" of the tape recorder signaling the tape's end. Often, the conversation continues long after the recording is finished. Many report, in widely different ways, that the conversations, surprisingly, were less dangerous in actuality than they feared in virtuality, and for many the conversations are remarkably liberating in ways that are difficult to come to terms with.

Participants then begin a lengthy process of transcribing their tape-recorded conversation. Most have no transcribing experience or any experience in listening closely, repeatedly, interruptedly, and reflexively to the sound production of their voices in conversation with the voice(s) of these particular interlocutors. Each participant begins with a relatively crude transcription that resembles script notes. From this draft transcript, participants continue listening to and transcribing successively microscopic and inevitably micropolitical planes of their conversations. The objectives are to transcribe all recorded sounds from the tape recording without resorting to technical linguistic/phonetic transcribing conventions and to deterritorialize one's conventional modes of listening to one's own as well as to one's interlocutor's conversational discourse production. Transcribing conventions and techniques are provided and suggested; additionally, participants are encouraged to invent their own transcribing conventions as necessary, making a record of their invented conventions and explaining the ways in which these were deployed. The objective is not to train technically competent linguistic transcriptionists; it is, rather, to listen deconstructively and repeatedly to one's conversational discourse production.

Participants are simultaneously apprehensive about and drawn into this work. The projects involve the often difficult, awkward, and vulnerable work of reflexing (i.e., theorizing one's practices retrospectively), indexing (i.e., identifying how one interprets utterances of one's interlocutor) and implicating (i.e., locating one's identity in the matrices of desire, experience, will, resistance, and resolve) by demonstrating how these strata inform, and in the same moment perform, relations with self and others as these relations are articulated with overdetermined social institutions and cultural formations. As the conversational discourse is transcribed into sequences of sounds and silences in the process of representing them as textual bits and pieces, identity becomes decoded and deterritorialized as well. How participants imagined themselves, their interlocutor, and their understanding of agency and choice (i.e., what is taking place as a product of their choices and how it is happening) becomes increasingly problematic. Time flexes, bends, dissolves, and reconfigures as the speed of experience varies in unconventional cadences. The attraction/repulsion of this work registers affectively as boredom, frustration, curiosity, vertigo, embarrassment, shame, narcissism, wonder, fatigue, disorientation, liberation, transformation, and futility (i.e., as forms and substances of desiring-production). Participants write of their transcribing experience, both during the transcribing process and during subsequent rehearsals. Transcribing is finished when it becomes all too apparent that transcribing is never finished once and for all; participants come to terms with the empirical fact that they could continue to fall into their dissolving conversational discursive sounds virtually and indefinitely.

On this micropolitical plane of conceptualization, participants begin to hear their complicities with and their collusions in the productions and reproductions of meanings, and they begin to ask how their conversations construct and locate their experience, identity, and agency within relatively fixed relations of power. What voices, forces, and agencies animate their subject positions, interests, and values? Which of these identified voices, forces, and agencies are they willing to interrogate? Whose voices are they, and what are they saying? In short, this reflexive, indexical, and implicative discursive work focuses on the relations between questions of power, knowledge, and practice—that is, questions of choice and selection, of content and expression, and of form and substance.

All participants continue writing and rewriting reflexions, indexes, and implications of their planes of experience and affect about a conversation that is no longer coherent as the form and substance of the conversation they experienced prior to transcribing it. Participants write whatever contents and expressions in whatever forms and substances make sense. This writing is usually nonlinear and temporally variable; it usually folds back and forth on itself in ways most participants have little or no experience writing about. Initially, their writing productions look incoherent to them—some have described it as schizophrenic, without knowing or necessarily referring to the *DSM-IV* clinical diagnostic category for that term. And at the same time, most find this writing liberating in surprising ways, even those who report not liking to write anything, much less something reflexive, indexical, and implicative. Participants eventually read aloud from their writing during the seminar at any time of their choosing.

Conversational transcripts are reformatted to specify what for some are a disconcerting assemblage of part-voices, certainly a heteroglossic experience for many. Richard Schechner (1985, pp. 16–21) describes this process of deterritorializing stratified assemblages as the workshop phase of performance, in which texts are reconfigured in novel and unconventional ways. Rehearsal is the place where these deterritorialized transcriptions are read reflexively, indexically, and implicatively, moving from common sense toward pure difference in order to interrupt, intervene, interrogate, embrace, and resist what otherwise passes as normal(izing) discursive practices. In the process of transcribing, reformatting, and rehearsing transcribed part-voices, the seemingly innocent and transparent ways families pass on and pass down their worlds of beliefs, values, prides, shames, pretenses, secrets, common senses, aphorisms, knowledges, resentments, sentiments, prejudices, and affects can be heard now as anything but innocent and transparent.

At this juncture of the seminar, each participant selects two other participants to reperform his or her transcribed conversation under his or her direction. In effect, each participant entrusts his or her conversation to two seminar participants who have never heard, and will not hear, the tape-recorded conversation. The transcript's author—one of the two tape-recorded interlocutors and the only one of the two who is participating in the seminar—is free to direct the two reperformers in any ways he or she desires. Each group of three participants then proceeds to rehearse the conversation by reading it aloud, asking questions about and making suggestions for how to rehearse the reperformance. There is no necessary expectation to reperform the tape-recorded conversation; in other words, the objective is not to copy and reproduce the tape-recorded conversation—as though that were even a possibility. In fact, these rehearsals are productive of surprises for the participant-becoming-director as he or she hears the two reperformers making discursive sense of his or her transcribed conversation. For the reperformers, initially, there is little that is familiar about this anonymous conversation. A tape-recorded conversation that the participant-becoming-director experienced as intensely angry, for example, may come to be reperformed as more detached and ironic, sometimes humorous, or even painfully nostalgic.

These rehearsals continue for three weeks. The participant-becoming-director experiences a range of affects with varying intensities as she or he comes to different terms with the recorded and transcribed, and now multiply rehearsed, conversation. Not only has each participant experienced falling into the microsonic abyss of their conversation as its sense dissolves into the imperceptible differences of sound fragments, but each also experiences listening to two others bring very different and singular reflexive, indexical, and implicative senses to that conversation. It is this relativizing of sense and affect that destratifies the limitations and constraints of contracted and centered meanings and their grounded and unitary identities, which are effects that also deterritorialize identity and agency. In such performative spaces, subjectivities becoming multiplicities open up previously bounded, unitized, and categorized senses to previously imperceptible differences, overlooked subtleties, and virtual possibilities.

In much of this work I am interested in how subjects identify agency and enact choices as alternative ways of intervening into and altering conversational flows and forces, ways that engage and transform unevenly distributed opportunities for relations of power. I am interested in when and how subjects surrender and when and how—with what forms and substances— they resist. Many of these lessons are already inscribed as flows of intensities and structures of feeling learned in the worlds of family—as newborns, infants, and children—long before these bodies are inserted, as becoming-subjects, into institutional(izing) worlds and their formal(izing) pedagogies. Listening reflexively, indexically, and implicatively to reperformances of their conversations, participants come to hear some of the voices of their histories and memories of their inherited traditions and conventional wisdoms.

The concerns subjects usually begin with are the practical, moral, political, aesthetic, and erotic issues entailed in the ethical dilemmas of producing an audiotape recording of a high-risk conversation. Subjects come to understand that they have remained in the territorialized spaces of their daily lives to record these conversations, only to experience some of the intensely held affectivities of identity and the collusive and complicitous ways they insist on the forces that hold them firmly in spaces that produce unwanted effects. There are, of course, the demanding tasks of transcribing and identifying (with) the voices, forces, and agencies of parents, teachers, authorities, guardians, oppressors, perpetrators, officials, and leaders, all of whom are coded in partial narratives as villains, heroes, victims, tricksters, allies, and strangers, as well as models of all sorts of prehuman forces. And there are the challenges of rehearsing and reperforming these part-voices, directing other subjects to reperform the conversation, coming to reflexive, indexical, and implicative terms with the inherent unresolvability and fluidity of identities while realizing previously virtual agentive possibilities and choices.

Most reperformances are readings from seated and standing positions, although some involve walking, movement, music, other sounds, or other nonspeaking bodies that may be motionless or in motion in various ways. The spaces of these reperformances vary from institutional university classrooms to small auditoriums and outdoor, open-air spaces. Following each reperformance, seminar participants engage the participant and the reperformers in dialogue—that is, questions, affirmations, reactions, affects, effects, interpretations, and associations. Reperformers often comment on their experience of bringing life to an anonymous transcript, how they came to find themselves in the various spaces of what seemed to be an incoherent conversation, how they struggled to familiarize themselves with it, brought their lived experience to it, and were terrified of, or repulsed by, attracted to, incredulous about, or all too uncomfortably familiar with what they experienced as subjectivities in these processes and whatever senses and values were produced as its effects.

Schechner (1985, pp. 35–115) refers to this work as *behavior restoration* and claims that restoring behavior is not a discovery process but rather a process of research and fieldwork and of rehearsals in the most profound sense. Theater, for him, is the art of specializing in the concrete techniques of *restoring* behavior. Conversation studies are performative as well as analytic in commitment and enactment. They produce conversational dialogues that transform discursive possibilities by peeling off strips of conversations, reconfiguring them as dialogical (con)texts of interiority, and then rehearsing them as (sub)texts of exteriority. In these senses, the seminar is a collection of practices of and processes for recording, transcribing, editing, deterritorializing, reterritorializing, and reformatting conversational discourses. This focus results in a dispersed sense of self (identity) and multiplied subjectivities (experience). It deterritorializes texts into more destratified assemblages of part-voices and discursive forces. To repress these knowledges and practices is to foreclose on virtual possibilities of and for subject groups (Colebrook, 2002, p. 60).

Finally, seminar participants write extended commentaries on their conversation projects. The objective is to encourage participants to think in a Deleuzian style and manner: to reflex, index, and implicate their thinking in a manner that is more nomadic, nonlinear, and fragmented than the thinking they have been taught for much of their lives (Deleuze, 1995; Deleuze & Guattari, 1988, 1994; Deleuze & Parnet, 1987, 2002). Said another way, the objective is for seminar participants to concretize and particularize their subjectivities, identities, and agencies. Immanent issues during this work are the commonsense dilemmas and paradoxes of daily life. The details and features of these everyday discursive practices are politicized in the course of the project's unfolding.

Conclusion

Schechner (1985, pp. 35–116) writes of the liminoid space of the not(me) . . . not (not me) produced during a performance following workshop and rehearsal preparation. Authors get senses of this liminoid space as they experience being at odds with their recorded voices. They begin to hear and to recognize the voices that articulate self with other, voices that speak presumptions of a unitary, univocal, singular identity. Bakhtin's treatments of *polyvocality* and the *inherent unfinalizability of the subject* can be understood this way. Participants begin to realize that these multiplicities and this destabilizing, deterritorializing experience are both unnerving and empowering. A conversation studied in these ways becomes a discursive reperformance enacted in the intensities and forces of the present.

Popular culture increasingly requires that subjects live spatially to cultivate alternative aesthetics and spiritualities befitting contemporary historical and material conditions. Conversations are the material media through which much of this gets worked out, even if never finally accomplished.

References

Bakhtin, M. M. (1981). *The dialogic imagination: Four essays by M. M. Bakhtin* (M. Holquist, Ed.; C. Emerson & M. Holquist, Trans.). Austin: University of Texas Press.

Bakhtin, M. M. (1984). *Problems of Dostoevsky's poetics* (C. Emerson, Ed. & Trans.). Minneapolis: University of Minnesota Press.

Bakhtin, M. M. (1986). *Speech genres and other late essays* (C. Emerson & M. Holquist, Eds.; V. W. McGee, Trans.). Austin: University of Texas Press.

Barthes, R. (1977). *Leçon*. Paris: Seuil.

Bateson, G. (1936). *Naven*. Cambridge, UK: Cambridge University Press.

Bateson, G. (1972). *Steps to an ecology of mind*. New York: Ballantine.

Bourdieu, P. (1977). *Outline of a theory of practice* (R. Nice, Trans.). Cambridge, UK: Cambridge University Press.

Bourdieu, P. (1990). *The logic of practice* (R. Nice, Trans.). Stanford, CA: Stanford University Press.

Brown, P., & Levinson, S. (1978). Universals in language usage: Politeness phenomena. In Esther N. Goody (Ed.), *Questions of politeness: Strategies in social interaction* (pp. 56–289). Cambridge: Cambridge University Press.

Certeau, M. de. (1984). *The practice of everyday life* (S. F. Rendall, Trans.). Berkeley: University of California Press.

Cohen, A. P. (1994). *Self consciousness: An alternative anthropology of identity*. London: Routledge.

Colebrook, C. (2002). *Understanding Deleuze*. Crows Nest, NSW: Allen & Unwin.

Csordas, T. J. (Ed.). (1994). *Embodiment and experience: The existential ground of culture and self*. Cambridge, UK: Cambridge University Press.

Deleuze, G. (1995). *Negotiations*. New York: Columbia University Press.

Deleuze, G., & Guattari, F. (1988). *A thousand plateaus: Capitalism and schizophrenia* (B. Massumi, Trans.). Minneapolis: University of Minnesota Press.

Deleuze, G., & Guattari, F. (1994). *What is philosophy?* New York: Columbia University Press.

Deleuze, G., & Parnet, C. (1987). *Dialogues* (H. Tomlinson & B. Haberjam, Trans.). New York: Columbia University Press.

Deleuze, G., & Parnet, C. (2002). *Dialogues II*. London: Continuum.

Foucault, M. (1979). *Discipline and punish: The birth of the prison*. New York: Vintage.

Foucault, M. (1986). *The history of sexuality: Vol. 3. The care of the self*. New York: Pantheon.

Foucault, M. (1988). *Politics, philosophy, culture: Interviews and other writings 1977–1984* (L. Kritzman, Ed.). New York: Routledge.

Foucault, M. (2001). *Fearless speech* (J. Pearson, Ed.). Los Angeles: Semiotext(e).

Garfinkel, H. (1967). *Studies in ethnomethodology.* Englewood Cliffs, NJ: Prentice Hall.

Giddens, A. (1979). *Central problems in social theory: Action, structure and contradiction in social analysis.* Berkeley: University of California Press.

Heritage, J. (1984). *Garfinkel and ethnomethodology.* Cambridge, UK: Polity.

Koelb, C. (1990). *Nietzsche as postmodernist: Essays pro and contra.* Albany: State University of New York Press.

Kristeva, J. (1975). The subject in signifying practice. *Semiotext(e), 1,*19–26.

Kristeva, J. (1984). *Revolution in poetic language* (M. Waller, Trans.; L. S. Roudiez, Intro.). New York: Columbia University Press.

MacIntyre, A. (1981). *After virtue.* London: Duckworth.

Martin, S.-P. (1988). *Open form and the feminine imagination: The politics of reading in twentieth-century innovative writing.* Washington, DC: Maisonneuve.

Miles, R. (1991). *Love, sex, death, and the making of the male.* New York: Summit.

Pomerantz, A. (1989). Epilogue. *Western Journal of Speech Communication, 53,* 242–246.

Sacks, H., Schegloff, E. A., & Jefferson, G. (1974). A simplest systematics for the organization of turn-taking for conversation. *Language, 50,* 696–735.

Sawyer, R. K. (1997). *Pretend play as improvisation: Conversation in the preschool classroom.* Mahwah, NJ: Lawrence Erlbaum.

Schechner, R. (1985). *Between theater and anthropology.* Philadelphia: University of Pennsylvania Press.

Schiffrin, D. (1994). *Approaches to discourse.* Oxford, UK: Blackwell.

Sudnow, D. (1978). *Ways of the hand: The organization of improvised conduct.* Cambridge, MA: Harvard University Press.

Sudnow, D. (1979). *Talk's body: A mediation between two keyboards.* New York: Alfred A. Knopf.

Taussig, M. (1993). *Mimesis and alterity: A particular history of the senses.* New York: Routledge.

Thompson, J. B. (1984). *Studies in the theory of ideology.* Berkeley: University of California Press.

Turner, V. (1969). *The ritual process.* Chicago: Aldine.

Turner, V. (1974). *Dramas, fields, and metaphors: Symbolic action in human society.* Ithaca, NY: Cornell University Press.

Turner, V. (1982). *From ritual to theater.* New York: PAJ.

Turner, V. (1987). *The anthropology of performance.* New York: PAJ.

Tyler, S. (1987). *The unspeakable: Discourse, dialogue, and rhetoric in the postmodern world.* Madison: University of Wisconsin Press.

Varela, F. (1979). *Principles of biological autonomy.* New York: Elsevier North Holland.

Volosinov, V. N. (1973). *Marxism and the philosophy of language* (L. Matejka & I. R. Titunik, Trans.). New York: Seminar.

Wittgenstein, L. (1963). *Philosophical investigations.* Oxford, UK: Blackwell.

2

Telling Twisted Tales

Owning Place, Owning Culture in Ethnographic Research

Contested Space and identity

Bryant Keith Alexander

I have a tale to tell. But this is not a tale to be *told out of school,* for the site of education is like a neighborhood: a social space and geographical location that both places and displaces bodies and cultures while it contains, conditions, and characterizes those on either side of its borders. This is not a tale that begins with "Once upon a time" and then bleeds over the divisions between there/then and here/now in a fantasy-farce, describing what occurred in an imagined place. The borders in this tale mark the boundaries of specific cultural performances, everyday performances of heightened competence. They mark the ways in which crossing the divides between campus and community demands awareness of shifting accountabilities for cultural capital, cultural knowing, and cultural doing. This is a true tale, an actual happening informed by critical reflection and the constraints of academic reporting. It examines how we are implicated in the cultural, performative production of our own shifting identities in space. It exposes the ways performance, as both *descriptive behavior* and a *regulative activity,* helps to negotiate conflicting dimensions of everyday practice.

This chapter examines the complexities involved in choosing local cultural sites, places, and spaces of everyday life, for ethnographic exploration,

preview...

and sharing ongoing research with students. It also explores how claims to knowledge and experience in a local ethnographic site shared by the professor-ethnographer and student-researcher become entangled, nay, twisted, in the tales they tell and perform both in and out of school. In this way the chapter addresses the contentious notion of *ethnographic authority* as it intersects with *cultural authenticity* and shifting value claims across the borders of the classroom and the community. Both the classroom and community are sites of everyday performance practice where particular "ways of operating" (Certeau, 1984, p. xi) establish "performance as situated behavior" (Bauman, 1977, p. 27). Certeau suggests that *space is practiced place.* This does not imply that location determines behavior. Instead, it imagines location produced by individual acknowledgments of particular social and political practices, performances that operate in the company of cultural familiars. In this case, "analysis [will] show that a relation (always social) determines its terms, and not the reverse, and that each individual is a locus in which an incoherent (and often contradictory) plurality of such relational determinations interact" (Certeau, 1984, p. xi).

Space and Relational Contingencies

So this tale begins, as all tales begin and as ethnography begins, in desire: the desire to know through experience and to tell of experience through "craft[ed] textual discourse" (Rose, 1990, p. 12). The act of telling fulfills the need of the teller to share experience and insights as either pedagogy, performance, or professionalism, with all the tensive entanglements of these efforts; it is an everyday practice of explaining realities. Yet, whether talking about performances in academic life or everyday life, "tellings" are performative displays of experience and competence. In other words, as Bauman (1977) suggests, these are necessary displays of a situated competency in cultural contexts. He writes, "Fundamentally, performance as a mode of spoken verbal communication consists in the assumption of responsibility to an audience for a display of communicative competence" (p. 11). In the telling of these tales the competing claims to competency and authority stand on grounds that shift in relation to the teller, the told, and the told to.[1]

There are a host of characters in this tale who mostly remain nameless; the nature of their acts and the roles they play in this social set of intersecting performances that are about to unfold are very important. Yet it may be that the major characters in this tale are not people at all, at least in the sense in which we invest people with traits that affect each other. Maybe the major characters are "space" and "place," each signaling how the nature of human engagement is contingent upon location and purpose. Space and place *can have character: those combinations of qualities or features that distinguish and dictate doing.* Yet the personal particulars introduced in this tale do also animate the story and *key the actual cultural performances* in these shifting cultural systems (Bauman, 1977). They reveal how assessments of the competency of our identity performances are *framed* as indigenous to shifting terrains of experience (Goffman, 1974).

A colleague of mine who taught a class in qualitative research methods directed one of her students to me in order to discuss aspects of a shared interest, transformed into an ethnographic project on black barbershops/salons. The student, a young black woman, entered my office. We began to talk in the middle of a conversation that seemingly had already started in a barbershop or salon, somewhere in a shared cultural memory. Yet the conversation was taking place in the reality of the university. My office is a synecdoche for the university at large and serves as an extension of the classroom. And while we spoke about the everyday practice of going to the barbershop/salon, the conditions of our predicament as teacher and student dictated a set of performances that held us in a tensive relational dynamic.

In our discussion we discovered that we were researching in the same site, Luke Walker's Beauty Care Center. While I had been attending the barbershop for the previous five years since my move into the area, this site was secondary to the memory of the barbershop of my childhood in another state, place, and time. On the other hand, the student claimed authority in this site as the primary location of her childhood and adult memories. The student asserted indigenous cultural membership specific to this space as she said something like "I grew up going to this salon . . . and the stories that I could tell!" She then began to rattle off the names of old and current barbers/stylists and the histories that she shared with them in and outside their business of doing hair.

In this act of telling, she claimed the "authority of experience" (Awkward, 1995, p. 28). Thus she exposed my migrated status to this community and placed me on the outside of the inside of this specific cultural site. While we were both black and making claims on this cultural location, it was the particularity of her experience, marked by longevity, relational ties, and the location of memory, that she used as the evidence of a situational authenticity. Her claim held me at attention and at a distance. As Clark (1962) observes, "[I]t is the associative qualities of our memories that beguile us as our feet or fancy carry us on our endless personal Odysseys" (p. 40).

In talking about procedural protocol, she asked if I had sought permission to do interviews. Her question engaged two communal performances, one from the university and the other from the neighborhood, one testing and applying her newfound knowledge of ethnography and the other declaring a kind of squatter's rights, checking my credentials and validating my pass to research a cultural site that she claimed. These are practices of *everyday life research*—both procedural and protective. I chose to interpret her question in terms of what was the *least* political in that moment and responded in terms of the wide variety of methods and approaches available to the person doing qualitative research.[2]

Yet in actuality I knew that my response could be highly politicized. It was a reflection of the contestatory nature of this encounter. Given that I was a black male teacher-researcher engaging a black female student-researcher in a struggle over issues of authority and authenticity, my move was an act of power. It was a *fallback performance,* a shift into the norms of daily interaction within the classroom that sought to discipline student voices in the academic arena. I engaged *the performance of knowledgeable authority,* in a location that sanctioned such a performance, as I perceived that her *cultural voice* sought to trump my experience in the ethnographic site we were both studying. In this particular relational dynamic, issues of race, culture, and gender were complicated by the specificity of our shifting locations and the values and power that we each wielded in both spaces/locations.

Somehow, in my discussion with the student, the energy and excitement that I had once felt about the shared interest turned into defensiveness as I sensed a competitive edge in her voice. And while it was hair care that linked our joint participation in this site, the roots of my hair did not extend as deeply as her localized cultural membership. She asked to see my notes, and I shied away from that, maybe for all the right and wrong reasons.

Ethnographic Disp(l)acement

Performance clarifies what ethnographies do in their descriptions of culture. They document social agents as performers in cultural arenas and their placements and displacements in assessments of performative competency. Ethnographies always signal issues of displacement; they are performative, instantiating identity and documenting cultural practice. Ethnographies illuminate relational issues of geographic location and the relational happenings of the culture reported on and the audience reported to, of the bodies represented in ethnographic reports and the bodies that present those reports. Writing about geography in her essay "Location, Place, Region and Space," Helen Couclelis (1992) offers a theoretical view of "experiential space" that I broadly apply to ethnography, and specifically to the research and relational endeavor of the tale I am telling. She writes,

Experiential space . . . is the space human beings actually experience before it is passed through the filters of scientific analysis . . . Experiential spaces also include the contemplative kinds of spatial experience inherent in the apperception of sacred and mythical spaces. (p. 229)

Such contemplative spatial experiences implicate bodies in the processes of teaching and researching, as well as in claims to cultural spaces like communities and neighborhoods.

These views of experiential spaces and spatial experiences support the conditions and perceptions that establish what I call *ethnographic disp(l)acement*. Ethnographic disp(l)acement is an instance in which the ethnographer doing observational research (or what Couclelis might refer to as observations of "behavioral space" and how people interact in particular places) is pointed out as *more researcher than observer*, more engaged in *the analysis of place and human activity* than in *actually experiencing social space as a sincere cultural participant*.

While Couclelis is talking about literal geography and how humans relate to physical space, any cultural terrain presents these same elements of point and counterpoint in establishing location and positionality. Such performative relational orientations establish the differences between the social, political, and cultural constructions of campus and community. Couclelis (1992) states, "The space people experience and in which they make daily decisions differs from the objectively definable, theoretical spaces that fall under rubrics of mathematical, physical, and socioeconomic space" (p. 225). This is because cultural performance is socialized embodied practice, influenced both in the specific moment of its engagement and in the wake of histories that narrate the life scripts of those involved in the encounter.

On a day when I entered the salon for my regularly scheduled appointment, the student was there. She stood with notebook in hand as she engaged the women who worked in the shop. Like old friends they engaged in *women's talk*—which is less about the subject matter than a stylistic, political, and intimately gendered engagement, a dialectic that seems to be unique to women in the salon. It is an overlapping of call and response and a mix of sex talk, politics, cultural critique, and black woman's-knowing. And in the brief moment of my observing her, before she saw me, she became a part of the cultural context of my ethnographic observance. She seamlessly blended into the cultural landscape of the salon.

While I recognized her and I knew of her project, she was also a member of this cultural community of women. I felt for the first time more of an observer than a participant. I felt that her sexed and gendered being, along with the sedimentation of her experience over years of participation, might allow her a more intimate engagement of the participant-observer role. I felt an odd moment of gender jealousy, as if my male body and maybe my male sensibilities could not engage what Michael Awkward (1995) refers to as "appropriate gestures" to describe what was happening in this site (p. 24). In this instance my insecurity was a kind of performance anxiety, linked to ethnographic observation as two acts of sense making that infused the known into the unknown.

I began to realize "the impact categories of difference, such as race and gender, can have upon the interpretive and artistic processes" of the ethnographer (Awkward, 1995, p. 25). I knew that we had entered this project from different places and maybe for different reasons. Our reciprocal surveillance in this situation might offer differing results based upon embodied presence and the very issue of longevity that we struggled over.

> Thus any mutual surveillance over "ways of seeing" is likely to circulate around the acceptance of certain key divisions with differences in the use of other divisions being overlooked or ignored, but with one important reservation. Members do not ever finally know how to do "member"; they are caught in the endless process of finding out. (Munro, 1997, p. 18)

While I was not a woman and did not seek to know or gain that kind of gendered understanding, I too was a customer and participant in this cultural arena. My perspective offered a different take. We, the student and I, were both in the process of understanding *how to do* and *know membership*, both from the inside of the outside and the outside of the inside. We used our own sensed ways of seeing and knowing based in our "dense particularities" as we engaged in the scholarly endeavors of our research and how that research was always already a part of our cultural process of understanding (Mohanty, 1989, p. 13). Maybe it was "this simultaneous division of labour over knowing" that would further illuminate the significance of this cultural site in our experiences of it (Munro, 1997, p. 17).

In the moment that the student saw me, we acknowledged each other and she hugged me. It was an embrace that seemed overly familiar, both because of our limited knowledge of each other and because of the ways in which teacher-student relations are carefully monitored and regulated. I knew that I was participating in the embrace both as a polite indulgence and in that way that people try to compensate in moments of discomfort. She said, "Hey, Professor Alexander! Are you working on your ethnography?" To the women in the shop she said something like, "Did y'all know that he was observing and writing about all of you?" And there was a moment of pause that was more than a dialectical tension. It was a moment when, if I had been drinking something, and if this had been a staged comedy sketch, I would have done a spit take: that act of spewing liquid mouth contents when shocked by hearing something, as if punched in the stomach (or maybe stabbed in the back). But instead, I just bit the inside of my lip and retreated into myself.

I experienced three forms of *ethnographic disp(l)acement* within this moment. The first was a form of *relational disp(l)acement*. These performances were about associational patterns of black intellectuals, and the academically cultivated components of their identities, in everyday performances of black cultural practice. The women in the shop knew that I was a college professor. They knew this from those initial strained moments of engagement that I experience in certain aspects of the black community, those moments when black people ask, "What do you do?" and I say, "I'm a teacher." And they ask, "Where?" By the nature of my response they then say, "Oh, a professor!" The phrase is delivered with a tone that is both a respectful acknowledgment and an alienating critique.

This tension involves a complex web of relational and perceptual values concretized in the very issues that undergird our personal differences and the necessary differences in performances between place and space, affiliation and disaffiliation. This is what Cornel West (1991) refers to as "the widespread refusal of [some] Black intellectuals to remain, in some visible way, organically linked with Afro-American cultural life" (pp. 134–135), and also what Phillip Brian Harper (1996) characterizes as "the unavoidable effect of inexorable social process . . . by virtue of their increasing engagement with the traditional (Euro-American) categories of intellectual endeavor, through which they largely and inevitably developed their public profiles in the first place" (p. 51). In this sense, there are questions of normative performances of racialized and cultural identity based, not only on education, but also on cultural circulation in spaces between campus and community.

Even though I resist the self-application of the critique within West's and Harper's statements, I must acknowledge that the elements of suspicion these statements reveal are clear. They circulate, not only as critiques from black cultural critics who have presumably maintained an *organic* connection to the black community, but also as attitude checks, warnings, and even calls to which black scholars must attend. This means attending to our social relations within the black community, and also to an acknowledgment of how the products and performances of our academic labor can be related or even translated back to our "home" communities. Maybe in more important ways the directionality of black intellectual labor might be focused toward illuminating the intricate layering of the black cultural community and the indigenous intellectualism that exists within the everydayness of the black cultural life.[3]

In his essay "The Fragmented Individual and the Academic Realm," Michael Curry (2001) states: "It is easy here to imagine that because the creations of the scholar are characterized in the law as *intellectual* property, they are conceived in the moral-right tradition strictly as intellectual." While Curry goes on to talk "about scientific knowledge as being a product of reason and scientific practice," I understand how these issues might translate to the relative nature of my project versus that of the student (p. 212). The perceived difference might be of my secretly corralling community and culture as intellectual property (the production of a published article or book chapter) for my own promotion. Her project might be perceived as celebrating culture by maintaining an authentic connection to her roots, even though she was a student at the university. But "[t]he two positions [the student's and my own] are not irreconcilable; a map can be considered a product of both scientific objectification and of the social and cultural circumstances in which it was made" (Woodward, 1992, p. 70).

These women had engaged me primarily as a customer and a community member. We would talk about hair and chat through social and cultural events. The reality of my professor status was not *real*, in that way that the black barbershop sanctions who you *are*, and not what you *do*, as you enter its space for service and communion. The women in the salon had not seen what they might construe as the evidence of my professor status (my business card, my faculty ID, a lecture, a publication, etc.). They had seen me reading nontrade books or writing notes, and maybe they had noted something in the tone or tenor of my voice, or in my language. I am not sure how they constructed that meaning. But there was never an *academic orientation* to our exchanges (e.g., a performative display of knowledge or bibliography, the citing of theory or principle, or an overextended use of vocabulary). This was not relevant to the primary nature of our engagement, or to *the nature of our relationship*.

I lived in the neighborhood—that geographical, social, and relational space. I attended the same church as many of them, and we often bumped into each other in the grocery store. And, as in the salon, these moments of recognition socialized us in space—and "little by little a *private, particularized space* insinuates itself as a result of the practical, everyday use of this space" and the people who practice a particular sociality (Certeau, Giard, & Mayol, 1998, p. 9). My membership in the neighborhood was garnered through both residency and social interaction. But it was the student's identification of me as *Professor Alexander*—that I taught at *her* university, and that *she* had recently been talking to me *in my office on campus*—that displaced me outside the neighborhood and into the university environment and a whole other set of social norms. My status as a college professor was made manifest in the salon only in the presence of the self-identified college student who established the reality of those pedagogical, performative, and political relations. In some ways her utterance revealed, or called into question, whether I was "absolutely integrated into the network of preferential human relationships" that was the *neighborhood collectivity* and more specifically, the salon (p. 15).

The second form of disp(l)acement is *intentional disp(l)acement.* This is not a question of why the student made the utterance as much as a description of how her comment called into question my intentions. The nature of her utterance was not "outing" me, necessarily, as the gay man that I was sitting in this salon filled with women; maybe a more immediate aspect of my identity was at risk in this moment. Her utterance called into question the sincerity or the primary purpose of my presence, as if I were a spy or a man who had infiltrated the secret world of women. And while ethnography is often about *infiltration* and *filtration,* entering of intimate spaces and the processing of substantive worth, I had not done this in drag. I had done this with my full self present, as much as anyone walks around *fully self-exposed* for all to see and negotiate an orientation accordingly, in the act of daily activities. I had attended the salon only in the times when I was seeking and receiving the services provided.

I know that my intention was not to exploit these women or this cultural site. I know that, while I had been privy to intimate disclosures in this space that was both public work and "private enclave," the specificity of their comments or acts was less important to me than describing the context in which they emerged (Adler & Adler, 1998, p. 102). I also know, as Frederick Erickson (1986) tells me, that "what makes [my] work interpretive or qualitative is a matter of substantive focus and intent, rather than of procedure in data collection, that is, a research *technique* does not constitute a research *method*" (p. 119). I was not revealing intimate practices as much as illuminating substantive worth. Like Harry F. Wolcott (1999), I feel and think that "[i]n my fieldwork and writing, I have sought to be objective but discrete . . . [knowing that] my discretion necessarily goes unremarked, while questions of possible indiscretion may arise for each reader anew" (p. 283).

I realize that I am in defensive mode. I realize that now, as I am documenting experience as I realized it then, in the moment of that experience, I was trying to link my intentions with that of the student, knowing that our embodied presences and political purposes might be different. That difference might be charted in the directionality of our travel, *from campus to community* and *from community to campus,* with the student using community as her base of reference while my experience was perceived solely as a research trajectory from an academic location. In "Praemia Geographiae:

The Incidental Rewards of a Professional Career," Andrew H. Clark (1962) acknowledges what all academic researchers must face. He writes:

> If the possession of an especially comprehensive place knowledge and the unquenchable desire to extend it, are the chief *raisons d'etre* of the geographer [/ethnographer] in the eyes of the man in the streets, it is nevertheless true that we are often uncomfortable and defensive about this conception of our primary intellectual role. Unhappy that the general public should think of us in such unsophisticated [and culturally isolating] terms, we are sometimes moved to a foolishly hasty denial of our basic heritage [as researchers]. (p. 232; italics in original)

Yet our performances as *researchers* cannot overshadow the desire that motivates our particular *research*. This is especially important if we perceive ourselves to be involved in research and performances that blend into, and bleed over, the borders between the places where we work and the spaces where we live.

In this research project, I was using what Antonia Darder (1991) might call my own "bicultural" status between campus and community to negotiate what was sometimes truly a tension. It was a tension between the educational terrain, which mandated a particular performance of professional productivity and sincere, yet staid, relationships with students, versus the cultural neighborhood, which demanded a performance of sociality rooted in geographic proximity, habitation, and the habituation of everyday communal practices. Campus and community both demand a performance of propriety. Propriety is "simultaneously the manner in which one is perceived and the means constraining one to remain submitted to it. Fundamentally, it requires the avoidance of all dissonance in the game of behaviors and all qualitative disruption in the perception of the social environment" (Mayol, 1998, p. 17).

My research in the salon signified a convergence of place, the materiality of bodies, and socialized norms. This is Certeau's (1984) definitional construction of space, and it demands particular attention to the processes by which black scholars mediate/migrate between the dominant discourses of educational institutions and the realities that they must face as members of subordinate cultures (p. 48). This involves bringing them together in meaningful dialogue, shifting tectonic plates to lessen the gaps between geographical location and racialized cultural practice.

The third form of disp(l)acement is *ethical disp(l)acement,* in which my ethnographic technique of unobtrusive and unannounced observation seemingly called into question the ethical nature of my process and thus questioned my character. In another visit to the shop, four weeks later, as I was sitting in the chair and the process was well under way, my hair stylist said, "Is it true that you've been writing about us without our knowing?" I felt trapped! It was in this moment that practical and ethical providence demanded that I reveal the nature and scope of my academic project, which was secondary to the ritual of getting my hair done.

I had to carefully negotiate language to explain the *what, why,* and *how* of the project in relation to the *who* and *where.* I found myself engaged in a *performative cultural semiosis.* "Semiosis is the process or activity of sign production—the signing rather than the signs themselves, the indicating rather than the indications, the inscribing rather than the inscription" (Silverman, 1998, p. 1). I was engaged in this treacherous negotiation of signifiers to explain. This is another example of Bauman's (1977) notion of performing situated competence. I was trying not to sound too professorial, but also trying not to reduce the significance of the project because I "recognize that [this] choice is never an easy one, for it [could] lead to isolation from locality and home" (Relph, 2001, p. 157). At stake in this moment was cultural acceptance and the viability of a research endeavor, which are never equal. They signal the conflicting dimensions of everyday practice and research protocol. They demand dueling performances of competency, each informing the other, and I could not fail in either.

The kernel logic of my explanation really involved a defense or a confession, an articulation of desire to celebrate the site and cultural tradition of this discursive space. I wanted to acknowledge and confirm that, unlike Laud Humphreys (1975) in his problematic ethnography *Tearoom Trade: Impersonal Sex in Public Places,* I had not been "disguised" or engaged in "covert research," *passing* as a *native* in order to watch their secret practices (Adler & Adler, 1998, p. 103). My membership in this cultural community was marked in my racial distinction, the texture of my hair, the method of processing my hair, and my full engagement in culture. All of these were present *before* my status as researcher and my impulse to research.

I had not broken the cardinal rule of observational research outlined so long ago by K. F. Erickson (1967); I did not "misrepresent [my] identity for the purpose of entering a private domain to which [I was] not otherwise eligible" or "deliberately misrepresent the characters of the research in which [I was] engaged" (p. 373). While I was a man sitting among women in this salon, my presence was primarily prompted by the hair care services that these women provided. In the sense of everyday cultural performances, I was truly both a participant and observer. I was not the "watchqueen," as Humphreys (1975) positioned himself in his research, not the one who surreptitiously gained a functional role in community by standing on the periphery of being both a participant and a "lookout" so that he could voyeuristically and politically claim the pleasure and assumed objective vantage point of insider/outsider status (p. 26). Nor was I the one who "shun[ned] involvement, desiring kicks without commitment," as Humphreys further characterized the men who frequented the cultural site of the gay tearoom (p. 2).

Cultural performance as a "directional movement occurs as a result of strategies that human agents operationalize and, further, these strategies operate either in the cultural performance themselves or in ancillary activities related to them, such as talking about performances prior to or after their occurrence" (Fuoss, 1993, p. 332). I fully participated in the relational intimacies, the cultural activities and performances in this location; the nature of my scholarly observational research aligned with my experience as a cultural member and client. It manifested itself as my desire to document and articulate the significance, the meaningfulness of this space, all of which I appreciated, celebrated, and extended into my research as a means of broadening the scope of research on black cultural experience. Yet, as a result of the student's utterance, I was forced to publicly negotiate the duality of my roles as cultural member and as researcher.

The woman to whom I was speaking, and the women who were surreptitiously listening to my informal research talk (explanation, excuse, confession, and defense), accepted and celebrated the project as important. They even began to chime in personal affirmations of their own perceptions of the space and experiences of being in the salon. In her subtle way, my stylist seemed to forgive me for not revealing my research "up front." But while I was grateful for the generosity and support of these women, I was in that uncomfortable position of having to apologize for someone else's problematic construction of my actions ("Did y'all know that he was observing and writing about all of you?"). I felt that I had been displaced, or maybe repositioned, within this cultural space and definitely in the very field of my own research project.

What I was doing, how I was doing it, and who I was—*Professor Alexander*—had now intervened in my process of observing. The eyes of the women in the salon seemed to gaze at my eyes gazing back at them. There was certainly an "observer effect," but this was not exclusively about how my presence was affecting their behavior. It also included the ways their observance of me affected and confused my level of comfort in both *observing and being observed* in this space (Adler & Adler, 1998, p. 89).[4] This was a very different feeling from when I had first entered, or even when I had first seen the student in this space.

> Epistemologically it is as though many strands of thought have simultaneously slipped anchor and are now drifting aimlessly, so that explanations about causes, and judgments about what is good or right or true, depend more on context than on universal principles of reason or logic. (Relph, 2001, p. 153)

My sensed knowing through the feeling of comfort that had always accompanied me in the barbershop/salon, and in many ways necessitated the research, was gone. In these ways the effect of disp(l)acement was a disjuncture of the *objective and intimate tones* that signified my orientation to campus and community, to research and the identity politics of cultural performance.[5]

Hyphenated Identity as Bridge and Border Guard

In her introduction to *Borders, Boundaries, and Frames: Cultural Criticism and Cultural Studies,* Mae G. Henderson (1995) offers a description that helps to establish the context for border crossing and cultural politics. She writes, "Forever on the periphery of the possible, the border, the boundary, and the frame are always at issue—and their location and status inevitably raise the problematic of inside and outside and how to distinguish one from the other"(p. 2). The phrase offers particular direction in those moments when the boundaries blur in research and cultural life, and in cultural life as research. The tale I have been spinning about the professor and the student is really *a perpetual tale,* one that is ceaselessly told by all who are bicultural, as well as sojourners, who venture forth and face having the complexities of their identities and intentions called into question. This, of course, includes us all because "cultural experience or indeed every cultural form is radically, quintessentially hybrid" (Said, 1994, p. 58).

Yet rather than approach this dilemma solely as one that is initiated from an outward projection being cast upon the traveler, I would like to also consider the dilemma as an intrinsic trait that we carry with us, centered within the intricacies of our hyphenated identities. Jennifer DeVere Brody (1995) offers a keen observation of the tensive character of the hyphen as it is linked with identities. Like an umbilical cord that conjoins, it is meant to be separated; the hyphen displays relationship and distinction. "Hyphens are [also] problematic because they cannot stand alone: in fact, they do not 'stand' at all; rather, they mark a de-centered if central position that perpetually presents readers with a neither/nor proposition" (p. 149).

If the tensiveness established by the hyphen is conflicted in some ways, it is also productive in that it signals the multiple realities (identities) that the hyphen holds in place. But unlike the figurative interlocking and overlapping circles that are often used to depict the multiplicity of roles we play in our daily lives, *this border bleeds.* And this interpenetration (and yes, even the seepage of knowledge), allows for an informed self-awareness that mediates the nature of our perceptions—as we cross the material and conceptual borders between place and space and make the necessary adjustments to the performative norms of particular social locations.

I know that, within the course of my study, when I entered the salon, I entered with a *configured identity*: no longer "just" a customer or someone who lived in the neighborhood but also a participant-observer, whose roles and labels could and could not distinguish between research and everyday cultural membership. I entered with the added intention of noting my *observations of,* sensate *reactions to,* and *engagement in* cultural performance. In entering the salon, I always assumed that I was cognizant of who I was: the adult man, the college professor-ethnographer, the cultural community member. I allowed those reduced aspects of my hyphenated identity to inform each other. But I also know that one always led the other.

In this way, I intentionally introduced the notion of the hyphen into performativity. While performative utterances do something (Austin, 1962), *hyphenated performative identities* do something while also revealing identity as complex and constructed. And, like the student who exposed my migrated status as professor, researcher, and cultural transplant, I exposed a hyphenated performative identity as facilitative. Like Turner's (1988) construct of *performative reflexivity,* hyphenated performative identities offer hyperawareness of competing identities as they move across cultural borders. This awareness illuminates the significance of *hyphenated performative competencies.* Recall Bauman's (1977) views of "performance as a mode of spoken verbal communication" (p. 11) and "performance as situated behavior" (p. 27). The awareness of hyphenated performative identities operates in a field of play that signals and signifies between the specificity of the cultural moment of its engagement and the coexisting fields of self-identity that provide a buffer and background for such performative range. They signal that one display of competence in the moment may stand in for a larger repertoire of identities and performances.

David Guss (2000) suggests that, in exploring cultural ethnography and the specificity of cultural performance, "what is important is that cultural performance be recognized as sites of social action where identities and relations are continually being reconfigured" (p. 12). In this situation, my status as professor-ethnographer established a certain performance of observation that marked my awareness of what happened and my presence in this space differently. In his essay "How Newness Enters the World: Postmodern Space, Postcolonial Times and the Trials of Cultural Translations," Homi Bhabha (1994) might refer to this intersection of space, identity, and intent as a display of *hybrid hyphenation*: "the performative nature of differential identities: the regulation and negotiation of those spaces that are continually, *contingently,* 'opening out,' remaking boundaries, exposing limits of any claim to a singular autonomous sign of difference—be it class, gender or race" (p. 219; italics in original).

So maybe it is fair that, through metonymy, the women in the salon saw me—or *Professor Alexander*—as the university itself. I became the ivory tower. I became a place set apart from their practices: a place where the features and performances they saw as most characteristic of academics—such as the use of language, educational attainment, class, attitude and intellectual power—could only make sense (Curry, 2001, p. 207). The student and I were positioned differently, and the women in the salon might "see a central feature of a work as its place within a community, so that a work created is a work that becomes part of one's identity" (p. 213). Indeed, they might see the creations of the student or scholar as products of a whole individual, who inhabited and represented a place. And in this sense, because of their long-term familiarity with her, they might ground the wholeness of her identity as *community member–student* and mine as *university professor–client*. The hyphen here not only connects but orders identity and directionality and thus foregrounds communal points of origin and significance. The women in the salon might reify/fortify the border between campus and community, allowing the student the freedom to migrate while restricting my movements to necessity and not desire, like a work visa that is designed for a job but not for claiming residency. But Patrick McGreevy (2001) tells me:

> There is a distinction to be made between the sort of boundary that defines a particular political/cultural domain *vis-à-vis* other cultures and the boundary that distinguishes the human from the nonhuman [me versus the ivory tower], but there is also a sense in which all that is beyond a cultural boundary, whether human or nonhuman, functions as a counterpart to group identity. (p. 248)

So while the women in the salon might support the student in her endeavor, and might support my "professor presence" as a sociocultural and professional possibility for the student and black people in general, a tensiveness might exist between her *being* (community member) and my *becoming* (academic-client), both infused with issues of authenticity and ongoing connections in the black community.

Homi Bhabha's notion of *hybrid hyphenations* and McGreevy's discussion of what I will call *boundary knowing* might represent the function of the hyphen in my experience as cultural member and ethnographer: Identity is not a unitary trait but a complex construction of competing and informing characteristics. The hyphen in the performative construction of identity might bridge oppositions in sites of individual agency where dimensions of identity are neither one nor the other but something else besides: in-between.

This *tensiveness* signals the contrasting rhythms that maintain a dynamic stasis (Bacon, 1979). This is in fact a natural component in the development-maintenance matrix of cultural communities where "performance reveals, shapes, and sometimes transforms personal and cultural identity" (Fine & Speer, 1992, p. 11). It is a dynamic in the process of being and becoming, as well as the attempt to maintain and appropriately perform cultural membership.

James Snead (1990), in his essay "European Pedigrees/African Contagions: Nationality, Narrative, and Communality in Tutuola, Achebe, and Reed," identifies *dedication* as the component that maintains culture in the midst of evolving and expanding performances, and maybe across the borders and boundaries of space and place. He states: "Dedication to the idea of culture provide[s] a kind of generalized coverage, insuring a group's identity against external or internal threat of usurpation, assimilation, or denaturement" (p. 235). His utterance helps to define my position, as well as my defense and desire to use my knowledge as the professor-ethnographer to display my dedication to those cultural practices that inform the fullness of my identity. Here, separate from the comments, questions, or critiques that I might receive about the nature of my work, I become the most important border guard of my own positionality. In this case the border is not that imagined invisible line that connects and divides geopolitical spaces, with agents empowered to check credentials and the suitability of passage. The border to which I refer is really operating inside my mind, like Augusto Boal's (1979) notion of "cops in the head." It might signal an ethical research strategy (a system of checks and balances, a list of dos and don'ts). Or it might represent a self-censoring act made manifest from my own internalized oppression of experiences in similar cultural contexts—like my desire *to be real* and my *need to pass*, held in place by a hyphen. Speaking of the art of Richard Rodríguez, Carlos G. Vélez-Ibáñez (1996) offers an important corollary to this thought when he says,

> The borders of the mind, of cultural boundaries, of marginal identities are often disassembled and reconstructed in creative epistolaries, painfully recalled childhood memories, and poignant and solitary monologues. . . . Such images take up the struggles of gender, race, culture, and class and contrast boldly to the borders created between the "public" and "private" worlds [that we inhabit]. (pp. 269–270)

Hence these borders and boundaries of place, identities, daily life, and research may be consciously and unconsciously constructed as I tentatively work my way through space: from the university to the salon, from campus to community. "Because boundary drawing is a process of limitation, what is excluded may be rendered a realm of infinite possibility. The space within the boundary may even seem confining, a cage" that I operate in, looking outward (McGreevy, 2001, p. 248). I begin to realize more than ever that these semipermeable containments of identity are always present. I begin to realize that external guards of cultural performances are also constantly enforcing the rules of cultural membership. I begin to realize that I have internalized many of those dictates as both reminders and regulators of who I am.

Helen Couclelis (1992) offers a similar construction when she says, "So place is both expanse and confine, both what is between things and what contains them, both empty of matter and defined by the presence of matter; space is even a period or interval of time" (p. 215)—the amount of time it takes to travel the distance of your own difference versus negotiating "the set of *habitualities*" in time that you spend before acquiring membership status (Casey, 2001, p. 409). This is about performance—both as the enacted presentation of self in everyday life and as an organizing framework for social interactions, norms of behavior, and categories of identity that establish "templates of sociality" (Hamera, 1999).

Points of Departure and Destination (a Conclusion)

In *Body, Self, and Landscape,* Edward Casey (2001) offers an interesting conundrum when he states: "Henry Lefebvre claims, 'the body serves both as point of departure and as destination.' But how can something that is normally beneath our notice be the pivot of the place-world?" (p. 413).[6] My own work as a professor/indigenous ethnographer asks me to negotiate the places, people, and practices I wish to study, with and against the cultural politics and performances that dictate my membership within those same communities. This membership is tied to racial specificity and shared cultural forms; it is mediated by both academic and social validations of cultural performances. In the processes of research and/as everyday life, I travel the distance between two cultures and my individual performances of membership in each, realizing that the border that exists between those places simultaneously connects and divides. The complexities involved in choosing localized cultural sites for ethnographic exploration become, in part, opportunities for allowing the multiplicity of cultural roles to influence the fullness of the researcher's identity and perception of the world. They require negotiations of the competing *rules of cultural engagement* in particular sites, with the knowledge that the circumstances of engagement may be further, and productively, complicated by the residual realities of other selves.

In such cases performance becomes both a paradigmatic lens and a literal checklist of accommodations, a helpful matrix used by cultural members and keen observers to identify, signal, and signify cultural membership. If performance is, in a reductive and catchall phrase, *enacted cultural behavior,* then such behavior finds the destiny and density of its purpose in place and space, and in the ways variables like race, gender, and sexuality are seen as *habitualities* used to organize social meaning through bodies. In this sense, performance becomes a means of assessing bodies in space as generative cultural sites that exist only in relation to the human social practices that mark their construction.

In the moment that I make objectifying descriptions of myself as researcher, scholar, or professor, I foreground the concerns and enacted behaviors of one cultural membership over another. I figuratively hold myself at arm's length in order to study myself in another context, knowing that the borders of my dual membership bleed; they affect and infect my positionality in both locations. In this moment my dual membership is no longer "beneath my notice"; it becomes "the pivot of the place-world[s]" that I attempt to negotiate.

I use one location to inform (or maybe reform) the other. With one foot firmly planted on the border, I find the focus that determines my direction. I then carefully shift my stance, knowing that I am grounded in certain traditions, or that certain traditions ground me: issues of the academy (teaching, writing, and research) and issues of culture (performance, race, and community). I know that I am always destined to travel the distance to find myself in the *dust tracks* that encircle me (Hurston, 1942/1996). Writing on Zora Neale Hurtson's hyphenated text *Dust Tracks on a Road,* Françoise Lionnet and James Buzzard suggest that I too, as *author-subject,* can "negotiate the terms of [my] insertion within and without the ethnographic field" (Lionnet, 1989, p. 115) and "into the identity-categories" that both research and culture impose on me (Buzzard, 2003, p. 73).

Maybe such "hyphenated" border work approaches *performance ethnography* through *grounded-theory methodology.* On one hand, performance ethnography is always a descriptive scrutiny and symbolic recreation of cultural practices, in either textual or embodied form: culture as embodied action; culture as practiced doing; culture as social relations that build and maintain community. And the task of the *indigenous performance ethnographer* in this situation is to describe culture in the act of performing it through participant-observation: not just a strategy of research but an embodied epistemology, a writing about doing and a doing in writing.[7] In such a case, this performative act becomes a form of grounded-theory methodology that involves "generating theory and doing social research [as] two parts of the same process" with a certain commitment to self-implication (Glaser, 1978, p. 2).

While the tale I have been spinning problematizes a particular happening between a teacher and student, it does not demonize such engagements or the consequences of such public and private encounters. I would like to reconstruct the student in this tale as an *innocent antagonist,* one who was not so much an opponent as engaging an imposing approach to a moment of chance encounter. The student was *right* in her methodological approach to the assignment, as well as at *home* in the space of the salon. I want to speculate on the nature of her actions and the reasons for my response. Through the encounter with the student in the salon and the reverberations that followed, I felt that my *ethnographic authority* had been challenged. But who, what, how, and when was that presumed authority bestowed upon me? And how was it taken away or threatened? ʂₑₑ Conquergood "dialogic relationship."

In her telling collection *When They Read What We Write,* Caroline Brettell (1993) states, "Ethnographic authority survived under the cloak of distance and difference because the 'natives' never knew what had been written about them" (p. 10).[8] Maybe they didn't even know that they were being written about. The student's public utterance about my project and method removed my cloak of distance by letting "the natives" know. Her utterance confirmed that a series of negotiations related to authority had to take place within this ethnographic endeavor.

These negotiations and this resulting ethnographic report are dialogical performances (a dialogical enterprise):[9] more hyphens that suture together my own multiple identities as well as relationships between me and the student, me and my informants (the women who work and frequent the salon), and me and my readers. While these negotiations oscillate between different modes of performance and different interlocutors, they are firmly linked to issues of accountability in shifting yet familiar territories. Accountability is related to performance competency in Bauman's sense and more: It is about revealing identity and purpose to informants, as well as justifying the significance of, and stakes in, the work to those who read this report. Here, accountability is evidenced as intense critical reflexivity on process, an activity in which I publicly process the mechanisms of my own labor, a process that is both a scholarly endeavor and a cultural performance.

The place of the hyphen in the role of the indigenous ethnographer, and in the construction of other complex identities, establishes a site of negotiation between place, space, and the politicized notion of situated location, *positionality.* In his essay "Aura and Agora: On Negotiating Rapture and Speaking Between," Homi Bhabha (1996) states:

Aligning negotiation with these systems of social exchange—language, action, signification, representation—places it as the center of modern life, at the cusp of the creation of commodities and the initiation of communication. Concerned primarily with the disclosure of human subject *as agent*, negotiation is the ability to articulate differences in space and signs and mediate what may seem to be incommensurable values or contradictory realities. (p. 8; italics in original)

Bhabha is actually discussing art, one quintessential expression of human desire; he uses the tensiveness that exists in the construction of *negotiating rapture* to generate an authoritative knowledge that embraces beauty. Yet these are the same variables that undergird the efficacy of ethnography, performance, and research. They are "incommensurable" relational values and "contradictory realities" that lie between intent and effect, between researcher and researched, between the perception of experience and the representation of experience, uneasily bridging gaps between the known and the unknown.

Conjoining these dynamics in a close analysis of any cultural site heightens the possibilities of knowing culture better. But this is not just culture as a marker of specialized practice informed by or cloistered within communities of particularly marked others, like black people in a black barbershop/salon. Culture is also an ensemble of everyday performance practices—life, research, and education—made up of diverse people who engage in performances based on location, commitment, and shared desire; all of them must attend to the multiplicity of roles and identities they carry with them across borders. All must negotiate the limits and possibilities of multifaceted performative identities and the shifting criteria on which those identities are evaluated in place and space.

The problem of ethnographic authority is sticky. In my encounter with the student in the salon, it involved claiming a positionality in a cultural site that established an approach to doing observational research and the ability to follow through, uninterrupted, with that research plan. This approach was simple because it was focused on opportunity and execution. It was complex because ethnographers can no more control the variables of their observations in the field than they can control their own responses to what happens there. This is the nexus of performance in everyday life ethnography: research that implicates the researcher as a cultural member with personal investments in a field that is as much about experience and location as it is about theory and methodology. The result is what Deborah Gordon (1990) describes as an ethnographic report in which authority is "dispersed [and] fragmented" (p. 162) and "polyvocal and conflictual" (p. 152).

Ethnographies of performance in/as everyday life are research and cultural engagements in which the complexities of identity politics complicate issues of membership and authority. They are processes in which the rules of engagement are known but cannot be predicted, where scripted social texts are performed improvisationally, known only in the moment of engagement with other texts that are always dialogically produced and messy.[10] This is all a part of the ethnographic moment and the inseparable positionality of participant-observer. And as James Clifford (1986) states in *Writing Culture*: "Here the ethnographer no longer holds unquestioned rights of salvage: the authority long associated with bringing elusive, 'disappearing' oral lore into legible textual form" (p. 17). In this case the lines between the researcher and the researched blurred and the issue of legibility was not of the story told but of who got to tell the story.

In the initial publication of my research in this site,[11] I chose not to include my encounter with the student. I chose to exclude the incident as a means of somehow recouping the integrity of the project, and because I did this, a certain "actuality of discursive situations and individual interlocutors [was] filtered out" (Clifford, 1983, p. 132). Later in consultation with the same colleague who directed the student to me, and in looking over my field notes, I realized the concentrated effort that I had put forth in avoiding a reality that had already affected the nature of my observational experience in the salon. While I tried to bracket the experience as tertiary to the observation and the writing of ethnography, it haunted me. The specter of that experience, and the apparent lack of resolution, beckoned me to revisit the meaningfulness of the event, how it served as an unexplored cultural artifact, and how I carried it with me each time I entered the site.

I came to understand that the nature of the encounter with the student in the salon was itself an aspect of the contestatory nature of cultural performance and everyday life research. "Performances articulate the divisions within a community by constructing, maintaining, reinforcing, or renegotiating the relationships amongst community's members" (Fuoss, 1995, p. 94). While we were teacher and student divided, we were also both black people joined in a cultural site that catered to black folk.

Maybe what she said (*"Did y'all know that he was observing and writing about all of you?"*) was intended as a playful acknowledgment of our common project?

Maybe it was meant as a friendly warning to the women in the shop of my *working presence* as participant-observer?

Maybe it was a method of confirming her legitimacy by questioning mine—maybe?

Maybe as we both entered this site, even with the knowledge of the other, the student and I assumed that the borders and boundaries of our own relational engagements would somehow allow us autonomy. But to what degree does any cultural member, ethnographer or otherwise, operate with autonomy, in isolation from the very mechanisms that dictate the doing and the culture that gives context to being and knowing? Like blood, cultural performance is a fluid connective tissue that links the body to community.

This has been a *twisted tale,* not in the sense of distortion or pathology, but in the way in which the hyphens in complex identities inserted themselves into the field of research. This resulted in descriptive entanglements, relational confusions, and desired deconstructions of cultural practices like the perceived impact and meaning of our encounter, which, in actuality, signaled a core characteristic of ethnography itself. For ethnography, like any good tale, is also interested in turning the external eye inward to penetrate cultural practices with understanding, sometimes twisting the continua of time and space, offering the reader/audience the opportunity to imagine him- or herself in the moment of the cultural experience.

In this tale I am implicated not only as the talebearer and ethnographer but also as an object lesson. In his introduction to Zora Neale Hurston's collection *Every Tongue Got to Confess: Negro Folktales from the Gulf Shores,* John Edgar Wideman (2001) says, "Language is treacherous, the tales school us. Interpretation, translation of words, leads to dangerous misapprehensions or not-so-funny predicaments" (p. xix). In the *telling of this tale*—I have been schooled. And I become both teacher and student, learning from my own lessons.

Notes

1. Here I am riffing on Della Pollock's (1990) "Telling the Told" essay, with the "told to" specifically referring to audience. I make another allusion to this text in the last sentence of the chapter.

2. I echo Denzin and Lincoln (1998) when they write: "Qualitative research involves the studied use and collection of a variety of empirical materials—case study, personal experience, introspective, life story, interview, observational, historical, interaction, and visual texts—that describe routine and problematic moments and meanings in individual's lives. Accordingly, qualitative researchers deploy a wide range of interconnected methods, hoping always to get at a better fix on the subject matter at hand" (p. 3).

3. I believe that this is what most of my work attempts to do.

4. Here I am making casual reference to two projects: first the edited volume by George W. Stocking, Jr. (1983) entitled *Observers Observed* that explores reflexive ethnography, and second the manner in which Michael Buraway (1991) writes about "observing the observers" and the fact that in ethnography, as "surveillers we do become visible and subject to countersurveillance, but it is not symmetrical.

Sooner or later we retreat behind the university walls, whereas our subjects remain to cope with the situation in which we found them" (p. 296).

5. About Zora Neale Hurston's *Dust Tracks,* Françoise Lionnet (1989) writes: "What the text puts in motion is a strategy of displacement regarding the expectations governing two modes of discourse: the 'objective' exteriority is that of the autobiographer whose 'inside search' does not bear out its promise of introspection, and the 'intimate' tone is that of the anthropologist who implicates herself in her 'research' by delving into Hoodoo, by performing initiation rites, and, in an ironic and clever reversal of the ventriloquism of ethnography, by letting her informants inform *us* about Zora's persona in the field" (p. 104).

6. Casey cites Lefebvre (1991, p. 62).

7. In some ways this construction signals Della Pollock's (1998) discussion of performative writing.

8. In writing about *ethnographic authority,* I struggle with the following constructions: a relational approach to interpretation using James Clifford's (1983) offerings of *experiential, interpretive, dialogical, and polyphonic* as stylistic guides or considerations; Clifford Geertz's (1973) use of *thick description* as a distancing positionality that foregrounds personal opinion and interpretation; and the way Richard Horwitz (1993) writes about issues of *accuracy* and *representation* in an attempt to capture experience.

9. Here I am alluding to Conquergood's (1985) "Performance as Moral Act" essay and also the manner in which Lionnet (1989) describes Zora Neale Hurston in *Dust Tracks* as being "[e]ngaged in a truly dialogical enterprise and not in the delusions of Boasian 'pure objectivity'" (p. 115) as she works in a field of some familiarity and identification.

10. Here I am referencing Denzin's (1997) construction of *messy texts*: "[M]any sited, [and] open ended, they refuse theoretical closure, and they do not indulge in abstract, analytic theorizing. They make the writer a part of the writing project. These texts, however, are not just subjective accounts of experience; they attempt to reflexively map multiple discourses that occur in a given social space. Hence, they are always multi-voiced, and no given interpretation is privileged. They reject the principles of the realist ethnographic narrative that makes claims to textual autonomy and to offering authoritative accounts of the processes being examined" (p. xvii).

11. See Alexander (2003), "Fading, Twisting and Weaving: An Interpretive Ethnography of the Black Barbershop as Cultural Space."

References

Adler, P. A., & Adler, P. (1998). Observational techniques. In N. K. Denzin & Y. S. Lincoln (Eds.), *Collecting and interpreting qualitative materials* (pp. 79–109). Thousand Oaks, CA: Sage.

Alexander, B. K. (2003). Fading, twisting and weaving: An interpretive ethnography of the black barbershop as cultural space. *Qualitative Inquiry, 9*(1), 101–128.

Austin, J. L. (1962). *How to do things with words.* New York: Oxford University Press.

Awkward, M. (1995). *Negotiating difference: Race, gender, and the politics of positionality.* Chicago: University of Chicago Press.

Bacon, W. A. (1979). *The art of interpretation* (3rd ed.). New York: Rinehart & Winston.

Bauman, R. (1977). *Verbal art as performance.* Rowley, MA: Newbury House.

Bhabha, H. K. (1994). How newness enters the world: Postmodern space, postcolonial times and the trials of cultural translations. In *The location of culture* (pp. 212–235). New York: Routledge.

Bhabha, H. K. (1996). Aura and agora: On negotiating rapture and speaking between. In R. Francis (Ed.), *Negotiating rapture: The power of art to transform lives* (pp. 8–17). Chicago: Museum of Contemporary Art.

Boal, A. (1979). *Theatre of the oppressed* (C. A. McBride & M. O. Leal McBride, Trans.). New York: Urizen.

Brettell, C. (Ed.). (1993). *When they read what we write.* Westport, CT: Bergin & Garvey.

Brody, J. D. (1995). Hyphen-nations. In S. E. Case, P. Brett, & S. L. Foster (Eds.), *Cruising the performative: Interventions into the representation of ethnicity, nationality, and sexuality* (pp. 149–162). Bloomington: Indiana University Press.

Buraway, M. (1991). Teaching participant observation. In M. A. Buraway, A. Burton, A. A. Ferguson, H. J. Fox, J. Gamson, N. Gatrell, et al. (Eds.), *Ethnography unbound: Power and resistance in the modern metropolis* (pp. 291–300). Berkeley: University of California Press.

Buzzard, J. (2003). On auto-ethnographic authority. *Yale Journal of Criticism, 16*(1), 61–91.

Casey, E. S. (2001). Body, self, and landscape: A geophilosophical inquiry into the place-world. In P. C. Adams, S. Hoelscher, & K. E. Till (Eds.), *Textures of place: Exploring humanist geographies* (pp. 403–425). Minneapolis: University of Minnesota Press.

Certeau, M. de. (1984). *The practice of everyday life* (Steven Rendall, Trans.). Berkeley: University of California Press.

Certeau, M., Giard, L., & Mayol, P. (Eds.). (1998). *The practice of everyday life: Vol. 2. Living and cooking* (T. J. Tomasik, Trans.). Minneapolis: University of Minnesota Press.

Clark, A. H. (1962). Praemia geographiae: The incidental rewards of a professional career. *Annals of the Association of American Geographers, 52,* 229–241.

Clifford, J. (1983). On ethnographic authority. *Representations, 1*(2), 118–146.

Clifford, J. (1986). Introduction. In J. Clifford & G. E. Marcus (Eds.), *Writing culture: The poetics and politics of ethnography* (pp. 1–17). Berkeley: University of California Press.

Conquergood, D. (1985). Performing as a moral act: Ethical dimensions of the ethnography of performance. *Literature in Performance, 5,* 1–13.

Couclelis, H. (1992). Location, place, region and space. In R. F. Abler, M. G. Marcus, & J. M. Olson (Eds.), *Geography's inner worlds: Pervasive themes in contemporary American geography* (pp. 215–233). New Brunswick, NJ: Rutgers University Press.

Curry, M. (2001). The fragmented individual and the academic realm. In P. C. Adams, S. Hoelscher, & K. E. Hill (Eds.), *Textures of place: Exploring humanist geographies* (pp. 207–220). Minneapolis: University of Minnesota Press.

Darder, A. (1991). *Culture and power in the classroom: A critical foundation for bicultural education.* New York: Bergin & Garvey.

Denzin, N. (1997). *Interpretive ethnography: Ethnographic practices for the 21st century.* Thousand Oaks, CA: Sage.

Denzin, N. K., & Lincoln, Y. S. (1998). Introduction: Entering the field of qualitative research. In N. K. Denzin & Y. S. Lincoln (Eds.), *Strategies of qualitative inquiry* (pp. 1–34). Thousand Oaks, CA: Sage.

Erickson, F. (1986). Qualitative methods in research on teaching. In M. C. Wittrock (Ed.), *Handbook of research on teaching* (3rd ed., pp. 119–161). New York: Macmillan.

Erickson, K. F. (1967). A comment on disguised observation in sociology. *Social Problems, 14,* 366–373.

Fine, E. C., & Speer, J. H. (Eds.). (1992). *Performance culture and identity.* Westport, CT: Praeger.

Fuoss, K. W. (1993). Performance as contestation: An agonistic perspective on the insurgent assembly. *Text and Performance Quarterly, 13*(4), 331–349.

Fuoss, K. W. (1995). "Community" contested, imagined, and performed: Cultural performance, contestation, and community in an organized-labor social drama. *Text and Performance Quarterly, 15,* 79–98.

Geertz, C. (1973). *The interpretation of cultures.* New York: Basic Books.

Glaser, B. (1978). *Theoretical sensitivity.* Mill Valley, CA: Sociological Press.

Goffman, E. (1974). *Frame analysis: An essay on the organization of experience.* New York: Harper Colophon.

Gordon, D. (1990). The politics of ethnographic authority: Race and writing in the ethnography of Margaret Mead and Zora Neale Hurston. In M. Manganaro (Ed.), *Modernist anthropology: From fieldwork to text* (pp. 146–162). Princeton, NJ: Princeton University Press.

Guss, D. M. (2000). *The festive state: Race, ethnicity, and nationalism as cultural performance.* Berkeley: University of California Press.

Hamera, J. (1999). Editor's note. *Text and Performance Quarterly, 19*(3).

Harper, P. B. (1996). *Are we not men.* Oxford, UK: Oxford University Press.

Henderson, M. G. (Ed.). (1995). *Borders, boundaries, and frames: Cultural criticism and cultural studies.* New York: Routledge.

Horwitz, R. P. (1993). Just stories of ethnographic authority. In C. Brettell (Ed.), *When they read what we write* (pp. 132–143). Westport, CT: Bergin & Garvey.

Humphreys, L. (1975). *Tearoom trade: Impersonal sex in public places.* New York: Aldine.

Hurston, Z. N. (1996). *Dust tracks on a road.* New York: HarperCollins. (Original work published 1942)

Lefebvre, H. (1991). *Production of space* (D. N. Smith, Trans.). Oxford, UK: Blackwell.

Lionnet, F. (1989). *Autobiographical voices: Race, gender, self-portraiture.* Ithaca, NY: Cornell University Press.

Mayol, P. (1998). Propriety. In M. de Certeau, L. Giard, & P. Mayol (Eds.), *The practice of everyday life: Vol. 2. Living and cooking* (pp. 15–34). (T. J. Tomasik, Trans.). Minneapolis: University of Minnesota Press.

McGreevy, P. (2001). Attending to the void: Geography and madness. In P. C. Adams, S. Hoelscher, & K. E. Till (Eds.), *Textures of place: Exploring humanist geographies* (pp. 246–256). Minneapolis: University of Minnesota Press.

Mohanty, S. P. (1989). Us and them: On the philosophical bases of political criticism. *Yale Journal of Criticism, 2*(2), 1–31.

Munro, R. (1997). Introduction. In K. Hetherington & R. Munro (Eds.), *Ideas of difference* (pp. 3–24). Malden, MA: Blackwell.

Pollock, D. (1990). Telling the told: Performing like a family. *Oral History, 18*, 1–36.

Pollock, D. (1998). Performative writing. In P. Phelan & J. Lane (Eds.), *The ends of performance* (pp. 73–103). New York: New York University Press.

Relph, E. (2001). The critical description of confused geographies. In P. C. Adams, S. Hoelscher, & K. E. Till (Eds.), *Textures of place: Exploring humanist geographies* (pp. 150–166). Minneapolis: University of Minnesota Press.

Rose, D. (1990). *Living the ethnographic life.* Newbury Park, CA: Sage.

Said, E. W. (1994). *Culture and imperialism.* New York: Vintage.

Silverman, H. J. (1998). *Cultural semiosis: Tracing the signifier.* New York: Routledge.

Snead, J. (1990). European pedigrees/African contagions: Nationality, narrative, and communality in Tutuola, Achebe, and Reed. In H. K. Bhabha (Ed.), *Nation and narration* (pp. 231–249). New York: Routledge.

Stocking, G. W. (Ed.). (1983). *Observers observed: Essays on ethnographic fieldwork.* Madison: University of Wisconsin Press.

Turner, V. (1988). *The anthropology of performance.* New York: PAJ.

Vélez-Ibáñez, C. G. (1996). *Border visions: Mexican cultures of the Southwest United States.* Tucson: University of Arizona Press.

West, C. (1991). The dilemma of the black intellectual. In b. hooks & C. West (Eds.), *Breaking bread: Insurgent black intellectual life* (pp. 131–146). Boston: South End.

Wideman, J. E. (2001). Foreword. In J. E. Wideman (Ed.), *Every tongue got to confess: Negro folk-tales from the Gulf states* (pp. xi–xx). New York: HarperCollins.

Wolcott, H. F. (1999). *Ethnography: A way of seeing.* Walnut Creek: AltaMira.

Woodward, D. (1992). Representations of the world. In R. F. Abler, M. G. Marcus, & J. M. Olson (Eds.), *Geography's inner worlds: Pervasive themes in contemporary American geography* (pp. 50–73). New Brunswick, NJ: Rutgers University Press.

II

Animating Locations

Introduction

Judith Hamera

In critical communication and cultural studies, space is not simply an inert context, a barren stage waiting for actors to show up. On the contrary, it is itself an actor, produced by and, in turn, producing communicative possibilities materialized by embodied subjects. In her study of the global city, Janet L. Abu-Lughod (1999) characterized the urban context in dynamic performative, communicative terms:

> The built environment is *not* organic, although it may often appear chaotically unplanned. It has been created and is continually being re-created, albeit by collectivities of social actors engaged in complex dances of successive and symbiotic interactions. These interactions continually weave together nature, materials, techniques, socioeconomic processes, and cultural forms to generate the urban fabric—a transitory expression in space that, like any work of art, derives its meanings more from observers' responses than from creators' intentions. (pp. 4–5)

But this is not only true of the built environment. Mark Neumann (1999) presents the Grand Canyon as a spectacular example of nature creating discourses even as it is created by them.

> I treat the Grand Canyon as a monumental space of public discourses spoken and written by planners, politicians, preservationists, institutions, artists, entrepreneurs, and commercial industries who treat the Grand Canyon as a tourist destination, a spectacle of nature, and a site for an expression of modern representational politics since the end of the nineteenth century. Since that time, commercial, scientific, and aesthetic discourses have framed and tamed the canyon's landscapes for tourists. . . . [C]ontemporary tourists make the scene by making it their own. (p. 11)

Space, writes Certeau (1984), is a practiced place. Space is multivocal, characterized by perpetual possibilities for transformation. Place is univocal, stable, proper. This distinction crosses both vernacular landscapes (Jackson, 1984) and official monuments; sometimes it describes the processes by which one insinuates itself into the other. Performance-based analysis offers a theoretical lens and a vocabulary for examining the communicative, cultural production and reproduction of place and space.

Here, the notion of the performative is especially useful. A performative does something. It makes something happen. It activates and creates. Judith Butler (1993) characterizes the performative as the "power of discourse to reproduce effects through reiteration" (p. 20); these effects constitute an iden-tity position, which repetition then stabilizes. Butler (1990) is reluctant to claim rhetorical power for the overtly theatrical (p. 278), but Elin Diamond (1996) opens up possibilities for a more expansive relationship between performance as a critical paradigm, performance per se, and performativity, one especially conducive to examining the social production of place. She writes:

> When performativity materializes as performance in that risky and dangerous negotiation between a doing (a reiteration of norms) and a thing done (discursive conventions that frame our interpretations), between someone's body and the conventions of embodiment, we have access to cultural meanings and critique. (p. 5)

"Doing" is an embodied utterance; it challenges or reinforces conventions of use, "things done." Performative "doings" produce place by tracing over prior acts to actualize specific possibilities and foreclose others in multivocal space. The reverse might also be true. We can imagine some doings that evade typical conventions of embodiment—discursive jaywalking—that erase stability in place (the "things done"); here multivocal space might be performatively produced. This productive "unmaking" of proper place is what Ash Amin and Nigel Thrift (2002) mean when they observe that "[e]ach urban moment can spark performative improvisations which are unforeseen and unforeseeable. This is not a naïve vitalism, but it is a politics of hope" (p. 4), and one not unique to urban analysis, as J. B. Jackson (1984) reminds us.

The two essays in "Animating Locations" analyze both of these operations. In "Looking for Stonewall's Arm," Michael Bowman examines tourists' productions of places even, indeed especially, when they depart from stable, proper itineraries. Such departures are inevitable and a form of critique, a way of unmaking official sites so as to hear other voices in different ways. Sonja Kuftinec explores the violent oscillations between space and place in

"Bridging Haunted Places." Here, during two upheavals in the recent Balkan civil wars, a literal bridge became the symbolic axis around which these oscillations from space to place, and the reverse, fluctuated. Kuftinec, with her collaborators, attempted to reproduce and interrogate these spatial dynamics, and their material consequences, with and for the residents of this city in Herzegovina using an actual performance.

In "Place in Fiction," Eudora Welty (1977) writes: "Location is the cross-roads of circumstance, the proving ground of 'What happened? Who's here? Who's coming?'–and that is the heart's field" (p. 118). Likewise, Alan Gussow (1971) observes, "A place is a piece of the whole environment that has been claimed by human feelings" (p. 27). *A performance approach* *recognizes the affective dimensions embedded in space and place.* Places of the heart and fantasy geographies have material and communal dimensions, as Bowman and Kuftinec remind us. Both offer arguments that resonate strongly with Edward W. Soja's (1996) conception of "thirdspace." Using the work of French critical cultural theorist Henri Lefebvre, Soja posits thirdspace to describe the embodied social and historical aspects of spatial production (pp. 50–51, 70–71); space is simultaneously lived, perceived, and conceived (p. 74). "Thirdspace" is his attempt to capture the material and affective complexities in "what is actually a constantly shifting and changing milieux of ideas, events, appearances, and meanings" (p. 2). This is precisely what Dolores Hayden (1997) means when she talks about the potential "power of place—the power of ordinary urban landscapes to nurture citizens' public memory, to encompass shared time in the form of shared territory" for working-class residents (p. 9). It also undergirds Neumann's (1999) reading of the Grand Canyon as a monumental performance venue.

> The Grand Canyon offers many *theaters* or *stages* for social display, consumption, and production where people seek experiences at a distance from the routines of everyday life. The Grand Canyon holds many geographies that appear at the intersections of lives as they are both lived and imagined—symbolic construction of public space and private life—where exterior and interior landscapes are dramatized in the interplay of space, time, and social performance. (p. 10)

Both Bowman and Kuftinec animate thirdspaces in their critiques. In them, history is inseparable from geography, and the rigors of "state" production or destruction meet the play of private consumption. Here, fantasies of what should or could be, or of what's left out or left over, meet the literal markers and residues that attempt to fix place in space. Moreover, both authors offer methodological tools—critical geography, tourist practice, performance per se—that illuminate and remake space and place as sites of scholarly inquiry.

References

Abu-Lughod, J. L. (1999). *New York, Chicago, Los Angeles: America's global cities.* Minneapolis: University of Minnesota Press.

Amin, A., & Thrift, N. (2002). *Cities: Reimagining the urban.* Cambridge, UK: Polity.

Butler, J. (1990). Performative acts and gender constitution: An essay in phenomenology and feminist thought. In S. E. Case (Ed.), *Performing feminisms: Feminist critical theory and theatre* (pp. 270–282). Baltimore: Johns Hopkins University Press.

Certeau, M. de. (1984). *The practice of everyday life* (Vol. 1; S. Rendall, Trans.). Berkeley: University of California Press.

Diamond, E. (1996). Introduction. In E. Diamond (Ed.), *Performance and cultural politics* (pp. 1–12). New York: Routledge.

Gussow, A. (1971). *A sense of place: The artist and the American land.* San Francisco: Friends of the Earth.

Hayden, D. (1997). *The power of place: Urban landscape as public history.* Cambridge, MA: MIT Press.

Jackson, J. B. (1984). *Discovering the vernacular landscape.* New Haven, CT: Yale University Press.

Neumann, M. (1999). *On the rim: Looking for the Grand Canyon.* Minneapolis: University of Minnesota Press.

Soja, E. W. (1996). *Thirdspace: Journeys to Los Angeles and other real-and-imagined places.* Oxford, UK: Blackwell.

Welty, E. (1977). Place in fiction. In *The eye of the story.* New York: Vintage.

3

Bridging Haunted Places

Performance and the Production of Mostar

Sonja Arsham Kuftinec

It is this bridge [the Stari Most] which became Mostar's symbol. Around this magnificent Old Bridge, the nucleus of the town developed forming a single architectural entity. . . . [D]espite all the misfortunes suffered, the Old Bridge has survived to grace the town to the present day. It is both a work of exceptional architectural beauty and a vibrant witness to the past.

Yugoslav Tourist Bureau, *Guide Book to Mostar*, 1989

(state produced)

On the 9th of November 1993, during the civil war, the bridge was destroyed by shelling, and, in a few hours, a masterpiece of the past times, an example of the ancient constructive technique, and an element of regional identity was definitely cancelled. . . . [N]obody, such as Bosnian people and Mostar citizens, is able to understand deeply the real meaning of such a loss.

M. Romeo and M. Mela, "Overview of Stari Most: Rehabilitation Design of the Old Bridge of Mostar"

post-war

It's true that the city is being reconstructed, but bridges, buildings, and parks never made a town; what made it was the people living in it.

Sonja Arsham Kuftinec, Scot McElvany, and
Geoff Sobelle, directors, *Where Does the Postman Go
When All the Street Names Change?* performed in Mostar, 1997

These three narratives, figuratively producing and reproducing Mostar's four-centuries-old Stari Most (Old Bridge), arise from a vast stream of rhetoric constituting the city's varied histories, cultural heritage, trauma, and projected recovery via the bridge. Like the stony fragments of the bridge, exhumed from the Neretva River for reconstructive analysis and later archival preservation, they tell a set of stories that reveal as much about those who use the bridge symbolically as about those who use it practically. The Stari Most figures tropologically as well as topologically in how individuals and the city identify, map, and remap themselves along the fault lines of a brutal internecine war.[1] As a multiethnic city located in Herzegovina, a region dominated in the early 1990s by the Croatian Defense Force (HVO), Mostar bore the brunt of two violent power struggles. In 1992, Bosnians with Croatian Catholic and Muslim affiliations fought together against aggressor Bosnian Serb forces. Shortly thereafter, the HVO turned against Muslims, destroying the Stari Most and resettling the city through an orchestrated campaign of terror. Following this campaign, the Neretva River, which once divided old east Mostar from its newer areas in the west, effectively divided Bosnian Muslims from Croats. This chapter works to illuminate the fault lines of this struggle, with particular attention to how spatial practices and stories—performance in the street and near the street—reshape the body and the body politic. The writing is fueled by my own past and attachments to a Croatian/Yugoslav ancestry, by memories of walking through Mostar, and by time spent forging performances such as *Postar (Postman)*—creating spaces of witness for others and attending myself to the stories that continue to haunt the city. I am driven to remember Mostar here by the question of how it will be remembered institutionally as well as through the bodies of those who continue to walk its streets and the most famous of its bridges.

It remains difficult to discuss the urban terrain of Mostar without referencing the destruction and reconstruction of the Stari Most, built under Turkish rule in the late 1500s. It is almost as difficult to avoid clichéd statements about the bridge's symbolic resonance. If the Stari Most had not been destroyed by HVO artillery in 1993, it might have collapsed under the figurative burden it bore in the years leading up to and following the war. But this same figuration offers a way into the various constitutions of Mostar before and after the rupturing event of the 1991–95 war and consequent destruction of the bridge.

The first epigraph above, from a state-produced tourist guide to Mostar, was written in English in 1989, on the cusp of war within a still nominally unified Yugoslavia. While pointing to the Stari Most as an aesthetic object of craft and grace, the guide foregrounds the bridge via its representational function as both an image of the city and its unifying center. Physical location links to structures of feeling; Mostar is cohesive and organic, a cell with the bridge as "nucleus." The purpose of the bridge appears metaphoric (nuclear), metonymic (symbolic of the city), and anthropomorphically historiographic (the bridge as survivor of and witness to history). Significantly, though the bridge figures both as a link to the past and as a unifying locus, its purpose as either a physical or a symbolic connector between two distinct sides of the city is not mentioned. In this prior era of official South Slavic unity, when many Serbs, Croats, and Muslims lived side by side in Mostar, the city officially imagined itself as a unified whole.

After the war, and particularly after the Stari Most's destruction, external accounts rewrite the city's heritage as one of divisions bridged. The United Nations Educational, Scientific and Cultural Organization (UNESCO), a key sponsor of the Stari Most's reconstruction, refers to a population that "saw the bridge as a symbol of peace and reconciliation between the peoples of Bosnia and Herzegovina."[2] Reconciliation implies something already torn apart. The unified organism imagined by the state-produced guide is here read back into history and reconfigured as a link between separate entities: east and west, Bosnian and Herzegovina, Muslim and Croat. The bridge additionally moves onto the (Western) world stage as a way to make sense of a war that implicated, before it directly involved, Europe and the United States. An October 2003 60 Minutes piece constructs a fairly typical narrative (Safer, 2003). Before the war, the bridge stands for ethnic unity and integration, linking the east and west banks of the city. During the war, the bridge, "battered, broken, but still standing," signifies survival, endurance, and the possibility of reconciliation. The destruction of the bridge then signals the collapse of common history, as its reconstruction evokes the possibility of a reintegrated future, "rebuilding the city's lost past."

But to focus on the bridge as either an architectural or a symbolic entity that can be physically and historically reconstructed neglects it as a void or site of trauma, a wound in memory surpassing rational understanding and descriptive language, denying the possibility of healing without a scar. The

Engineering Workgroup's narrative of events on its reconstruction Web site evokes this loss but does not seem to know how to build it into their reconstructed bridge (Romeo & Mela, n.d.). Michael Ignatieff, a cultural theorist speaking on *60 Minutes,* indirectly acknowledges their flaw, and that of the United States in pushing the bridge's reconstruction as a form of nation building. "Don't think you can impose reconciliation. Bitterness runs very deep, you can't plaster over that stuff." Personification of the bridge in various accounts further underlines the trauma suffered by Mostar's citizens. An anonymous comment on Mostar Online (1998) on the damage done to Mostar during the war slips between depiction of the city's symbolic rape and the actual rape and destruction of its citizenry. The writer records his inability to document the destruction witnessed, feeling as if he were taking a photo of a woman who had been brutally raped and butchered. He castigates those who would erase these wounds of memory in a blindly optimistic goal of reconciliation. "Now the foreigners come telling [Mostar's citizens] don't worry, be happy, live together again and be reconciled." But you can't plaster over this stuff. A rebuilt bridge won't heal a traumatic wound.

In response to the dilemma of resisting the total erasure of unrepresentable absence, architects such as Daniel Libeskind and Lebbeus Woods have structured voids into their edifices. Libeskind's Jewish Museum in Berlin and design proposal for a new World Trade Center both conjure that which can be neither represented nor forgotten. Inaccessible yet visible columns of space loom throughout the Jewish Museum. The tension between memory and movement grounds Libeskind's WTC design, which seeks to emerge from rather than replicate the destroyed towers. In his essay "No-Man's Land," Lebbeus Woods (2000) refers to voids as "spaces of crisis" where "the entire elaborate superstructure of social and personal relationships, built up over lifetimes, is called into question" (p. 199). Woods speaks from a perspective familiar to human geographers who propose that *who* we are intimately connects to *where* we are, construing space as a network of relationships and connections rather than as a set of boundaries and exclusions. Phenomenologists such as Yi Fu Tuan (1977) cite place as space transformed by memories and feelings accrued over time. For Mostarians, the Stari Most embraces a series of attachments, rituals of walking, the feel of stone under feet, the sensation of height over the river below. The violent rupture of those perceptions and relationships, coupled with the material destruction of place, physically and psychically remapped the city.

Trauma can lead to at least temporary psychic erasure, an effort to repress the memory of the wounding event. Woods (2000) implies that spaces of crisis may, in contrast, lead to revelation rather than erasure. The collapse of a structure can lay bare its inner workings. Within Mostar's dissolution the cultural, legal, and political disciplinary systems struggling to forge new identities and histories through the city were rendered visible. At the same time, individual, tactical resistances to these systems emerged, particularly relating to the control over and production of space.

Michel de Certeau (1984) proposes a distinction between these kinds of tactical resistances and more authoritative strategies in analyzing the relationship of behavior to power and place. Strategies refer to those actions undertaken by subjects within a *"propre"* (p. xix), a physical location established in part by discourses of legitimacy (a proprietor, a city). Strategies to define (or redefine) Mostar include the printing of city maps, the establishment of a postal service and its limits, and the renaming of city streets. Strategic power, however, is bound by its very visibility in space, as in order to function effectively, this kind of power must be easily perceived. Tactics, in contrast, depend on time, on subjects without a "proper" place recognizing opportunities for interventions to play in the foundations of visible power, to literally walk a different path from that which is formally laid out. Henri Lefebvre suggests that these authoritative foundations and frameworks negotiate among various modes to produce space.

In *The Production of Space* (1991), Lefebvre posits that space is actively created through negotiations among the conceived, the perceived, and the lived. He identifies conceived space as dominant, tied to the production of order. This is the realm of strategies: of urban planning, bureaucracy, and surveillance, of maps, capital, and visual control. In Mostar the struggle for power over conceived space revealed itself in hastily constructed official maps of "Croatian" west Mostar, visibly erasing the city's mostly Muslim east side. Perceived space, produced by memory, routine, and social relationships, remains the traditional focus of human geographers such as Tuan. Lefebvre details this mode as the domain of spatial practices that "secrete society" (p. 33) by forging routes, networks, and patterns of interaction among locations of work, play, and leisure. The performance of everyday life in Mostar both conformed to and tactically resisted the boundaries delineated by the west side's conceptual maps as individuals chose to cross or avoid particular streets and bridges.

Lived space overlays physical space; it is the locus of "passion, action, and of lived situations" that conceptual space seeks to dominate and rationalize (Lefebvre, 1991, p. 42). Within lived space, the cultural geographer Edward Soja (1996) identifies what he terms a "thirdspace" of struggle and resistance to the conceived order. The thirdspace embraces the realm of art, in which representations of power signal the power of representation. When the real and the imagined intersect, as in the space of theater performed in the city, a "counterspace" may emerge in relation to the centrally ordered conceived space. Michel Foucault (1986) describes this kind of counterspace as a heterotopia, a site related to other sites in a way that reflects and inverts them, "a simultaneous mythic and real contestation of the space in which we live" (p. 24). An outdoor theatrical performance such as *Where Does the Postman Go When All The Street Names Change?*, which I co-directed in 1997, most directly inhabits this counterspace of myth and materiality. Yet Lefebvre's understanding of how intersections of the conceptual, the perceptual, and the corporeal produce space suggests multiple roles for performance as a paradigm and particularly as a practice. These include performance in everyday life, performance as a rhetoric of confrontation and resistance, performance as art, and combinations of all three. Apprehending the interactions among these various performances remains key to understanding the production of power and identity, as well as space, in Mostar.

"Producing" Mostar

Grounded in Marxist theory, Lefebvre (1991) proposes that the conceptual and material separation of spatial modes ensures mass consent. Neglecting the connections among conceived, perceived, and lived space obscures how the production of space also reproduces the status quo, thus eliding the intersubjective relationships that forge authority and power. A map of a city cannot exist without the authority to produce it and the schematics to read it. Lefebvre warns, however, that "once construction [of a certain kind of power and authority] is complete, the scaffolding is taken down," thus concealing its origins (p. 113). In a space of crisis, however, as in a state of war, the scaffolding as well as the inner workings of power may visibly reemerge.

In the mid-1990s Mostar could be perceived as a palimpsest of spatial contestation that rendered visible operations of power within the city. Hastily redesigned urban architecture and changing street names (conceived space), redefined pedestrian routes (spatial practices), and a youth theater festival reappropriating bombed-out buildings and street corners (spaces of representations) negotiated the production of space, meaning, and memory in Mostar. The destruction of the Stari Most is only the most obvious, symbolically laden example.

Spatial control in Mostar can seem deceptively easy to read if one accepts notions of bounded, cohesive ethnic identity, a corollary to assuming clearly defined nation-state borders. The 1993 bridge shelling did work to enforce division within the city, but only when accompanied by aggressive resettlement and the forced rethinking of identity. This physical violence, coupled with symbolic violence, draws attention to the complexity of identity in Mostar and the persistence of enforced taxonomies of difference.[3] Assumptions of equivalence between subject and label, territory and ethnicity, make little sense in Bosnia. This systemization reflects the thinking of a "Classical" episteme, which Foucault (1970) describes as obsessive in utilizing difference to establish identity. But differential systems held little currency in the actual practice of forging relationships and self-identities in former Yugoslavia. Before the war, few of the youth I worked with even knew the religious affiliations of their peers; under Marshall Tito's totalitarian socialist regime (1946–80), few urban Bosnians actively practiced their religions. The youth saw themselves less as Croat or Muslim than as Bosnian or Yugoslav, or, more frequently, as poets, musicians, spurned lovers. But violence can remake even the most hybrid and open identities.[4]

While the bridge's destruction marked a split between "Muslim" east and "Croat" west Mostar, social and spatial practices continued to complicate this reading. Intermarriage, prewar friendships, and the presence of Muslims in west Mostar, and Bosnian Serbs on both sides, rendered enforced conceptual boundaries more fluid. Spatial practices also continued to defy conceptual mapping as old "Muslim" Mostar, and Mostarians crossed the Neretva, spilling onto the "Croatian" west side of the bank. Additionally, an urban site on the conceived west draws a different line through the city—the front line of the war fought between nominally Muslim and Croat forces. This street of bombed-out, crater-marked building shells runs parallel to the Neretva, marking with blood and bullet holes the city's division against itself.

The shifting names of a street near the front line offer yet another site from which to read the dynamics of change in the city. Before 1992, the street was known as "Santiceva," after a Serbian poet. Following the Bosnian Serb army's aggression against the city in 1992, Mostar's then Muslim-Croat coalition renamed the street "Ricina," after a former community leader. After nationalist HVO forces claimed the west side of the city, they renamed part of the street "Dr. Mile Budaka," after a Croatian man known as a hero to nationalist Croats and as a fascist war criminal to others. Yet, as Tuan notes, attachments to place can supersede their official conception, and differential usage marks both the persistence and erasure of meaning as each name haunts the others. Nationalist Croats inscribe their affiliation by renaming the streets of west Mostar with their heroes. Others persist in calling the streets by their prewar Yugoslav names or by their remembered use. Each practice defies the others, disrupting efforts to maintain or erase a cohesive past.

Absences and presences such as these evoke the Derridean notion of "hauntologie," in which present meaning and use are always already haunted by a past, by the attachments of memory (Derrida, 1994). The street once had a very different use value, serving as a main thoroughfare and pedestrian route in the city. By 1997 it stood as a "no-man's land," a void haunted by the presence of potentially live grenades in its ruins. The former everyday performances that defined the street as a thoroughfare, a route from home to school, ghost its present decay, just as the shell of a school bus once carrying children of both "sides" to undivided schools shadows the street, a material sign of both unity and division.

Conceptual and practiced remappings of the city accompany its physical reconstruction, underlining interactions between the material and the symbolic, the pedestrian and the political. Jean Baudrillard (1983) discusses this interaction in terms of the "precession of the simulacra," in which symbols become detached from and potentially redefine their social contexts and references. Baudrillard suggests that in this world of the "hyperreal," the simulacrum guides the reformation of that which it purports to represent: "the map precedes the territory" (p. 2).

This dominance of conceptually produced space had material consequences for all Bosnians. Following a 1992 conference in London to work toward a peace negotiation, the international community appointed Lord Owen of Great Britain and former Secretary of State Cyrus Vance of the United States to work out a plan for the reconstitution of Bosnia. In October 1992 Vance and Owen drew up a map of Bosnia-Herzegovina that divided the country into 10 regional cantons. When they presented their map at the Geneva Conference in early 1993, the cantons had been labeled "Serb," "Croat," and "Muslim," with one "Muslim-Croat" canton and one "mixed" canton around the capital city of Sarajevo. While appointing policing powers to each individual canton, the Vance-Owen plan also called for the return of refugees. Thus, in their thinking, the cantons were not to be pure ethno-religious states but simply "under the control" of the groups labeled on the maps. Rather than representing any kind of present or historical reality, however, the map preceded the territory.

The map unintentionally encouraged further land grabbing that essentially cleansed cantons of inhabitants other than those labeled as the majority. Ethnologist Michael Sells (1996) asserts, "[W]hen the [Bosnian Croat forces] saw that the Serb army would be [territorially] rewarded for its [cleansing of Muslims], it began copying them" (p. 101). According to Sells, after the Bosnian Serbs rejected the original Vance-Owen map, Thorvald Stoltenberg and Owen produced a new map that, in Owen's words, recognized "reality on the ground" (p. 100). This "reality," marking Serb and Croat-held territory in Bosnia-Herzegovina, was in fact preceded and guided by the Vance-Owen map. By September of 1995, the territory again matched the map. Reporters Laura Silber and Allan Little (1997) affirm, "The map that emerged from September's battles—or, at least, the share of territory that it allocated—was consistent with the peace plan that had been put together by [U.S. diplomats]" (p. 368).

The map produced by west Mostar shortly after the U.S.-sponsored Dayton Peace Accords offers yet another example of symbolic power and the production of conceptual space. One of the principles signed by the Bosnian representatives in Dayton called for the reunification of Mostar. From license plates, to currency, to language, schooling, and maps, not a single official sign in the decidedly separate west Mostar conformed to this principle. Instead of reconnecting what had been blown apart, west Mostar officials sought to merge with the pseudostate of Herceg-Bosna, a unified string of municipalities in Herzegovina with its own armed forces. Founder Mate Boban imposed Croatian-style government and schooling; the Croatian dinar (later kuna) became the official currency of the territory, and "Croatian" its official language.[5] While the Dayton Accords formally erased Herceg-Bosna, its not-so-spectral remains continued to haunt Mostar and the de facto reality of the accords.[6]

Baudrillard (1983) elaborates on the paradoxical relationship between simulation and reality, pointing out that simulated illness can produce "real" symptoms (p. 5). In the case of Herceg-Bosna, simulations of its existence combated the international community's dissimulation, or pretense that the para-state did not exist. Herceg-Bosna did not in fact legally exist. Nor was it internationally recognized as a state. Yet in 1997 simulations of its existence and ties to the Croatian government were literally everywhere, situating and defining both Herceg-Bosna and "west" Mostar. ID cards issued on the west side identified individuals as living in Herceg-Bosna. Radio and television stations announced news "from the Herceg-Bosna region." The Croat Sehovnica, a red-and-white checkered crest, hung from lamp posts and in shop windows and was stamped on buildings. Cars registered on the west side sported Croat rather than Bosnian license plates. Banks announced themselves as "Croatian National" and changed kuna, deutsche marks, and most major international currency but would not change these currencies to Bosnian dinars. Xeroxed photos posted around west Mostar celebrated the ultranationalist Bosnian Croat Mafia Godfather "Tuta" as "our hero." Police officers from the west wore Herceg-Bosna patches.

Yet despite efforts to create a Herceg-Bosna and Croatian west Mostar, everyday spatial practices and representations of space also participated in the ongoing production of Mostar. Traces of traumatic memories broke through their repression, reemerging in ghost-written graffiti that challenged officially conceived space. A sign near the absent Stari Most warns pedestrians, "Don't Forget." The bridge reappeared in representational forms sketched out on the city walls with a caption insisting, "Ovo je Mostar!" (This is Mostar). Pedestrians as well as politicians remapped the city. While most inhabitants changed their spatial practices during the war, altering patterns of walking to conform to officially enforced divisions, the presence of a multiethnic youth center in west Mostar defied the conceptual border drawn between Mostar's teenagers.

Though located on the "Croatian" west side of Mostar, Mladi Most functions as an open center for youth of all backgrounds to mix in a social setting. The name, meaning "Youth Bridge," references the center's purpose as it recalls the absent "Old Bridge." In 1997, when I worked with youth at the center, Mladi Most incorporated a game room, weekly meals and movies, football tournaments, a magazine, and theater workshops, all of which blended "Croat" with "Muslim" and "Serb." In all of these lived spaces, the youth made a point of not asserting divisions of identity among themselves. These less bounded social relations, alongside the spatial practices of gathering at the center, threatened those whose power and identity derived from the city's division. They assaulted Mladi Most with rocks, verbal insults, gunfire, and grenades. In a personal e-mail (Feb. 2, 1997), volunteer Scot McElvany reported, "Tonight we were threatened by a crazy drunk bastard roaming the streets shouting, 'This is Croatia! I want to see a Croatian flag in front of your house in 15 minutes or I'll call everyone I know in the Croatian Defense Council!" This cry for a marker to clearly define "Croatian" Mostar once again draws attention to the need for power to locate itself strategically—visibly and symbolically.

While Mladi Most thus functioned as a resistant oasis to conceived spatial authority, it also led to the production of an even more provocative countersite. A theatrical heterotopia represented, inverted, and reproduced Mostar while simultaneously reflecting on the city's dissolution. This imagined construction of the city, *Pisma (Letters)* or *Where Does the Postman Go When All the Street Names Change?*, premiered at Mostar's International Days of Youth Theater Festival in August 1997. Presented near the street, outside any officially constituted theatrical places, with selected debris from the city its only stage props, *Postar (Postman)* worked to simultaneously engage an actual and a fictional Mostar, reproducing and producing the city through a set of stylistically varied spatial stories.

Performance Near the Street: Reproducing Mostar

I had been creating original performances with youth in the Balkans since 1995, when the idea for *Postar* arose from a walk in the city. As I stood with

McElvany, my artistic collaborator, on a small stone bridge overlooking the city's remains, we discussed theater as a site of remembering, envisioning an original performance that could momentarily put together Mostar for participants and audience. Over several months in 1997, McElvany and I worked with eight youth from Mladi Most and a third collaborator, Geoff Sobelle, to develop a piece that bore witness to the youths' experience while seeking to avoid a replication of their trauma. As architects of the project, we worked to build a performance with a void.

In generative workshops, participants decided that the piece would be about Mostar without directly referencing the city or the war that had divided it. A simulacrum, a "not-Mostar," would take Mostar's place, as the structure of the piece followed life in "the City" before, during, and after an event that was "not-the-war." This mythic Mostar, performed in the "real" Mostar, evolved around signs of the city and communication within it: maps, street signs, and the delivery of letters. Postar thus engaged conceptual, perceived, and lived space, alluding to while often inverting a variety of sites in the city. Stylistically, the piece worked to defamiliarize individuals, objects, and signs of power. Actors created archetypal characters, masked figures, transformative images, and enactments of their own histories in a sometimes chaotic mix of the allegorical, expressionist, symbolic, and surreal.

As relative outsiders to the city, we as directors tried to point toward the operations of our own power in constructing the piece, to maintain some of the show's scaffolding. We each entered the stage space at select moments to add costume pieces, manipulate props, or narrate a particular passage from inside an empty television set, further framing the fictional terrain through our introduction and construction of archetypal characters. The ensemble developed these characters with broad physical gestures and little psychology, featuring exaggerated movements that drew attention to vocations rather than inner lives. A Map Maker and Sign Maker signified the city's conceptual space-makers. A mafioso-like Café Owner, a Banker, and Woman With Money stood for systems of capital control within the city, the People With Influence. A Herzegovine Housewife and her Street Kid daughter represented the everyday life of the city. And an Everyman Postman navigated his way through its shifting terrain.

In the "pre-event" section of the piece, the Postman established the representational space, setting up character relationships through the delivery of letters. While he was instrumental in mediating this space, events soon undermined the Postman's agency. Other actors donned masks and variously represented their character/archetypes and past selves, while the Postman remained the one figure who did not undergo a physical transformation. He seemed acted upon rather than acting in the events surrounding him—similar to how the young participants had themselves experienced the war. Too young to fight in or to comprehend events, they could only bear witness to the moment when their identities violently shifted, when the war ruptured their senses of belonging. One particular shared memory served as the basis for representing this shift in *Postar*: our effort to point toward a traumatic break without directly reproducing the experience for participants.

According to ensemble members, even during fighting in other areas of Yugoslavia, no one in Mostar believed there could be a war. One actor, Kenet, explained, "We used to go outside and wave at the JNA [Yugoslav army] airplanes as they passed overhead. This was our army, and we were so proud of it. How could our army shoot us? We never believed it would happen until it did." Violence transformed Kenet's metonymic identification of the planes with Yugoslavia, from "our army" to "our enemy." Reference to this shift and the consequent sense of absurdity experienced by participants commenced in *Postar* with a comic brawl. The Postman's delivery of letters not only established an initial setting and social relations in the piece but also reflected the external rise in tensions leading up to the war, particularly over the control and production of space. The Banker and the Café Owner disagreed over the naming of the café: Would it signify conceptual, capital control (the Banker, Lana's Café) or lived, proprietary control (the Owner, Bambo's Café)? Other characters aligned themselves with opposite sides of the dispute until a physical fight broke out. The Street Kid brandished her squirt gun, the Sign Maker threatened all with her menacing paintbrush, the Banker and the Woman With Money hauled chairs above their heads as the Sign Maker and Map Maker swung two wooden boards up toward each other. At this point, the action slowed to reveal an image of the Old Bridge, constructed from pieces of the set that were themselves debris from the city. The image held for a moment until the Street Kid shot three times at its center. As the bridge collapsed, the Street Kid picked up a paper airplane, one she had constructed earlier from a letter stolen from the Postman, and floated it toward the now cheerily waving crowd. The sound of the plane transformed to a menacing drone as formerly waving hands began to shield faces. The crowd stumbled backwards, knocking over elements of the set and scattering pieces of the city, while donning featureless masks for the "after event" portion of show.

The violent transformation of identity experienced by participants, signaled by the masks, arose from a representational rupture. In the terrain of memory, the JNA plane had stood in for the country, for a unified, protective state of Yugoslavia founded on Tito's platform of unity and brotherhood. In the spatial story related by participants and alluded to in *Postar*, the jet as metonym was displaced from an association of the individual with a particular national identity ("our army") and veered instead toward an association of absence, to a voided identity.[7] This metonymic shift from "Yugoslav" to "Other" signaled not only a transference of signification but also a manipulation of ideology. The newly produced conceptual space of Yugoslavia literally and figuratively displaced young Bosnians.

As an emblem for the individual loss of control experienced by ensemble members during the war, the Postman referenced this shift in identity and the violence that produced it. At the same time, the character alluded to everyday impacts on communication in the official drive to segregate and conceptually reproduce Mostar. After fighting and mapmaking in the early 1990s effectively partitioned Bosnia into three political entities, telephone and postal systems split up as well. Phone companies charged international rates for calls across Mostar's east/west border, and letters from one side of Mostar to the other were rerouted through distant cities in Serbia and Croatia. Postmen in Mostar had to navigate the city's changing street names. It remained challenging for a theatrical representation to match this level of everyday absurdity, but we tried. In *Postar's* representational space, the Postman had a nightmare following the brawl, in which the People With Influence transformed into more surreal, threatening figures, opening and discarding all of his letters. The Postman awakened to find himself in a pile of undelivered mail. He tried desperately to distribute the letters, but changes within the city thwarted his efforts. Mailboxes no longer functioned, everyone had moved (or been moved), and all of the street names had changed. The Map Maker stoked the Postman's mounting frustration by handing him an updated city plan each time he passed. After finally resorting to calling names aloud, the Postman eventually stumbled across three letter recipients: Iris, Lana, and Hajdi. They proceeded to remove the signs of their archetypal characters to read these letters as "themselves," as other ensemble members reconfigured the stage space with their bodies.

McElvany and I had worked over several years with participants to create allusory performances rather than direct testimonials, in part because of the ineffectiveness of language to access the past several years. "So much of the experience was impossible to articulate, impossible to describe," explained Mesa, the actor portraying the Postman. Physical metaphor became a way for participants to express impressions rather than recreate experiences, with associative resonances beyond individual stories. In *Postar,* for example, Iris created an image expressing both the physical location of her imprisoned brother and the emotional separation she felt from him. Four women wearing featureless masks stood side by side with arms raised as another actor peered through, searching for but unable to meet Iris's eyes. This image, like others generated for *Postar,* arose from workshops focused on letters, objects of communication signifying physical absence. We asked participants to bring in their favorite line from a letter that they felt comfortable sharing with the group. Working with masks and physicality, we developed and incorporated several of these moments into the show, all of which represented the difficulty of communication across boundaries during and immediately after the war.[8]

One ensemble member, Lana, received her letter after a brief visit with a friend from across the city's new dividing line. During the war, the Red Cross intermittently set up a tent in the border zone, allowing women only to meet in this literal no-man's land. Visitors had to follow strict procedures, signing in and getting stamped and numbered before spending a few minutes with each other, a strategy that defined them within their distinct, proper spaces. But Lana's theatrical retelling resisted that which was deemed proper. In her impressionistic representation, two young women located each other across a distance, then came together to collapse into each other's arms, taking in details of each other's faces, and finally exchanging letters. Time allowed them this moment of resistance, conceived space forced them to separate, and they reached for one another while moving backwards out of the tent space, defined and guarded by two masked officials. In this spatial story and its retelling, the letter bridged a void while remaining a template of division. Hajdi's scene worked more directly with physical metaphor to tell a story of political separation from and momentary connection to an actress she had worked with from the Bosnian Serb Republic.[9] The ensemble created a linked wall through which she and the letter writer struggled to grasp hands. As they touched, the wall broke briefly apart. Hajdi (as herself) and Minja (as Sanela) then shared lines from Sanela's letter about the difficulty and importance of communicating across borders. The wall snapped back into place as the two young women backed away from each other, eyes locked. Both stories produced a kind of relational topography, mapping out and acting out the connection between two politically separated individuals. Their representation provided an opportunity for the letter writers to experience the space they had written into, to create a tangible connection to that which separated them, and to experience in representation that which was impossible to articulate, impossible to describe.

Letters functioned as witnesses to absence and as efforts to transcend conceptual borders—as real objects laden with symbolic attachments. But *Postar* also worked with what theater director Tadeusz Kantor (1993) refers to as "REAL OBJECTS." Kantor, a painter, writer, and director in post–World War II Poland, insists that abstraction "disappeared in the period of mass genocide" (p. 211). Mere representation lost its power, and artists had to work with the "Real or POOR object," one "almost bereft of life," about to be discarded, functionless, and therefore artistic (p. 211). Kantor offers several examples of such objects: a cart wheel smeared with mud, a decayed wooden board, a scaffold spattered with plaster, a kitchen chair. Without having read Kantor before developing *Postar,* we happened upon a selection of remarkably similar objects discovered in Mostar's streets: a rusted bicycle wheel, two decayed wooden boards, a paint-smeared stepladder, two kitchen stools, and a broken picture frame. These poor, real objects hearkened toward rich, lived space that existed outside the representational frame, but also to a past life that existed only in memory. Thus, while Kantor's objects retained their tangible object-ness, we chose to suggest a possibility of transformation in our space of representation. The stepladder served as the Housewife's window, the Postman's bookshelf, and a giant chicken in the Postman's nightmare. The window frame changed from the Woman With Money's mirror, to a picture in the Housewife's home, to the Housewife's new doorway after "the event." The objects brought pieces of Mostar into the theatrical counterspace, suggesting through their imaginative transformations various possibilities for rebuilding the city. In the final scene, the actors proposed both a material and a social reconstruction, using pieces of the set as well as verbal set pieces from the show to call for a mutually enacted rebuilding.

After establishing their sense of displacement, the nightmare that followed the war, and fragmented attempts at meaning making through a series of spatial stories told through undelivered letters, the actors removed their masks. Together they picked through assorted debris on the stage—broken boards, an old television, envelopes, a ladder on its side. They reconstructed the demolished set, and as they did so one actor stood to recall lines from a poem that had opened the show (translated from Bosnian):

> What is this city? City of poets, jokers, thieves . . .
> It is true that the city is being reconstructed,
> But bridges, buildings, and parks never made a town;
> What made it was the people living in it.

The poem arose from a workshop exercise about Mostar that led to a depiction of the city, and its theatrical simulacrum, as a negotiation of history, architecture, and daily activities—of lived, conceived, and practiced space. To the ensemble members, the city embraced Turkish and Austro-Hungarian occupation, elements of eastern and western European culture and design, swimming upstream in the Neretva River, the art of wit and verbal trickery, and the ongoing practice of living its borders. The poem called for this lived spatial practice to continue, to produce a new city. In performing the poem, the actors extended their address to *Postman's* audience, crossing the representational frame to call for a practiced reconstruction of Mostar. They asked the audience to transfer their agreement, the agreement that allows for the production of fictional space, to produce a nonfictional space. Working together outside the representational terrain, this counterspace of possibility, audience, and actors might together produce a different "real" Mostar.

Audience makeup and reaction to the show rendered this potential agreement even more possible. Though the performance and festival took place in east Mostar, several of our actors and their friends lived on the west bank. *Postman* thus brought together individuals from both sides of the city and indeed from throughout Bosnia, eliciting a series of spatial practices that resisted the new order in Mostar and Bosnia. Over the summer, McElvany, Sobelle, and I had worked in the Bosnian Serb Republic as well as within the Muslim-Croat Federation, using theater as a means to bring together youth, mainly through shared videotapes of their performances.[10] The process had proved difficult, particularly in the more ultranationalist and closed areas of the Bosnian Serb Republic. When invited to attend our Mostar performance, Kile from Banja Luka, who had served in the Bosnian Serb army, claimed that he would require a battalion of tanks to accompany him. Danka from Srbinje ("place of the Serbs") had not left that city for six years and cited fear of Muslims and Croats as the reason she would not be present at our performance. Much to our surprise, both Danka and Kile appeared at the show's opening, their attendance helping to yet again reimagine Bosnia. They joined youth from Sarajevo and other areas of Federation Bosnia, German students, international volunteers working in various organizations in Mostar, and teenagers from east Los Angeles participating in the festival.[11] This diversity of attendance at least temporarily remapped the conceptual dividing lines of the city. The audience makeup also conspired with location to further negotiate identity and meaning in Mostar. We performed on the steps of the newly rebuilt puppet theater, which was haunted by its past as a Jewish synagogue. The hillside location overlooked the Neretva River and west Mostar: All of Mostar framed *Postar* as the show reciprocally framed and potentially reproduced the city.

Producing "Mostar"

Our performance was not, of course, the final word on Mostar's ongoing production. In a peculiar addendum to *Postar,* a documentary film about our rehearsals produced yet another version of the city. The filming of our practice occurred as part of a contest for two-minute features about European countries. In this somewhat unconsciously poststructural event, the most semiotically dense production of place would triumph. The Sarajevo film-maker Benjamin Filipovic required even more extreme visual density for his two minutes, as he documented eight different border-crossing youth projects in Bosnia-Hercegovina for 15 seconds each. He framed our project in Mostar with four shots, averaging less than four seconds apiece.

Filipovic began by shooting our ensemble walking down the street, bear-ing masks and musical instruments, as Spanish tanks carrying deadly serious soldiers drove beside us. We proceeded to our outdoor rehearsal space, a shelled statue conveniently located next to Mostar's frontline street. Filipovic then cut to a shot of ensemble members Mesa and Hajdi crossing this border from east to west Mostar in order to join our rehearsal. The next shot featured a performer drumming as two tanks pulled away behind him. In the fourth shot Mesa and Hajdi crossed a rebuilt chain bridge, temporarily filling the space of the Stari Most, just as a young Mostarian jumped from its tremendous height into the chilly waters of the Neretva below.

We conspired with Filipovic to fake almost every element of this docu-mentary. To "establish that we were a theater group," we grabbed whatever instruments and props we found in our indoor rehearsal space. We never worked outdoors in the west, as this could have endangered our mixed group of participants, but ensemble members had agreed to a one-day sus-pension of this rule. The tanks, conveniently passing by as we strode to our conveniently fragmented space, had actually been precisely directed. The sol-diers, who normally lounged lazily atop the tank, smoking and chatting with passersby, now performed a sterner, more "soldierly" stance, rifles raised to attention. When we reached our fake site, the tank driver radioed his col-leagues so that two other armored personal carriers would pass through the next shot. Though Mesa lived in east Mostar, and indeed had to cross the frontline street to reach rehearsal, Hajdi lived on the west and did not. Finally, Filipovic paid the young man to jump from the temporary Old Bridge at the precise moment that Mesa and Hajdi began to cross to Hajdi's nonexistent home. Despite the illusions and fakery, the resultant documen-tary, replete with gutted buildings, armored tanks, fragments of the old bridge, and theatrical border crossings, conveyed "Mostar" more strongly than any 15-second framing of real time in the city would.

But what is this city?

Filipovic had neither the time nor the capacity to wait for Mostar to emerge, so he forged an image of Mostar predetermined in his imagination, reproducing a space that had already been mediated by mapmakers and image makers. The pedestrians and performers in this movie had no choice in the path laid out, the audience no input into Mostar's future. The filmic image froze the city through an illusion of movement.

Postar was not innocent of image manipulation. Like the conceptual production of space, theater achieves its power by declaring one thing another, by changing signs and names. Mostar becomes "the City." The space in front of the puppet theater becomes a living room, a café, a nightmare, a jail, a memory. This infiltration of space does not guarantee resistance; indeed, the theater often operates strategically as a cultural institution fashioning and reinforcing a particular identity and heritage, an operation that requires visibility, stability, and often a theater building. One of the first edifices to be constructed in west Mostar was a national theater. In a village near Mostar, amateur performers revived a historical play hearkening to and forging ties to a particular Muslim past. In its "proper" place, theater creates and maintains culture. Outside this propriety, performance can invert official culture in a more nomadic, tactical manner; performance can become a practiced space of resistance.

Prior to the war, the Youth Theater of Mostar had sponsored an International Theater Festival. For two decades the festival had brought together performers from throughout Europe and Yugoslavia in Mostar's numerous theater buildings. After several years' hiatus the festival returned, though the proper places for performances, the theater buildings, had all been destroyed. So performances borrowed space in the haunted shells of former Mostar: a bombed-out cinema, the husk of a luxury hotel, the steps of an old synagogue. Playing in these gutted foundations, the festival celebrated a different conception of the city, temporarily envisioning a new space. As part of this festival, our performance of *Postar,* of a postwar *Postman,* played with the foundations of power, producing a variety of spaces filmic, theatrical, and imaginary. But was it just an exercise?

Seven years after our performance, the actor who had played the Postman posed this question as we walked the streets of Mostar. Now a published poet, translator, and teacher of the blind, the post-Postman turned to me and asked, "What do you really think about this performance? Was it just some kind of exercise?" We skirted bulldozers, upturned cobblestones, and forbidding fencing. The city was again under reconstruction in preparation for the July 23 bridge reopening, and there was so much symbolic residue to exhume on our journey. I thought about the last time I had seen Mesa cross the bridge, in a filmic reconstruction. I thought about our recent trip to Sarajevo and about a man who just keeps running, running through the city.[12] How can I answer such a question? It was an exercise, but not only that. It was an exercise in imagination, an effort to produce an image of the city that did not preexist and was not officially conceived. This imagining undergirds the power of tactical theatrical representation.

The city is again changing, upended in preparation for the new Old Bridge's reopening. Pedestrians are now warned against crossing this bridge when they come to it, as the space must first be marked by official narrative before individuals initiate their own spatial practices. The material underwriters of the project, the United Nations, will feature prominently in defining the new city through its new bridge. Secretary General Kofi Annan will narrate the bridge's reopening, marking its presence as part of a new world order of international reconciliation. George Bush may make an appearance, perhaps hoping that the image of a reconciliatory bridge between the west and its Muslim neighbors might replace that of tortured Iraqi soldiers. Whatever occurs, the city will be reproduced yet again, awaiting further production through performance, practice, and the exercise of everyday power.

Notes

1. The wars in former Yugoslavia were, for the most part, neither civil nor ethnic. Drawing on and responding to past conflicts, oppressions, and anxieties, the Serbian leader Slobodan Milosevic acted in the name of the Yugoslav National Army to initiate aggression against the breakaway Slovene and Croatian republics in 1991, then later in 1992 against Bosnian Muslims and any Bosnian who supported Bosnia as an independent multicultural state. The differences among "Croats," "Serbs," and "Muslims" in former Yugoslavia stem from historical religious affiliations and imperial alignment rather than ethnicity; Croatians affiliate with Catholicism, Serbs with Eastern Orthodoxy. All are South Slavs, speaking basically the same language. Many Bosnian Muslims, who are mostly secular, now prefer the appellation *Bosniak*. The terminology I choose in this essay shifts depending upon context and the historical moment about which I am writing.

2. As might be imagined, delicate geopolitical negotiations are required to reconstruct the Stari Most, highlighted by the plethora of stolidly named international bodies associated with the project. Shortly after the bridge's destruction, UNESCO launched an appeal for its rebuilding. About eight years after this appeal, reconstructive work actually commenced. UNESCO oversees the project along with an International Commission of Experts (ICE) and the grudging support of the Project Coordination Unit (a carefully mixed board of Mostarians). Funds are provided by several European countries and managed by the World Bank. In 2002, the oversight committee selected an Italian design firm, General Engineering, to take on the material reconstruction of the bridge. By ICE mandate, General Engineering must work alongside a German construction company providing materials, a Turkish company in charge of geological surveys, and a Croatian company responsible for designing the bridge's towers.

3. The sociologist Pierre Bourdieu (1985) identifies symbolic violence as that which occurs when one group imposes a set of ideas and symbols on another through, for example, education, enslavement, or colonization.

4. Early one morning in 1992, one of the actors in our production of *Postar* was awoken by an armed Bosnian Serb militia group and informed at gunpoint that he and his family had five minutes to leave their home in Caplina, about 30 minutes south of Mostar. Mesa does not consider himself Muslim or practice Islam in any way; he sees himself as a partisan and poet. Though he did not identify himself foremost by his Muslim religion, it was for his name, Mesa—Mehmed, Mohammed—that he was forced to leave his home, his identity forged externally through violence.

5. Before the war, residents of Serbia, Croatia, and Bosnia spoke regional dialects of the language then known as "Serbo-Croatian." After the territories descended into war, each region began redefining its language as "Serbian," "Croatian," or "Bosnian," often fetishizing minor differences among them. These efforts toward linguistic distinctions are complicated by the fact that Bosnian Serbs and Bosnian Croats spoke the Bosnian rather than Serbian or Croatian dialect of the former "Serbo-Croat" language. Most Bosnian Serbs also wrote with Latin rather than Cyrillic script, though political authorities have now enforced changes in many Serb-controlled areas of Bosnia.

6. Though January 2004 marked Mostar's formal municipal reunification, and the Convertible Mark can now be spent throughout the city, west Mostar still maintains its own phone and primary school system.

7. The psychoanalytic theorist Jacques Lacan (1986) asserts that metonymy inherently implies a veering from signification, allowing for a displacement rather than replacement of meaning. In a system of power that relies on the production of signs, the ability to manipulate language becomes a key to discerning how power operates. Thanks to Geoff Sobelle for pointing me toward ideas about metonymic displacement and the infiltration of theatrical space.

8. Another communication difficulty we negotiated involved language. I speak a minimum of Bosnian, and co-directors Sobelle and McElvany speak practically none. We relied on English as a common language among participants and ourselves, though actors performed in Bosnian.

9. The Dayton Accords allowed for two political entities within the state of Bosnia-Herzegovina: the Bosnian Serb Republic and the Muslim-Croat Federation. Herceg-Bosna existed as an additional shadow state in federation territory.

10. For additional depiction and analysis of these workshops in the Bosnian Serb Republic, see Kuftinec (1999).

11. Co-director Geoff Sobelle, originally from west Los Angeles, commented on the parallel between Mostar and Los Angeles. Though there are no border guards, residents from east and west LA rarely mix.

12. There is an older man in Sarajevo who dresses in jogging gear from the 1980s and runs and runs all over the city with a piece of fruit in his mouth. He just runs. And, apparently, he has been doing so since the war ended. It seems to me an evocative emblem of the inexplicable trauma of three years of siege.

References

Baudrillard, J. (1983). Precession of simulacra. In *Simulations* (pp. 1–58). New York: Semiotexte.

Bourdieu, P. (1985). *Language and symbolic power*. Cambridge, UK: Polity.

Certeau, M. de. (1984). *The practice of everyday life* (S. Rendall, Trans.). Berkeley: University of California Press.

Derrida, J. (1994). *The spectres of Marx* (P. Kamus, Trans.). New York: Routledge.

Foucault, M. (1970). *The order of things*. New York: Random House.

Foucault, M. (1986). Of other spaces (J. Miskowiec, Trans.). *Diacritics, 16,* 22–27. Originally published from a 1967 lecture as "Des espaces autres," in *Architecture-Mouvement-Continuité* (October 1984).

Kantor, T. (1993). The Milano lessons 1. In M. Kobialka (Ed. & Trans.), *A journey through other spaces: Essays and manifestos, 1944–1990* (pp. 211–212). Berkeley: University of California Press.

Kuftinec, S. A. (1999, Summer). Fighting fences: Theatrical rule-breaking in the Serbian Republic of Bosnia," *South East European Performances, 19*(2), 50–57.

Kuftinec, S. A., McElvany, S., & Sobelle, G. (Dirs.). (1997). *Where does the postman go when all the street names change?* Original theatrical production staged in Mostar, Bosnia.

Lacan, J. (1986). The agency of the letter in the unconscious or reason since Freud. In H. Adams (Ed.), *Critical theory since 1965* (pp. 738–756). Tallahassee: Florida State University Press.

Lefebvre, H. (1991). *The production of space* (D. Nicholson-Smith, Trans.). London: Blackwell.

Mostar Online. (1998). Anonymous comment in user thread. Retrieved March 28, 2004 from www.geocities.com/Heartland/1935/start.html.

Romeo, M., & Mela, M. (n.d.). Overview of Stari Most: Rehabilitation design of the Old Bridge of Mostar. Retrieved March 28, 2004, from www.gen-eng .florence.it/starimost/00_main/main.htm.

Safer, M. (2003). Mostar: Nation-building. Retrieved March 27, 2004, from www.cbsnews.com/stories/2003/10/17/60minutes/main578648.shtml.

Sells, M. (1996). *The bridge betrayed: Religion and genocide in Bosnia*. Berkeley: University of California Press.

Silber, L., & Little, A. (1997). *Yugoslavia: Death of a nation*. New York: Penguin.

Soja, E. (1996). *Thirdspace*. Oxford, UK: Blackwell.

Tuan, Y. (1977). *Space and place: The perspective of experience*. Minnesota: University of Minnesota Press.

United Nations Educational, Scientific and Cultural Organization. (n.d.). Mostar. Retrieved March 28, 2004, from /www.unesco.org/opi2/mostar/stari_most.htm.

Woods, L. (2000). No-man's land. In A. Read (Ed.), *Practices of art, architecture, and the everyday* (pp. 199–210). London: Taylor & Francis.

Yugoslav Tourist Bureau. (1989). *Guide book to Mostar*. Mostar: Author.

4

Looking for Stonewall's Arm

Tourist Performance as Research Method

Michael S. Bowman

> *Tourist sites are an appropriate place for locating the broad debate over self and society. . . . Tourism is a metaphor for our struggle to make sense of our self and world within a highly differentiated culture . . . it directs us to sites where people are at work making meaning, situating themselves in relation to public spectacle and making a biography that provides some coherency between self and world.*
>
> M. Neumann, "Wandering Through the Museum: Experience and Identity in a Spectator Culture"

Tourism has become the locus of an emerging body of research where the interests of scholars in performance, communication, and cultural studies intersect. Such research has shown us that while tourism is, of course, a popular leisure pursuit for increasing numbers of people around the world, it is also a complex form of communication and performance

(Kirshenblatt-Gimblett & Bruner, 1992). In much of this work, tourism is conceptualized in terms of a "semiotics of nostalgia" (Frow, 1991), where the interactions among tourists and the people and places they visit are shaped and practiced so as to reproduce both the longing for and the absence of some authentic "other." Critical/cultural studies in tourism have focused *Lit* heavily on the "tourist gaze" (Urry, 1990) and on a separation of tourist *review* from tourist production, while other, related research points to the consequences of tourism on tourist destinations themselves: the alterations in the landscape or environment needed to accommodate tourists, which often contribute to the erosion or vulgarization of a site, sometimes turning people and places into caricatures of themselves. In most ideological critiques of tourism, the sense of sight is particularly important—sight*seeing*—and given the "hegemony of vision" (Levin, 1993) that has characterized Western philosophy and social thought over the last few centuries, this is not surprising. As Urry (1990) has suggested, perhaps the most important cultural work done by tourism—as a set of processes, practices, and products—is the reinforcement and reproduction of gazing-as-knowing, and the dissemination of particular kinds of seeing as the predominant way of engaging the world for growing numbers of people.

It is almost obligatory in tourism studies to point out that tourism is, or will soon be, the largest industry in the world. Consequently, the vast majority of tourism research has focused on its economic consumptive and productive aspects. Much of this research is produced by and for students, workers, and managers in the tourism industry and relies on quantitative data gathering and statistical analysis. Although investigators have looked at a wide range of subjects—recreation, development, historical preservation, environmental impact, economic sustainability, globalization, and so forth—they tend to rely on conceptions of the tourist as a universalized, contained, rational, and self-knowing bundle of innate or preexisting "preferences." Certainly, economic analysis of the tourism industry can be informative, but such studies tell us little about tourist experiences. Thinking about tourism is confined to studying and manipulating various economic indicators, and making policy decisions often becomes a marketing issue of finding ways to appeal to tourists' preferences.

Taken together, both of these major strands of research create a view of tourism as a disembodied practice. In the first, the tourist is a pair of eyes; in the second, tourists are sets of integers. Researchers know who travels, where and when people travel, and what sorts of purchases they make when they travel. However, what tourists actually *do* when they travel, besides spending money and looking at things, and the significance or meaning of their travel to them are relatively neglected questions in tourism studies in

research gap

both the qualitative and quantitative traditions. Because little attention has been paid in tourism studies to the actual "doing" of tourism by tourists (Crouch, 2002), they are construed as "sightseers" (sometimes more honorifically as "readers" or "semioticians") or "consumers," which places them in the position of distanced, disembodied decoders of the authenticity or worth of a given text, object, or site.

More recent performance-centered research in tourism has sought to redress this tendency to "disappear" the tourist into abstractions. Metaphors of performance, drama, and theater have been integral to tourism research since MacCannell's (1976/1989) seminal work in the 1970s. Though social dramaturgical studies have been useful in both structural-functional and ideological analyses of tourism, more specifically performance-centered research that has emerged in the last decade seeks to reorient the researcher's gaze from looking at tourism in terms of performance metaphors to looking at the actual performances and theatrical displays that commonly constitute tourist "destinations" (Kirshenblatt-Gimblett, 1998). When tourists travel to see the sights, in other words, what they see isn't merely *like* a performance; it *is* a performance insofar as the sight/site is often composed of live bodies engaged in acts of "restoring behavior" (Schechner, 1985) that are put on display for the tourists' consumption (Desmond, 1999). From this standpoint, tourists are not so much "readers" of "texts" as they are audiences of the "imagetexts" (Mitchell, 1994) that they experience as multimedia, oral-dramatic events. By attending to the different genres, modes, and styles of these events, we find that *spectator*, with its connotations of passive viewing, is a less accurate descriptor for tourist behavior than something like Augusto Boal's (1985) "spect-actor": an interactive co-creator of the performance who may take a more or less important role in it. Indeed, as Kirshenblatt-Gimblett (1998) has convincingly argued, many of the productions that are staged for tourists are formally more akin to happenings, environmental theater, or other styles of avant-garde performance than they are to conventional theater, with its physical separation of and clear demarcation of roles for actors and onlookers. While it may be true in some sense that tourists are often cast in the roles of "spectators" by the productions that are mounted for them, such productions often encourage tourists to become co-performers in the events they visit or witness. In any case, as Schieffelin (1998) warned, "[T]he exact nature of the performative relationship between the central performers and the other participants (including spectators) in a cultural event cannot be assumed analytically, but must be investigated ethnographically" (p. 202).

Historically, at least, travel has been recognized as a performed art for centuries, and contemporary tourism may be recognized as a manifestation of this art (Adler, 1989). Indeed, Ulmer (1992) reminds us that there are a number of links between tourism and the arts, beginning with the ancient Greek practice of *theoria,* which of course is the etymological root of our words *theory* and *theater.* The practice of *theoria* involved travel to foreign places, to oracles, to sites where strange or marvelous objects, people, or activities were rumored to be. The *theoros* would venture to such places in order to see what could be seen, to get the lay of the land, to investigate the rumors, and so forth, and then he would return home and appear before the public to give an account of his travels. Tourism, theory, and theater come together in the ancient practice of *theoria,* considered as a mode of creative research that relies on performance as its method. Because of the stigma associated with the position of "tourist," Ulmer proposes the neologism "Solonist" to revalue the practice in honor of the wisest of the Greek *theorein,* Solon, the first "tourist-as-theorist."

To explicate this move from tourism to "Solonism," I examine, primarily through a representative account of my own visits to sites of historical trauma and violence, such as battlefields and military parks, how tourism often prompts performances that are more complex than merely gazing or consuming, and how such performances produce other meanings and pleasures than the preferred ones of such sites. I begin with an account of one visit to a Civil War battlefield. Treating that account as a representative anecdote, I extract from it a lesson about tourism as a performance art, showing how tourist behavior may "breakthrough into performance" (Hymes, 1975) in several ways. I conclude by extrapolating from that lesson a methodological discussion, arguing for the generalizability of the experience I had and the lesson I derived from it, foregrounding its resemblance to other forms of creative research. As Urry (1990) has pointed out, "[P]eople are much of the time 'tourists' whether they like it or not" (p. 82). But what we have chosen to make of our identities as tourists is, judging by the bulk of scholarly studies of the subject, regrettable. My overarching conviction throughout this chapter is that the remedy for "bad" tourism isn't *no* tourism but *better tourism.* And the path I want to sketch toward "better tourism" is to reconsider and revalue what it is we do as tourists.

Looking for Stonewall's Arm

Men can see nothing around them that is not their own image; everything speaks to them of themselves. Their very landscape is alive.

Karl Marx, quoted in G. Debord, "Theory of the Dérive"

In one of his essays on surrealism, Walter Benjamin (1999b), attempting to bring home the lessons of Breton, Aragon, Apollinaire, et al., poses the question: "What form do you suppose a life would take that was determined at a decisive moment precisely by the street song last on everyone's lips?" (p. 210). One of the decisive moments in my life was when I learned how to read. That moment was marked for me by a gift from my parents of two books— books that I could call my own, books that would never be *read to* me, books that I would not have to share with my siblings. At the time, around 1960, one of the songs that happened to be on everyone's lips involved the U.S. Civil War, as the country was preparing to commemorate its centennial. Consequently, the books I received from my parents were both about the Civil War. I don't recall their titles, but they were something like "The Civil War for Boys Who Just Learned How to Read"—that kind of thing. They were oversized books with large print and lots of illustrations. I loved those books.

They told me stories about things that had happened long ago when groups of blue- and gray-clad men came together at places named Bull Run, Shiloh, and Gettysburg to fight each other. The scale of the fighting was difficult to imagine. I had seen TV cowboys fight groups of men in black hats, but I couldn't conceive of anything so terrible as the stories this book told me: of fields strewn with more dead people than lived in my hometown, of a conflict that had lasted as long as I had been alive. The illustrations were especially fascinating to me: ghosts, abstractions; a few pencil strokes suggesting thousands of men marching down a road, snaking back and forth from the foreground to the vanishing point; or the drawings of tiny blue and gray figures on a watercolor battlefield, a bird's eye view, so pretty to look at that I wished I could live there.

One illustration in particular has stayed with me always: a black and white line drawing of a great general named Stonewall Jackson riding a horse. In the drawing, Jackson and his horse were presented in profile. The horse's legs and mane were rendered in such a way as to suggest that it was running. Jackson was bent back on his horse, arms outstretched and head thrown back as if appealing to Heaven, and his eyes were squinted shut and his mouth was twisted in an expression of agony. It looked as if he had just been shot and might be about to fall off his horse. I knew from the text that he was in fact shot by mistake by some of his own soldiers, and, knowing nothing about "friendly fire" in those preschool, pre-Vietnam days, I found the story and the picture to be very sad.

I have devoted a healthy percentage of my leisure time during the last 45 years to the Civil War: reading many more books about it, looking at photographs and other documents from the time, watching films and television programs, and visiting museums, battlefields, and other sites *[personal interest]* associated with it. I never made a conscious decision to study the Civil War as a scholar, an enthusiast, or a "buff" might, and when I was beginning to contemplate a career in academia, it never occurred to me that I already knew more about the Civil War than anything else and might have become a Civil War historian. But I suppose it was inevitable that I would try to mix my professional and amateur interests at some point in my life.

In May–June of 1997, I made the first of a series of trips through the states of the old Confederacy to visit a number of historical sites, the majority of *[Scholarly interest]* which were Civil War related. These trips were motivated in part by my ongoing scholarly interest in how history is used in the contemporary enactment of southern identity (see, e.g., Bowman, 1998). But they were also, quite frankly, pleasure trips insofar as they were partly motivated by my desire to experience what some Civil War reenactors call a "Civil Wargasm."

The term *Civil Wargasm* is used in two different ways. The first and most common usage, as the name suggests, refers to a peak experience in the reen- *(1)* actment of a battle, a moment when the sensory experience of simulating a battle produces in the reenactor a sensation that time has slipped, that this is "how it really was," that *this* is what it felt like for those men in the 1860s to be in battle. I have heard other reenactors refer to this experience as a "time warp" (cf. Turner, 1990), and the equation of time travel with sexual climax is an indication of how prized the experience is to reenactors. As one reenactor told me, "When most people think of taking trip or a vacation, they only think in terms of geography, going somewhere different in space. When I take a vacation, I want to go somewhere different in time" (D. Cheatham, personal communication, June 1997). The second usage for the term is to describe an extended period of immersion in Civil War sites and Civil War–related activities (cf. Horwitz, 1998). For the hardcore reenactor, this means wearing hot, dirty, smelly woolen clothing, sleeping out of doors, eating rancid pork fat, and so on, for several weeks at a stretch in hopes of experiencing the time warp in other ways besides the simulation of battle. It is in the second sense of immersion in Civil War–related things that I was searching for a wargasm. But because I wasn't about to go the hardcore route, I suppose I could be accused of trying to fake a wargasm, for I was going as a tourist/ethnographer.

There is an area in northern Virginia in and around the town of Fredericksburg, about halfway between Richmond and Washington, D.C., where four major battles of the Civil War were fought. The names of those battles are Fredericksburg (December 1862), Chancellorsville (May 1863), The Wilderness (May 1864), and Spotsylvania (May 1864). On that relatively small patch of land there were approximately 125,000 casualties in those four battles. Today, a little over 8,000 acres of this land have been set aside as a national park, the Fredericksburg and Spotsylvania County Battlefields Memorial National Military Park. On each of my trips, Fredericksburg was my primary destination. While Gettysburg is the battle that everyone knows and the battlefield that is the most visited (nearly 2 million visitors in 2003), I had already been there too many times and found the place too hideously crowded with tourists and kitsch to hope to achieve a wargasm there, although I have met others who claim to have done so. But the area in and around Fredericksburg, the site of four major—and in their way equally legendary—battles, the most blood-soaked real estate in North America, would be prime wargasm territory, I thought. For those who may not recall what happened there, allow me to summarize a portion of the story that bears on my own.

After the battle of Antietam in western Maryland in September, 1862, Robert E. Lee ended his first attempt to carry the war into the North and withdrew his forces south of the Potomac River back into Virginia. When the Union commander at Antietam, Gen. George McClellan, failed to pursue the badly damaged and outnumbered Confederate army, Lee retired his Army of Northern Virginia to Fredericksburg on the Rappahannock River to establish winter quarters. Frustrated by McClellan's inaction, President Lincoln dismissed him (for the second time) and appointed Gen. Ambrose Burnside as the new commander of the Union's Army of the Potomac.

Burnside's Fredericksburg campaign in December of 1862 was a disaster. Indeed, the Fredericksburg campaign failed so miserably that Lee was able to send two divisions of his already-outnumbered army, along with his second-in-command, Gen. James Longstreet, south to counter a developing Union threat in the Tidewater region of Virginia and North Carolina. In January of 1863, Lincoln dismissed Burnside and appointed yet another commander, Gen. Joseph Hooker, who was known as "Fighting Joe." Hooker spent the winter reorganizing his army and restoring the morale of his troops,[1] and then in April he went into action. Using part of his army to screen the Confederates at Fredericksburg, he marched the bulk of his forces a few miles upriver and crossed the Rappahannock in force, effectively flanking Lee's army. But, having gained the advantage, Fighting Joe suddenly grew timid when Lee reacted quickly and aggressively, attacking Hooker's lead units near Zoan Church outside of Fredericksburg. Instead of pressing the attack against Lee when he had the advantage, Hooker reformed his army into a defensive position near a place called Chancellorsville.

When Hooker paused, Lee again took the initiative, pulling off what many regard as the most daring and spectacular victory of his storied career. After learning from his scouts that Hooker's own right flank was "in the air" (i.e., unsupported and unanchored by a natural defensive barrier or obstacle such as a river or mountain), Lee consulted with Gen. Thomas J. "Stonewall" Jackson, and the two formulated a plan. Having already split his forces in the face of the superior Union numbers—a cardinal error in military thinking—Lee did so again, sending Jackson and nearly 30,000 men on a forced march through the densely wooded area known as "The Wilderness of Spotsylvania" around the Union army, where they would fall upon Hooker's vulnerable right flank. Jackson's successful maneuver and attack on May 2, 1863, caught Hooker by surprise, routing an entire Union corps.

However, as darkness fell over the battlefield, Jackson and his aides and subordinate commanders rode out between the disorganized Union and Confederate lines to reconnoiter the terrain in preparation for a night attack. As the group rode back toward their own lines, an understandably nervous North Carolina regiment mistook them for Union troops and opened fire. Jackson and Gen. A. P. Hill were both wounded, and four other members of the party were killed. Jackson was removed to a field hospital where his shattered left arm was amputated before he was taken farther behind the lines to recuperate. When Lee was informed, he was said to have remarked, "He has lost his left arm, but I have lost my right." Although Jackson was expected to survive his wounds, he contracted pneumonia and died a few days later on May 10. Historians, armchair generals, and apologists for the "Lost Cause" have speculated ever since what might have happened two months later had Lee's "right arm" been with him at Gettysburg.[2]

There was no "ville" at Chancellorsville, just an inn called the Chancellor House located at an intersection of two roads known as the Orange Turnpike and the Orange Plank Road where Hooker made his headquarters. In addition to its mythical status as the site of Lee's greatest victory—and loss—Chancellorsville was also the unnamed battle of Stephen Crane's *The Red Badge of Courage* (1894/1951), which described the landscape as "some little fields girted and squeezed by a forest" (p. 42). For the most part, that descriptor is still accurate, although most of the original battlefield is privately owned or is being sucked into the vortex of Fredericksburg's expansion and development (O'Brien, 2004). The first time I visited the battlefield, I arrived at the small visitor's center, which is located adjacent to the spot where Jackson was mortally wounded, early one cold, drizzly Saturday morning in May. I thought I might have arrived too early. Although the building was unlocked and the lights were on, no one else seemed to be inside. I spent a moment looking through a rack of postcards, figuring someone would show up eventually to take my entrance fee, and that was when I first saw it: a photo of a stumpy, grayish-white tombstone inscribed, "Arm of Stonewall Jackson, May 3, 1863."

[handwritten marginal notes: Jackson + friendly fire, arm amputated, died, changed course of war?]

Arm's
tombstone

I knew, of course, that Jackson had lost his arm at Chancellorsville, but the notion that someone had taken the trouble to find it—save it, bury it, and buy it a gravestone—struck me as morbidly comic. I had visited the house where Jackson and his family had lived when he taught at VMI before the war, as well as the cemetery where (the rest of) his remains are buried— along with the tomb of Lee, the grave of Lee's horse, and the stuffed hide of Jackson's horse—in Lexington, Virginia, just a few days prior to my visit to Chancellorsville. I was certainly aware of the saintlike veneration of the two Confederate generals in the decades following the war. But until that moment, I had no idea that a "relic" of Jackson existed or that I might visit it. I could feel my interest in the battlefield begin to slip. I had wanted to visit this mythical place for most of my life, but in an instant, my lifelong inter- est in Civil War history, my pilgrimage to the sacred, "hallowed ground" where the legendary battle was fought, my search for the image of Jackson's mortal wounding from my boyhood book, my desire for a wargasm—all that became less important than finding Stonewall Jackson's arm.

A sleepy, teenaged youth appeared when I began laughing at the postcard, and he assumed a position behind the counter. I went to the counter and paid my admission fee, and he handed me the slick National Park Service pam- phlet that marked the important sites of the Fredericksburg and Spotsylvania National Battlefields Military Park as a whole, along with a Xeroxed sheet or two describing the driving and walking tours of the Chancellorsville battlefield in particular. I glanced through them quickly, looking for an "X" marking the spot where Jackson's arm was buried, but it was not to be found. I got one of the postcards and showed it to the boy and asked him to point out its location for me. He shrugged his shoulders and apologetically confessed that he didn't really know much about the place. The park wasn't yet on "summer hours," so there were no guides or staff available; he was still in high school, I learned, and running the register was just a part-time weekend job for him. The ranger would probably know, he added, trying to be helpful, but the ranger had just left to give a tour to a group of soldiers. If I hurried, I might catch up with them.

I asked him if he had any other information about the battlefield than the two Xeroxed sheets of paper he had given me, and he pointed to a small stack of audiocassettes on a shelf behind him and said they were for the dri- ving tour. He told me the price of the cassettes, and his manner suggested that he would be ashamed to take so much money for one. I offered to allow him to give me one, but that only seemed to confuse him. Eager for any clue as to the whereabouts of the arm, I purchased a tape, along with a couple of the postcards. Given how miserable the weather was, the driving tour of the battlefield seemed like a good idea, anyway.

I stepped outside and walked around the building to look at the large, obelisklike boulder that had been placed at The Spot where Jackson was said *experiencing* to have been when his troops opened fire on him. Suffice it to say that this *iconic image* wasn't the spot as I'd imagined it all my life, nothing remotely like the iconic image I'd carried in my head from my picture book. The building was in the *dissonance* way, for one thing, and a split-rail fence had been erected around the whole *"The* area. The monument rested only 10 to 20 yards from the road where the *Spot"* Confederate lines had been reforming after the initial assault, by my calculation, and if his troops opened fire on him here, <u>assassination would be a better term for what happened than *accident*,</u> I mused. Of course, given the confusion at the time and the conflicting reports of who was where and what had happened, it is unlikely that this really was The Spot. But it's an impressive rock nonetheless, completely overwhelming the nearby stone cross that marks the grave of an unknown Union soldier, with convenient bathroom and parking facilities just around the corner.[3]

I returned to my car and drove off, back in time, passing the ruins of the old Chancellor inn, to the first stop on the tour: the pine grove where Lee and Jackson met on the night before the battle to plan their attack. Their parting the next morning, known as "the Last Meeting," is one of the more sanctified moments in Lost Cause mythology, reproduced in countless romantic paintings and prints—with reproductions of those reproductions available for purchase in the visitor's center, of course. It had begun to rain more heavily now, and the temperature was a wintry (to me) 40 to 50 degrees. There was a bus parked at the stop, painted in camouflage, and a couple dozen soldiers dressed in camouflage field uniforms were standing around the clearing listening to someone I took to be the missing park ranger and another man who must have been their commanding officer. I got out of the car just as the ranger was ending his spiel, and the officer began trying to impress upon his men and women the audacity of the plan, its brilliance and its stupidity.

It isn't uncommon to see military personnel on a Civil War battlefield. When the first national military parks in this country were established in the *battlefield* 1890s, they were designed to serve three purposes: (1) to preserve and pro- *preservation* tect land that had become, to echo Lincoln's famous words, "hallowed ground"; (2) to commemorate the participants in the battle; and (3) to provide field classrooms for the U.S. military's officer corps. The "staff ride" around a battlefield is a traditional way of teaching military leaders in the *staff* U.S. armed forces, especially in times of peace when the gap between com- *ride* bat training and combat experience is great. The staff ride consists of three phases: (1) a preliminary study phase involving readings and lectures about a given battle; (2) the field study phase, consisting of the actual ride around the battlefield itself; and (3) an integration phase, conducted on the field, in which the facts and inferences drawn from the past are projected as lessons for today's military (Stoft, 1998).

This was my first experience witnessing a staff ride at such proximity. But as I listened to the officer's lecture, I couldn't help thinking of those "don't try this at home" disclaimers that were part of so many TV programs and commercials when I was growing up. Although much of it emphasized the technical or logistical problems of the plan, the "lesson" seemed to be: *It's okay to pull a stunt like this if you're a genius like Lee and have a genius field commander like Jackson to execute your harebrained ideas, but if any of you maggots ever tried this . . .*

I felt a little uncomfortable wandering around the clearing among the soldiers, eavesdropping on their lessons. Half the soldiers were African Americans, and I wondered what they must have thought of me, a lone white guy making a pilgrimage to a shrine devoted to two Confederate generals. I caught the eye of a couple of them, and they looked at me as if to say, "We *have* to be here—what's your excuse?" Others were shifting around, shooting longing glances at the dry, warm interior of their bus. My own discomfort led me to get back in my car and wait for them to depart. I popped the tape I'd purchased into the tape player and listened to the story of the Last Meeting one more time. The tape was typical of the genre. It featured, along with background music and sound effects, a narrator, with a more euphonious voice than either the ranger's or the officer's, who was also attempting to convey the prebattle drama of that brilliant, audacious, desperate Last Meeting. Save for the periodic instructions to pause the tape and drive on to the next stop on the tour, it could pass as the soundtrack for a History Channel program or a Ken Burns film.

I waited until the soldiers had piled onto the bus and driven off, and then I hopped out of my car again so I could look more closely at the small granite block telling me that this was indeed where Lee and Jackson had met on the night of May 1, 1863, and the other sign replicating one of the well-known Last Meeting paintings. There was also a tree stump in the clearing. I looked at the tree stump and then back at the picture. Was this the stump on which Jackson sat before leading his men on that famous march before he got shot? I began to put pieces of the story together in my head in a kind of "This is the house that Jack built" fashion, trying to trace the logic of the tour ahead, which would take me back eventually to the visitor's center where I'd just been—"this is the stump that stands on the spot . . ."—but, no, in the picture Stonewall isn't sitting on a stump. It looks more like an ammo crate or cracker box. I sat down on the stump, smoked a cigarette, and tried to let myself drift off to imagine the two great men huddled together in

More dissonance in experience

this very spot 134 years ago almost to the day, hoping to get a little wargasm groove going. But the rain and cold were not conducive to communing with the dead, so I tossed my cigarette aside—tobacco is, after all, a traditional gift to leave at such places—and got back in the car.

From the Last Meeting site, the driving tour of the Chancellorsville battlefield follows the route of Jackson's march, winding down narrow, unpaved country roads, through those little fields that are girted and squeezed by forest. Evidently, the narrative of the march on my tape was not quite as detailed as the one the soldiers were getting on the bus. I'd given them a good 10- or 15-minute head start, but it only took about 30 seconds to catch up to the bus, which was crawling along at a speed undetectable by my speedometer. The road was so narrow that I could do nothing but crawl along behind them, and my propensity for road rage began to grow. When the bus finally pulled over at the next marked stop on the tour, I made the decision to bolt and run: To hell with it, I thought, I'll do the tour later. *I had to find that arm!*

Mentally cross-indexing the map of the battlefield with my knowledge of the battle, I had drawn some inferences about where the arm should be. In 1863, there were a couple of noteworthy "farms" (i.e., plantations) and another inn known as the Wilderness Tavern farther out along the Orange Turnpike that figured in the battle of The Wilderness a year after the Chancellorsville battle, and those were highlighted on the maps I had. I knew that Jackson had been taken to this area after he was wounded, and if I could find those landmarks, I felt sure that something—a sign, a marker, voices in my head—would lead me to the arm.

Well, I spent the next six hours driving around Spotsylvania, Stafford, Orange, and Caroline Counties, Virginia—traversing state routes, county roads, farm access roads, a few driveways, and even a short section of Interstate-95—but I never did find it. With four major Civil War battlefields in the area, there are plenty of signs, markers, and monuments to see, along with a few of the obligatory cannons and unknown soldiers' graves sprinkled here and there. I think I saw every one of them, some of them several times. I would drive a few hundred yards, pull over to read a sign, and zoom off to the next one. I let the tape play through, although I was on my second lap around the tour by the time it finished, and nothing it described corresponded with what I saw outside my window. Not that it made much difference. I had tossed the maps in the back seat and so was lost a lot of the time, drifting back and forth between sections of the four battlefields. In most cases that which was marked by a sign or by the tape's narration was just a little field or part of the forest that girted and squeezed it, and it was difficult to say whether I was looking at an 1862 little field, an 1863 little field, an 1864 little field, or a 1997 little field.

As the day wore on, the Talking Heads, Tom Jones, Frank Sinatra, and Motown replaced the Chancellorsville tape as the soundtrack of my tour. The temperature rose, the rain tapered off, and I would pull over and get out of the car every now and then to look at a little field, some girting and squeezing forest, or a mound of dirt that could have been Union or Confederate trench works or someone's sewer line. I drove the entire route of Jackson's march three times—once in reverse order, just to see if I could do it—and ended the day with a blow-by Grand Tour (interrupted by a stop at the gas station I'd passed several times for fuel, a bathroom visit, and a cup of something they said was coffee) of all four battlefields that, by this point, had become jumbled together in one big Civil War Battlefield Land Self-Amusement park.

At the end of the day, I knew exactly where the arm had to be, since it was practically the only bit of Spotsylvania County I hadn't seen. There was that one driveway with a chain across it that I'd passed several times situated right where I thought the arm might be when I'd set out to find it that morning. But I was tired and hungry and in such a good mood that driving all the way across the county again to pull off a B&E job was less appealing than stopping at that crab shack down by the riverfront in Fredericksburg that I'd reconnoitered the previous day. Looking for Stonewall's arm had been so thoroughly enjoyable that finding it would only be a letdown.[4]

Tourists as Performers

Those who fail to reread are obliged to read the same story everywhere.

Roland Barthes, *S/Z: An Essay*

Like other physical pursuits, the pleasure of tourism is often in the chase rather than in the actual capture of the object of one's desire. In his seminal study *The Tourist*, Dean MacCannell (1976/1989) approached the matter from a social dramaturgical perspective, showing how the tourist embarks on a quest for something perceived as more authentic than what he or she finds in everyday life. MacCannell shows how a sense of "staged authenticity" is created through a process of "sight sacralization," a communicative process of naming and framing objects, places, people, cultures—"sights"— so that tourists will know when they have arrived at the "real thing." The movement of tourists hoping to see the sights helps to elevate their importance, to enshrine them as "sites," but it also threatens to undermine the sight/site's authenticity or specialness owing to the profusion of signs, markers, and other tourists that begin to collect there. Furthermore, tourists know that the sights/sites that have been presented to them are mediated, framed, or packaged for their consumption, much like a theatrical production. While some are undoubtedly content to sit and watch the show, perhaps lose themselves in staged illusions of authenticity, others believe that the authentic lies elsewhere, backstage, behind the scenes. As Culler (1988) pointed out, the irony of tourism is that, for a sight/site to become authentic, it must be marked, but our very conception of the authentic equates it with the *un*marked.

[margin handwriting: marked/unmarked sites]

Consequently, tourists appear to be caught in a spiral of semiosis where the relations between sight and marker become confused and inverted, such that the markers become more important than the sights/sites themselves. As we approach the condition of the simulacral, we find sights/sites being remade so as better to conform to their markers (Dorst, 1989; Kirshenblatt-Gimblett, 1998; MacCannell, 1992). I have heard tourists in New Orleans commenting, for example, on how much cleaner or "nicer" the French Quarter is at Disneyworld. Because the French Quarter is such a boon to the city's economy, political initiatives to "clean up the Quarter" so as to make it more attractive to tourists and businesses are easily understood by opponents and critics as an effort to remake the city into an image of itself made popular and more palatable to middle-class tastes by Disney.

[margin handwriting: Remade sites]

The tendency in some early critical and cultural studies of tourism was to blame the "victims" in this semiotic shell game: the tourists themselves. Tourists were often represented either as dupes who don't know they've been duped, or else as dupes who have learned to enjoy being duped, have become content to find pleasure in fake or simulated culture when the "real thing" could be had for free if they were just to step outside their little tourist bubbles (see Boorstin, 1962/1987, pp. 77–117). In either case, the tourist's pursuit of something—whether it be authenticity or the extraordinary—is interpreted as a kind of social neurosis, a psychopathology of modern life, a repetition compulsion or form of "deep play" that drives us to wander the globe in search of something that does not exist except as a projection of our own collective fantasy life.

[margin handwriting: Tourists: seeking something that only exists in fantasy]

As I indicated earlier, metaphors of theater and performance have been used most commonly in tourism studies to foreground the production of tourism, both as a series of staged events and places and as an array of performative techniques and dispositions. Influenced by Goffman's (1959) analysis of everyday social interaction, such work treats tourists as "performers" by calling attention to the conventions and shared norms that govern their self-presentation in order both to manage others' impressions of them and to achieve certain instrumental goals. The emphasis on the instrumentality of tourists' social performances helps capture some aspects of the habitual, normative, or scripted character of tourist behavior, particularly *postmodern tourist*

the canalization of individual tourists into stock "roles" or "types" or "styles." But it also conjures images of the tourist as another example—perhaps indeed the prototype—of the (post)modern, alienated, overly calculating individual who goes on tour precisely to escape the artificiality of everyday life, only to find him- or herself failing, falling ever deeper into the abyss of the simulated, the fake.

Tourism as ethnographic performance

restoring agency to tourists

More recently, however, some scholars have begun to examine the actual "doing" of tourism by tourists as performance in ethnographic and aesthetic terms. Rather than deploying the term metaphorically to call attention to the artifice of the interactional order, performance has become important to restore a sense of agency to tourists; to counter the emphasis on tourism as product, package, or production by foregrounding its processual elements; to call attention to the embodied nature of tourists' movements and encounters; to explore how such embodiment creates other than imagistic, ocular-centric forms of knowledge; and to reconsider identity performance, not simply as the reiteration or repetition of behavioral norms or scripts, but as opening up the possibility for emergent authenticity (see, e.g., Bruner, 1994; DeLyser, 1999) and becoming (Bruner, 1991).

re-envisioning tourism

As Edensor (2001) suggests, tourism is too often, perhaps, represented as removed from the quotidian, as an attempt to "escape" from the routine or the mundane, as offering opportunities for "play" rather than "work," and as occasions where tourists seek to cast off their everyday masks and set free their "authentic" selves. Because notions of an "escape" or "getaway" are heavily coded culturally, because tourists invariably carry their daily habits with them on tour along with their other baggage, and because their behavior on tour reflects commonsensical understandings of how to act like a tourist, critics operating from such assumptions have found it easy to criticize tourists as acting in bad faith. To do so, however, is to ignore how tourism is imbricated in the everyday, as well as the practical advantages of the role of habit in the practice of daily life. Such habits "strengthen affective and cognitive links, constitute a habitus consisting of acquired skills which minimize unnecessary reflection every time a decision is required" (p. 61). But of course everyday life is never simply a robotic repetition of the habitual. The *performance* of habit, the immanent embodied experience of the everyday—its disruptions, distractions, daydreams, and sensual engagements—always threatens to undermine its *performativity*, the structural, structuring force of habit.

Everyday performance

Tourism may be viewed as productive in this sense because it often provides the motive and the means for intensifying this potential for breaking the performative force of habit. First of all, tourism brings people together in "contact zones" (Pratt, 1991/1999) or "behavioral vortices" (Roach, 1996) with others who have *different* habits—whether they be people from another nation or culture altogether, or simply other passengers from one's own country who happen to be on the same package tour. Sitting in the breakfast room of a Scottish B&B with other travelers from the United States, Canada, Germany, and Australia a few years ago, I recall that much of our conversation revolved around our assessments of the "full Scottish" breakfast in comparison to the "full English" breakfast, as well as confessional tales about our breakfasting habits in our own countries. Second, tourism often makes habits tough to maintain. The most ordinary of activities—taking a walk, having a conversation, eating a meal, going to the bathroom, sleeping—can become strange or difficult when one is on tour. Indeed, the strangeness of such activities often becomes the grist of our travel narratives and reminiscences. Most anyone who has traveled abroad will have several tales of the "foreign toilets I have known" variety. The point in both these instances is that such encounters often make it necessary for us to verbalize precisely that which we ordinarily consign to the realm of "common sense," of things that "go without saying." And once a habit has been described, put into discourse, it becomes something one must reconsider or take a stand on: Do we stick to our habits, or do we change them?

Performative norms need to be continually reiterated through repeated performances to retain their power, and the prescriptive conventions and values that inhere in them are rarely disrupted if they are performed unreflexively. It is common to assume that an unreflexive disposition characterizes much of tourists' performances, and, where this is not the case, where reflexive improvisation and a critical disposition are mobilized, the resultant ambiguity or difficulty can threaten the sense of well-being or pleasure that is presumably one of the goals of tourism: to relax and let go. Self-surveillance engenders self-doubt, which is not usually considered conducive to having a good time, and such experiences occur frequently in tourism. Anyone who has ever spent time around tourists has had to listen to their constant carping and grumbling—I have done my share of it, certainly—and heard their common complaints of "This is too much like work" and "I'm on vacation, I don't want to have to think." The tourism industry seems bent on making it easy for tourists to retain an unreflexive disposition by the creation of "enclavic" tourist spaces (Edensor, 1998)—tourist "bubbles"—and by the "McDisneyization" (Ritzer & Liska, 1997) of those spaces—that is, the creation of a global monoculture where no one ever need worry about being surprised or having to work or think too hard.

Contemporary "post-tourists," those who find pleasure in the pure kitschy-ness of McDisneyized tourism and thereby perform a cynical or playful detachment from it (Feifer, 1985; Ritzer & Liska, 1997), are imbued with their own conventions and habits, of course, their own unreflexive assumptions about what distinguishes them from "conventional" tourists. It would be as easy to exaggerate the nature and import of tourists' reflexivity as it has been to overstate their unreflexivity. If we follow the line of cultural populist thinking that reinscribes popular cultural consumption as cultural production, it is no great feat to see tourists as a "bricoleurs" or "poachers," subversive rewriters of, rather than mere passive recipients of, the productions and products that are marketed for them. As Neumann (1999) observes, "Seeing tourists as 'nomads poaching their way across fields they did not write' is an appealing and appropriate analogy" in some instances. But to imagine or celebrate tourists "as engaged in semiotic combat on a politicized battlefield drawn by critics of popular culture is, perhaps, to set the stakes too high for people taking a vacation" (p. 187; cf. Morris, 1990). Nevertheless, the degree of reflexive awareness mobilized by the performers, their level of detachment or involvement, influences the range of an actor's repertoire and the scope for improvisation. Thus one of the sources of tension and contestation in tourist performance—that which defines it—is that between unreflexive and reflexive dispositions: between tourist performances that occur in a state of everyday, habitual "flow," where tourists share conventional ways of doing and thinking in relatively unchallenging contexts—often as strategies to minimize disorientation or dissonance in unfamiliar settings—and performances that seek to test conventions.

The particular direction of a given tourist performance will be shaped in part by the nature of the space or stage on which the performance occurs and the degree of control or direction given by the producers or stage managers. As Edensor (2001) notes:

> Tourist epistemologies are shaped by an orientation towards the kinds of experiences that are available [on a given site], how they can be achieved and what is appropriate in their execution. . . . Tourism is constituted by an array of techniques and technologies which are mobilized in distinct settings. Thus when tourists enter particular stages, they are usually informed by pre-existing discursive, practical, embodied norms which help to guide their performative orientations and achieve a working consensus about what to do. (p. 71)

Regardless of how incoherent or heterogeneous a given site or production may be, a set of preferred meanings usually may be inferred from it, and tourists often modify their performances in accordance with the inferences they draw about such meanings. Performance in this sense becomes a "discrete concretization of cultural assumptions" (Carlson, 1996, p. 16).

In the case of "sacred" national sites, such as Civil War battlefields—sites that are always framed as "hallowed ground" (Foote, 1997; Linenthal, 1993; Thomas, 1987)—the predominant response one sees enacted is a kind of hushed awe or respectful, meditative silence, displays similar to shame in many cases—an affect that, as Sedgwick (2003) notes, is often contagious in its performative force. At some places, like the American Cemetery above Omaha Beach or on some World War I battlefields, this contagion of affect moves people to weep openly. And while I have never seen anyone weep at a Civil War battlefield, the most common verbal response I hear when I ask people how their visit made them feel is the simple phrase (or some variant of it): "It gets to you." Many of those I've spoken with seem surprised by their own responses, as if they had anticipated being bored or unmoved by the visit. Battlefields and military parks are designed to "get to you," of course, and one of the most important ways they get to you is by stage-managing your performances on them.

Everyone has felt the force of public history, written in stone or bronze, or on the buildings and parks and battlefields preserved for us today. Being at a place where "history happened" has a certain power. The feelings of pride, regret, elation, sorrow, remorse, and rededication we feel when we visit national shrines and monuments can be linked in part to the techniques and technologies used in the process of sight/site sacralization, as MacCannell (1976/1989) so powerfully demonstrated. But we must understand that those technologies are also enmeshed in certain embodied dispositions and performances of those who visit the site. In other words, the process of sight/site sacralization is not simply a semiotic affair of creating a readable, meaningful "text"; it is more akin to a directorial affair where actors are put into motion, prompted to say and do things that will allow them to experience and enact the tacit meanings and values of the sight/site. Visiting the Lincoln Memorial, for instance, isn't a matter of standing back, gazing at it, and trying to decipher its meaning: "Oh, I get it!" Rather, the Lincoln Memorial "gets" you by virtue of your enacting a tacit "script" in order simply to be in its presence and then to behave appropriately once you get there. The behavioral routine imagined for visitors requires them to expend money, time, and effort to travel, of course, but it also requires a number of decisions or, as we say in the theater, "performance choices": choosing the appropriate clothing or costume to wear; learning certain styles of movement and gesture and affect display; determining how and where to look and whether and what to photograph; and making appropriate forms of speech, both during and after the visit.

In terms of its general structure, at least, the visitor's performance at a Civil War battlefield mimics the military staff ride. The preliminary study

[handwritten margin note: sacred sights: set in motion by actors under direction]

phase may be more or less prolonged, ranging from the lifelong study of the Civil War by amateurs such as myself or the intensive study of a battle by *preliminary* professional historians to the ad hoc "briefings" tourists receive from pamphlets, guide books, short films, models, dioramas, or informative speeches at or near the visitor's center. The second phase is virtually identical. Because battlefields usually are spread out over several square miles, people tend to ride to major points of interest in their automobiles, following the route of a carefully mapped-out driving tour, perhaps with an accompanying audiotape, to numbered stops at places where key moments of the battle occurred. Visitors drive to each stop, park their cars, check their pamphlets, read the information on signs of various sorts, look at monuments if those are present, perhaps listen to a presentation by a park ranger or interpretive guide, wander around a bit to examine the terrain, snap a couple of photos, converse quietly with others, get back in their vehicles, and move on to the next *Integration* stop. The third phase, the integration phase, is also performed, although in a much less programmatic way than in the military staff ride. The lessons drawn from the visit may well concern military matters, and mimicking the staff ride can be pleasurable for what one may learn about the events of the battle, the people who fought there, how they fought, and why they fought as they did, given the state of military technology and tactics at the time. In the case of Chancellorsville, the main impression is one of awe: Lee's decision to split his forces in the face of superior numbers was so audacious as to seem suicidal, and Jackson's ability to sneak 30,000 men through that "wilderness" around the Union army camped only a few hundred yards away is simply breathtaking.

Yet the principal lesson of such visits is, of course, an ideological one, *ideological* never so well expressed, perhaps, as in the words many of us had to commit to memory as children:

We are met on a great battlefield of that war. We have come to dedicate a portion of it as a final resting place for those who here gave their lives that the nation might live. It is altogether fitting and proper that we should do this.

Gettysburg Address

But in a larger sense, we cannot dedicate, we cannot consecrate, we cannot hallow this ground. The brave men, living and dead, who struggled here have consecrated it far above our poor power to add or detract. The world will little note nor long remember what we say here, but it can never forget what they did here. It is for us the living rather to be dedicated here to the unfinished work which they who fought here have thus far so nobly advanced. It is rather for us to be here dedicated to the great task remaining before us—that from these honored dead we take increased devotion to that cause for which they here gave the last full measure of devotion—that we here highly resolve that

these dead shall not have died in vain, that this nation under God shall have a
new birth of freedom, and that government of the people, by the people, for
the people shall not perish from the earth. (Lincoln, 1863)

It is virtually impossible to visit a Civil War battlefield and *not* hear these
words, or at least phrases from this speech. They echo softly in your head as
you stare shamefacedly out at a little field and contemplate the thousands
who died on it; they are printed on pamphlets, signs, and monuments all
around you; they are spoken by park personnel and interpretive guides in
their presentations, and they are reiterated by tourists when they chat softly
among themselves or explain to their children why they have come here
instead of going to the beach or the amusement park. Phrases from Lincoln's
speech serve as linguistic shortcuts—"ideographs," in McGee's (1980) sense—
that can be dropped easily into our conversations to convey a host of ideas
and beliefs and attitudes about what Bellah (1980) calls our civil religion.
Uttering those phrases is part of the performance of veneration of our government, ourselves: *It is proper for us to do this, to come here to hallow the
ground that we cannot hallow because it is already hallowed by the blood of
the fallen, but at least we can rededicate ourselves and strengthen our resolve
and commitment to government of, by, and for the people. Amen.*

Performatively, the tautological nature of this civic prayer becomes "taute-
gorical" (see Edwards, 1999), insofar as it achieves a particular form of
forgetting-as-memorializing that Kammen (1997) dubs the "heritage syn-
drome" (p. 220), an approach to the presentation and performance of history
at or of a cultural landscape that usually results in "commercialization, vulgarization, oversimplification and tendentiously selective memories—which
means both warping and whitewashing a fenced-off past" (p. 221). The most
conspicuous form of "forgetting" involved here is that which occurs when
words uttered for a very specific occasion—the dedication of a cemetery for
Union soldiers who died at Gettysburg—are applied to *all* soldiers from *both*
sides of the conflict who fought in *any* battle in the Civil War. The battlefield
tour and its performances stress the extraordinary events of the battle as a
whole, as well as the extraordinary feats and sacrifices of combatants. Two
other sorts of "forgetting" seem immediately apparent: strategic or operational blunders that resulted in the slaughter that was most Civil War battles
are reinterpreted as unfortunate but understandable given the tactical situation (or vice versa); and the whole reason for the war is forgotten in favor of
the human drama of ordinary people facing extraordinary circumstances.

Why were they fighting in the first place? This is a complicated question to
which thousands of people have devoted millions of pages. Battlefields and

war memorials ignore the questions in favor of proclaiming that whatever happened was, in the end, good; they convert problematic things into appropriate, commendable, preordained things—of, by, and for the people. It is hard for us to interrogate why people fought and died for the Confederacy, much less to reproach them for doing so, when every battlefield sanctifies the mere fact that they did so and when most of the monuments on those battlefields conflate the Confederate cause with "freedom" and "fighting for their country" and "states' rights." Indeed, as Mayo (1988) noted in his examination of the monuments and memorials placed at the major battlefields of Gettysburg and Vicksburg, "The visitor unaware of history could just as easily perceive that the South had won these major battles" (p. 176). The visitor looking for some symbolic proclamation of Southern guilt or Confederate defeat must search for it outside the battlefield proper.

At the conclusion of his analysis of the end of the Confederacy and the development of the Lost Cause mythology in the New South, my colleague, the historian Gaines Foster (1987), observed:

> The rapid healing of national divisions and damaged southern self-image . . . came at the cost of deriving little insight or wisdom from the past. Rather than looking at the war as a tragic failure and trying to understand it, or even condemn it, Americans, North and South, chose to view it as a glorious time to be celebrated. Most ignored the fact that the nation had failed to resolve the debate over the nature of the Union and to eliminate the contradictions between its equalitarian ideals and the institution of slavery without resort to a bloody civil war. Instead, they celebrated the war's triumphant nationalism and martial glory. (p. 196)

The creation of battlefields and military parks, together with the erection of thousands of Civil War monuments in the late 19th/early 20th century, was part of that effort. Civil War battlefields invite us to perform and perpetuate our historical failure to examine the contradictions in our society, particularly the racial questions that remain unresolved nearly a century and a half later, providing us instead with occasions and stages wherein the ideological may pass unreflectively into the physiological, where nationalism and militarism and the willed amnesia regarding the causes of the war need not be contemplated as ideas but experienced and felt as a great collective wargasm. I could understand Gaines's reaction when I mentioned in casual conversation with him shortly after returning from my trip how I'd spent my summer visiting and doing research at the battlefields. He rolled his eyes, shuddered theatrically, and groaned: "I think they all ought to be turned into parking lots" (G. Foster, personal communication, October 1997).

Tourist Performance as Invention

My impression is that American culture easily encourages people to assume that a first-person anecdote is primarily oriented toward the emotive and connotative functions, in Jakobson's terms, of communication: that is, toward speaker-expressive and addressee-connective activity, or an I/you axis in discourse. However, I take anecdotes, or yarns, to be primarily referential. They are oriented futuristically towards the construction of a precise, local, and social discursive context, of which the anecdote then functions as a mise en abyme. That is to say, anecdotes for me are not expressions of personal experience but allegorical expositions of a model of the way the world can be said to be working.

M. Morris, "Banality in Cultural Studies"

I would like now to return to the story of my search for Stonewall Jackson's arm, to reread it not as a sample of the genre of tourist performances of narrating/reminiscing but as an allegorical model of tourist performances of a different sort than the one described in the preceding section. More specifically, I would like to suggest that some tourist performances resemble a research method of simulation and experiment suggested by Walter Benjamin, among others. I might define that method by saying that it has as its goal *the staging of knowledge*—a phrase that I hope will serve as an attention-getter, and that takes as its immediate source Jean-Luc Godard's (1972) well-known statement about his aims as a filmmaker: "Cinema, Truffaut said, is spectacle—Méliès—and research—Lumière. If I analyse myself today, I see that I have always wanted to do research in the form of a spectacle" (p. 181).

By proposing that the key to the 19th century lay in the Arcades of Paris and their spectacle of consumerism, with their flâneurs and shop windows and gas-lit evenings, and by further outlining a historical method that seems both the extreme of scholarly research—"[E]verything one is thinking at a specific moment in time must at all costs be incorporated into the project at hand" (Benjamin, 1999a, p. 456)—and its negation—"I needn't *say* anything. Only show" (p. 460)—Benjamin (1994) anticipated Godard's concerns. In *The Arcades Project,* which he called "the theater of all my conflicts and all my ideas" (p. 359), Benjamin's efforts to stage knowledge provide a solution to what he called "a central problem of historical materialism": "Must the Marxist understanding of history necessarily be acquired at the expense of the perceptibility of history? Or: In what way is it possible to conjoin a heightened graphicness to the realization of the Marxist method?" (Benjamin, 1999a, p. 461).

In *The Pleasure of the Text*, Roland Barthes (1975) takes a similar tack, noting that philosophical knowledge becomes more receivable, more pleasurable, when grounded in the presentation of details of everyday life he called "the novelistic": "Why do some people, including myself, enjoy in certain novels, biographies, and historical works the representation of the 'daily life' of an epoch, of a character? Why this curiosity about petty details: schedules, habits, meals, lodging, clothing, etc." (p. 53). In his autobiography, Barthes (1977) recognized that this matter went beyond the tactics of presentation, that it was itself a mode of cognition, a way of conducting research, creating knowledge and not just representing it:

> The Lacanian subject (for instance) never makes him think of Tokyo, but Tokyo makes him think of the Lacanian subject. This procedure is a constant one; he rarely starts from an idea in order to invent an image for it subsequently; he starts from a sensuous object, and then hopes to meet in his work with the possibility of finding an abstraction for it, levied on the intellectual culture of the moment: philosophy then is no more than a reservoir of particular images, of ideal fictions (he borrows objects, not reasonings). Mallarmé speaks of "gestures of the idea": he finds the gesture first (expression of the body), then the idea (expression of the culture, of the intertext). (p. 99)

Fifty years earlier, looking for a way to formulate the rhetorical complement to this epistemology, Benjamin (1996) wrote that "[t]o convince is to conquer without conceptualization" (p. 446), an aphorism suggesting knowledge's dependence on something other than abstractions—on, for example, a chance encounter with a postcard in the visitor's center at a Civil War battlefield. As Benjamin (1996) further noted, "To someone looking through piles of old letters, a stamp that has long been out of circulation on a torn envelope often says more than a reading of dozens of pages" (p. 478).

The problem, of course, is that it is often difficult to notice the stamp when your focus is on the project of looking through the letters. Freud (1989) knew the problem too, proposing as a solution the sort of attentive inattention that was the hallmark of his analytical sessions and that he believed allowed analysts to listen differently. The surrealists, who borrowed from Freud's method, proposed to offer training in how to notice something like Benjamin's stamp. For the surrealists, film was a crucial site, both the miracle cure and the old problem writ large. By virtue of its capacity to extract people and things from the world, film had the capacity to make them visible as never before. However, by making every detail of a film subservient to the narrative, cinema discouraged the kind of distracted attention that allowed one to notice the stamp instead of the letter. At every moment, an isolated image fragment threatened to become more interesting than the film of which it was a part, hence the need to integrate or subsume those fragments into the linear, forward-moving structure of the film's narrative. As Mulvey (1975/1990) pointed out in her influential essay "Visual Pleasure and Narrative Cinema," for example, images of women are crucial to the scopophilic pleasure offered in film but also its potential undoing: "The presence of woman is an indispensable element of spectacle in normal narrative film, yet her visual presence tends to work against the development of a story line, to freeze the flow of action in moments of erotic contemplation. This alien presence then has to be integrated into cohesion with the narrative" (p. 33). Finding ways to resist such integration, of course, became the favored tactic of feminist filmmakers and critics.

In all these cases—Benjamin, Barthes, Freud, the surrealists, feminist film critics—the method of producing new knowledge relied heavily on fragmentation, the interruption of narratives, habits, routines, by allowing oneself to follow random or chance encounters with whatever objects, images, gestures, or petty details one might be drawn to at a given moment. Breton, for example, recommended walking into the middle of a film and leaving when the story began to become too comprehensible. And Barthes (1982) was fascinated with Japan precisely because he did not understand it, had little prior knowledge of its language, history, or culture. As a result, he was "delivered of any fulfilled meaning" (p. 9)—freed from the responsibility to integrate what he saw and experienced into a preexisting conceptual framework—and thus able to experience a magical defamiliarization of the world around him. The trick for Barthes then became one of transposing or reproducing this experience within his own culture, hence his later experiments with fiction, romance, film, and photography. And it was this reenchantment or, better, repoeticization (see Benjamin, 1999b, p. 208) of the world—what he described as its "profane illumination" (p. 209)—that Benjamin discovered in the writings of the surrealists and in the practices of the flâneur and the collector.

As I suggested earlier, and as Barthes's experience in Japan reminds us, tourism presents us with innumerable opportunities to estrange ourselves from our habitual perceptions, interactions, and understandings of the world. Indeed, as Urry (1990) has argued, the promise or hope of such encounters is what often drives us to travel in the first place. Tourism promises transformation into, or self-actualization of, a more authentic self by virtue of contacts or encounters with extraordinary phenomena. Like film to the surrealists, it promises to lift the veil from our eyes, reminding us of the marvelous, intoxicating character of the world around us. It has the capacity to make ordinary things—walking, eating, sleeping, looking at other people or the environment—strange, difficult, unfamiliar. Yet, like film, which subordinates the individual shot or frame to the narrative, tourism offers us plenty of material to construct our "alibi" (Barthes, 1972) for denying the surreal evidence of our experience.

In addition to the tacit scripts tourists are invited to perform, such as the staff ride–like performance of a Civil War battlefield tour previously discussed, performers are also subject to the disciplinary gaze of co-participants and onlookers, including especially the locals and workers at tourist sites (Crang, 1997), and the appropriateness of tourists' performances will depend as much on the ability of their audiences to share the meaning the actors hope to transmit as on their understanding of the script. This internal and external surveillance may restrict the scope of tourists' performances and help to underscore communal conventions about "appropriate" ways of acting as a tourist. As Goffman (1959) would have it, social actors frequently aim for coherence, so that their characters can be understood as consistent and predictable and ambivalence and ambiguity may be reduced. Saving face and maintaining one's "cool" in the presence of sights or encounters that should astonish us, the "hipness unto death," as Miller (1988) called it in another context, is so much a part of our habitual social performance that displaying any affect whatsoever is often considered bad form, especially to the "post-tourist."

However, rather than being fixed, performance is always an interactive and contingent process. Even the most carefully rehearsed and repeated social performance must be reenacted in different conditions, and its reception may be unpredictable. Each performance can never be exactly reproduced, and fixity of meaning must be continually striven for. As Schechner (1985) noted, every effort to "restore" or reiterate some earlier behavior is always a reinvention of that behavior (pp. 36–37; see also Schieffelin, 1998, pp. 196–199). Everywhere there are gaps, interruptions, and distractions as we confront other people, practices, and sights that confound our own habitual, unreflexive way of doing things. Even within the most conscientiously sustained effort to replicate the scripts that have been laid out for them, tourist performances break through constantly into other registers, other keys—tentative, fleeting moments of improvised resistance to or freedom from the performative force of habit.

Where, for instance, does a visit to a Civil War battlefield fit within the plot of a family vacation? What may be a desire for a Civil Wargasm for one member of the family may be to others the bit of "history" that is dropped into the mix with the "nature" or "culture," like the roughage in the diet, because it's thought to be "good for you." As Neumann (1999) reminds us, the family vacation is often an occasion for split-second performances of an idealized version of self and of family identity in which the expectations for the journey and the experience of living through it create gaps and fissures that are difficult to mend or conceal:

The inherent pushes and pulls that inevitably accompany actually spending an extended time together can quickly dissolve and reconstitute on vacation. "Can we at least try to look like a family?" a wife says, frustrated. I watch the instantaneous retrieval of postures and smiles, a fatherly hand placed on a son's shoulder in the pause before the camera shutter opens and lifted off when it closes. Such moments give us a glimpse of the gaps that open up between the lived and the imagined, a canyon of divided selves, a ritualized dwelling in double consciousness, a time for seeing with split vision. Tourists tack back and forth between the ideals and the realities of their vacations, and also of the selves and families who live in each. In the struggle to keep it all together, they shape-shift into various "possible families," resurrected by the rites of vacation time and the occultlike power of photo opportunities. And in this pursuit of the vacation as an ideal family time, one for making and collecting material fictions, desires not only get expressed but continue to flourish. Sometimes the quest for freedom may become encumbered by the very weight carried in expectations for the journey. (p. 272)

The problem, in short, is not one of forcing a shift from flow to reflexivity or of creating gaps—that happens routinely—but of recognizing them, taking advantage of them, figuring out what to do with them once they occur.

The story of my search for Stonewall's arm, though it happens to be a true story, is intended as an allegorical model of what can happen (and what, I am convinced, does happen) when tourists take advantage of such moments. Clifford (1988) has written of how people increasingly produce creolized practices through their use of an expanded range of cultural resources, they "improvise local performances from (re)collected pasts, drawing on foreign media, symbols and languages" (p. 14). Rojek (1997) draws an analogy between tourist performance and the active receptivity of Internet browsing, where individuals "index and drag" materials from a variety of sources into an original composition of their own, a practice Rojek calls "collage tourism" (p. 62). Besides these mergings, contesting performances take place on the same stage, perhaps expressing different dispositions and identities informed by class, gender, age, and ethnicity. As other studies have shown, there are multiple ways of carrying out particular kinds of actions, such as walking, gazing, making photographs, or narrating/reminiscing, that seem to constitute the bulk of tourists' performances (see, e.g., Crawshaw & Urry, 1997; Edensor, 1998, 2000, 2001; MacCannell, 2001; Neumann, 1999; Urry, 1999).

It would be easy to stop right here, as many others do, and simply celebrate such things in the cheery "voxpop" way of some cultural studies researchers by noting that, in all the aforementioned instances, tourists can be seen not simply as consumers of others' performances and representations but as producers of their own. But I want to go a little further and extend the conclusion to my own story.

In the particular case of my search for Stonewall's arm, I might say that the chance encounter with a postcard prompted a performance of battlefield tourism that contributed, not to "sight sacralization," but rather to what I might call "site de sacralization" in its refusal of the tour's imperatives—imperatives, I must stress, that I was fully prepared to obey when I arrived—and a cognitive and geographical "remapping" of the battlefields themselves. Moreover, it forced me to reckon with my own assumptions regarding the "tourist gaze" and its role in tourism. While tourism does permit moments of concentrated gazing, and while it may appear that certain styles of gazing seem prevalent among tourists, a more appropriate descriptor for how tourists interact with sights might, as Chaney (2002) recently pointed out, be "glancing" rather than gazing (pp. 200–201). As a metaphor for tourists' participation in or consumption of the sights/sites they visit, the gaze is "masculine in the presupposition that it articulates normality, and imperialist in the way it appropriates other cultures. . . . This way of understanding tourist experiences cannot be accepted. It makes all tourism intrinsically and irretrievably morally repugnant" (p. 199). While the scopophilic pleasure of voyeuristically gazing at things you believe cannot look back at you may operate in some sightseeing activities and venues, staring long and hard at things can get you in trouble. Recognizing this, tourists' mode of interaction with the environment is more usually to glance around and fleetingly note different things around them, an implicit acknowledgment that they are simultaneously seeing and being seen.   *to break out of the routine*

Along with Rojek (1997), I think what tourists seek are "distractions" rather than "the extraordinary" or "the authentic," although, like Chaney (2002), I do not believe that we are obliged to turn such an observation into a mass culture critique that says this is all tourists are good for: "It is rather that 'distractions' is a good term for the heterogeneous jumble of tourists' experiences" (p. 205). It is this experience—of being distracted from my original intentions by a chance encounter with a postcard, and then of allowing myself to exist for a day in a state of distractedness—that I prize from my search for Stonewall's arm, precisely because it enabled me to map a new relation to the U.S. Civil War, rather than follow the maps I had been following my whole life. To put the matter another way: Thinking critically about Civil War battlefields did not make me search for Stonewall's arm; rather, looking for Stonewall's arm led me to think critically about Civil War battlefields as a way to account for, to understand, the profane illumination that I had already performed that day.

Notes

1. Although the term is not eponymous, *hooker* became a popular synonym for *prostitute* during the Civil War because of Hooker's own proclivities and the reputation of his encampment during this time, when the "working girls" in Washington's large red light district became known as "Hooker's Division."

2. While the preceding account is my own synopsis of the events at Fredericksburg and Chancellorsville, those interested in more detailed accounts might consult Furgurson (1992) and Sears (1996).

3. During subsequent visits to the battlefield and in conversations with some of the rangers and interpretive guides, I discovered that, no, it couldn't be the spot where Jackson was wounded, although it might be the spot where he was carried immediately after he was wounded. An interpretive presentation about Jackson's shooting is given at a new "spot" perhaps 50 yards from the old "spot" (summer hours only, of course). It talks about archival references to and recent archeological excavation of a long-overgrown trail known as the Mountain Road that passed through the area where the visitor's center now stands, which the park is working to excavate and reconstruct. The presentation endorses the view that Jackson and his entourage must have been riding along this trail when the fatal shots were fired, although, if pressed, the guides will admit that, no, the new spot probably isn't "The Spot," either, and that no one knows where it might be.

4. Two years later, during my next visit, I drove right to Stonewall's arm, in fact. The National Park Service in partnership with the Friends of Wilderness Battlefield organization acquired the Ellwood property, where the arm is buried, in 1998, and had erected signs for it, opened it to the public, and was beginning restoration of the Lacy House and grounds. In 1997, the place was closed, and I couldn't have gotten on the property to see it even if I had found it.

References

Adler, J. (1989). Travel as performed art. *American Journal of Sociology, 94,* 1366–1391.

Barthes, R. (1972). *Mythologies* (A. Lavers, Trans.). New York: Noonday.

Barthes, R. (1974). *S/Z: An essay* (R. Miller, Trans.). New York: Noonday.

Barthes, R. (1975). *The pleasure of the text* (R. Miller, Trans.). New York: Hill & Wang.

Barthes, R. (1977). *Roland Barthes* (R. Howard, Trans.). Berkeley: University of California Press.

Barthes, R. (1982). *Empire of signs* (R. Howard, Trans.). New York: Hill & Wang.

Bellah, R. N. (1980). *Varieties of civil religion.* San Francisco: Harper & Row.

Benjamin, W. (1994). Letter to Gerhard Scholem (M. R. Jacobson & E. M. Jacobson, Trans.). In G. Scholem & T. W. Adorno (Eds.), *The correspondence of Walter Benjamin, 1910–1940* (pp. 358–360). Chicago: University of Chicago Press.

Benjamin, W. (1996). One-way street (E. Jephcott, Trans.). In M. Bullock & M. W. Jennings (Eds.), *Walter Benjamin: Selected writings: Vol. 1. 1913–1926* (pp. 444–488). Cambridge, MA: Harvard University Press.

Benjamin, W. (1999a). *The arcades project* (H. Eiland & K. McLaughlin, Trans.). Cambridge, MA: Harvard University Press.

Benjamin, W. (1999b). Surrealism: The last snapshot of the European intelligentsia (E. Jephcott, Trans.). In M. W. Jennings, H. Eiland, & G. Smith (Eds.), *Walter Benjamin: Selected writings: Vol. 2. 1927–1934* (pp. 207–221). Cambridge, MA: Harvard University Press.

Boal, A. (1985). *Theatre of the oppressed* (C. A. McBride & M-O. L. McBride, Trans.). New York: Theatre Communications Group.

Boorstin, D. (1987). *The image: A guide to pseudo-events in America.* New York: Vintage. (Original work published 1962)

Bowman, M. S. (1998). Performing southern history for the tourist gaze: Antebellum home tour guide performances. In D. Pollock (Ed.), *Exceptional spaces: Essays in performance and history* (pp. 142–158). Chapel Hill: University of North Carolina Press.

Bruner, E. M. (1991). The transformation of self in tourism. *Annals of Tourism Research, 18,* 238–250.

Bruner, E. M. (1994). Abraham Lincoln as authentic reproduction: A critique of postmodernism. *American Anthropologist, 96,* 397–415.

Carlson, M. (1996). *Performance: A critical introduction.* New York: Routledge.

Chaney, D. (2002). The power of metaphors in tourism theory. In S. Coleman & M. Crang (Eds.), *Tourism: Between place and performance* (pp. 193–206). New York: Berghahn.

Clifford, J. (1988). *The predicament of culture: Twentieth-century ethnography, literature, and art.* Cambridge, MA: Harvard University Press.

Crane, S. (1951). *The red badge of courage: An episode of the American Civil War.* New York: Modern Library. (Original work published 1894)

Crang, P. (1997). Performing the tourist product. In C. Rojek & J. Urry (Eds.), *Touring cultures: Transformations of travel and theory* (pp. 137–154). London: Routledge.

Crawshaw, C., & Urry, J. (1997). Tourism and the photographic eye. In C. Rojek & J. Urry (Eds.), *Touring cultures: Transformations of travel and theory* (pp. 176–195). London: Routledge.

Crouch, D. (2002). Surrounded by place: Embodied encounters. In S. Coleman & M. Crang (Eds.), *Tourism: Between place and performance* (pp. 207–218). New York: Berghahn.

Culler, J. (1988). The semiotics of tourism. In J. Culler, *Framing the sign: Criticism and its institutions* (pp. 153–167). Norman: University of Oklahoma Press.

Debord, G. (2000). Theory of the dérive (K. Knabb, Trans.). Retrieved April 11, 2004, from www.cddc.vt.edu/situationist/si/theory.html. (Original work published 1958)

DeLyser, D. (1999). Authenticity on the ground: Engaging the past in a California ghost town. *Annals of the Association of American Geographers, 89,* 602–632.

Desmond, J. C. (1999). *Staging tourism: Bodies on display from Waikiki to Sea World.* Chicago: University of Chicago Press.

Dorst, J. D. (1989). *The written suburb: An American site, an ethnographic dilemma.* Philadelphia: University of Pennsylvania Press.

Edensor, T. (1998). *Tourists at the Taj: Performance and meaning at a symbolic site.* London: Routledge.

Edensor, T. (2000). Staging tourism: Tourists as performers. *Annals of Tourism Research, 27,* 322–344.

Edensor, T. (2001). Performing tourism, staging tourism: (Re)producing tourist space and practice. *Tourist Studies, 1,* 59–81.

Edwards, P. (1999). Neuschwanstein or the sorrows of Priapus. *Text and Performance Quarterly, 19,* 271–306.

Feifer, W. (1985). *Going places.* New York: Macmillan.

Foote, K. E. (1997). *Shadowed ground: America's landscapes of violence and tragedy.* Austin: University of Texas Press.

Foster, G. M. (1987). *Ghosts of the Confederacy: Defeat, the lost cause, and the emergence of the New South, 1865–1913.* New York: Oxford University Press.

Freud, S. (1989). Recommendations to physicians practicing psycho-analysis. In P. Gay (Ed.), *The Freud reader* (pp. 356–363). New York: W. W. Norton.

Frow, J. (1991, Summer). Tourism and the semiotics of nostalgia. *October, 57,* 123–151.

Furgurson, E. B. (1992). *Chancellorsville, 1863: The souls of the brave.* New York: Alfred A. Knopf.

Godard, J. L. (1972). *Godard on Godard* (T. Milne, Trans.). New York: Viking.

Goffman, E. (1959). *The presentation of self in everyday life.* New York: Anchor-Doubleday.

Horwitz, T. (1998). *Confederates in the attic: Dispatches from the unfinished Civil War.* New York: Pantheon.

Hymes, D. (1975). Breakthrough into performance. In D. Ben-Amos & K. S. Goldstein (Eds.), *Folklore: Performance and communication* (pp. 11–74). The Hague: Mouton.

Kammen, M. (1997). History is our heritage: The past in contemporary American culture. In M. Kammen, *In the past lane: Historical perspectives on American culture* (pp. 213–225). New York: Oxford University Press.

Kirshenblatt-Gimblett, B. (1998). *Destination culture: Tourism, museums, and heritage.* Berkeley: University of California Press.

Kirshenblatt-Gimblett, B., & Bruner, E. M. (1992). Tourism. In R. Bauman (Ed.), *Folklore, cultural performances, and popular entertainments: A communications-centered handbook* (pp. 300–307). New York: Oxford University Press.

Levin, D. (1993). *Modernity and the hegemony of vision.* Berkeley: University of California Press.

Lincoln, A. (1863, November 19). Draft of the Gettysburg address. (Hay copy). [Electronic version]. Retrieved January 27, 2005, from the Library of Congress Web site: www.loc.gov/exhibits/gadd/gatr2.html.

Linenthal, E. T. (1993). *Sacred ground: Americans and their battlefields.* Urbana: University of Illinois Press.

MacCannell, D. (1989). *The tourist: A new theory of the leisure class.* New York: Schocken. (Original work published 1976)

MacCannell, D. (1992). *Empty meeting grounds: The tourist papers.* New York: Routledge.

MacCannell, D. (2001). Tourist agency. *Tourist Studies, 1,* 23–37.

Mayo, J. M. (1988). *War memorials as political landscape: The American experience and beyond.* New York: Praeger.

McGee, M. C. (1980). The ideograph: A link between rhetoric and ideology. *Quarterly Journal of Speech, 66,* 1–16.

Miller, M. C. (1988). The hipness unto death. In M. C. Miller, *Boxed in: The culture of TV* (pp. 3–27). Evanston, IL: Northwestern University Press.

Mitchell, W. J. T. (1994). *Picture theory: Essays on verbal and visual representation.* Chicago: University of Chicago Press.

Morris, M. (1990). Banality in cultural studies. In P. Mellencamp (Ed.), *Logics of television: Essays in cultural criticism* (pp. 14–43). Bloomington: Indiana University Press.

Mulvey, L. (1990). Visual pleasure and narrative cinema. In P. Erens (Ed.), *Issues in feminist film criticism* (pp. 28–40). Bloomington: Indiana University Press. (Original work published 1975)

Neumann, M. (1988, Summer). Wandering through the museum: Experience and identity in a spectator culture. *Border/Lines, 15,* 19–27.

Neumann, M. (1999). *On the rim: Looking for the Grand Canyon.* Minneapolis: University of Minnesota Press.

O'Brien, T. (2004, May 19). The second battle of Chancellorsville. *Christian Science Monitor.* [Electronic version]. Retrieved May 29, 2004, from www.csmonitor.com/2004/0519/p14s02-trgn.html.

Pratt, M. L. (1999). Arts of the contact zone. In D. Bartholomae & A. Petrosky (Eds.), *Ways of reading: An anthology for writers,* 5th ed. (pp. 582–596). Boston: Bedford/St. Martin's. (Original work published 1991)

Ritzer, G., & Liska, A. (1997). "McDisneyization" and "post-tourism": Complementary perspectives on contemporary tourism. In C. Rojek & J. Urry (Eds.), *Touring cultures: Transformations of travel and theory* (pp. 96–109). London: Routledge.

Roach, J. (1996). *Cities of the dead: Circum-Atlantic performance.* New York: Columbia University Press.

Rojek, C. (1997). Indexing, dragging and the social construction of tourist sights. In C. Rojek & J. Urry (Eds.), *Touring cultures: Transformations of travel and theory* (pp. 52–74). London: Routledge.

Schechner, R. (1985). *Between theater and anthropology.* Philadelphia: University of Pennsylvania Press.

Schieffelin, E. L. (1998). Problematizing performance. In F. Hughes-Freeland (Ed.), *Ritual, performance, media* (pp. 194–207). London: Routledge.

Sears, S. W. (1996). *Chancellorsville*. Boston: Houghton-Mifflin.

Sedgwick, E. K. (2003). *Touching feeling: Affect, pedagogy, performativity*. Durham, NC: Duke University Press.

Stoft, W. A. (1998). The staff ride and Civil War battlefields. In F. H. Kennedy (Ed.), *The Civil War battlefield guide*, 2nd ed. (pp. 16–17). Boston: Houghton-Mifflin.

Thomas, E. M. (1987). *Travels to hallowed ground: A historian's journey to the American Civil War*. Columbia: University of South Carolina Press.

Turner, R. (1990). Bloodless battles: The Civil War reenacted. *TDR: The Drama Review, 34*(4), 123–136.

Ulmer, G. (1992). Metaphoric rocks: A psychogeography of tourism and monumentality. Retrieved August 19, 2004, from www.clas.ufl.edu/CLAS/Departments/Rewired/ulmer.html.

Urry, J. (1990). *The tourist gaze: Leisure and travel in contemporary societies*. Thousand Oaks, CA: Sage.

Urry, J. (1999). Sensing the city. In D. R. Judd & S. S. Fainstein (Eds.), *The tourist city* (pp. 71–86). New Haven, CT: Yale University Press.

III

Interrogating Histories

Introduction

Judith Hamera

I n "Making History Go" (1998), the introduction to her volume *Exceptional Spaces: Essays in Performance and History,* Della Pollock poses a series of questions that lie at the heart of history's "crisis in representation":

> What does it mean to represent the past? How have politics shaped the traditions of representation? What are the appropriate objects of historical analysis (whether from the prospective of the art, literary, or social historian)? Who are the subjects of history—and are they agents or subjects only? How can the representational tactics of scholars across the disciplines restore and enable historical agency? To what extent is history writing itself an exercise in history making? (pp. 3–4)

These questions vex all critical historians, but, on the surface, they would appear especially challenging for performance-based analysis. This work, as we've seen, takes the multisensory embodiment of/in experience as a fundamental element of research. Yet, for some performance theorists like Peggy Phelan (1995), "The moving body is always fading from our eyes. Historical bodies and bodies moving on stage fascinate us because they fade" (p. 200). This leads Pollock to propose one more very bracing question for performance-based critical historians: "How do we make history *go* when it seems to be *going away?*" (p. 16).

Performance-based historians are particularly attuned to the complex interplay of remembering and forgetting that makes history go, whether as lived experience or as monument. For many, this interplay means that the bodies of/in history do not simply fade; they enter representation in multiple and sometimes contradictory ways. These bodies may leave the stage, but they don't disappear. In *Cities of the Dead* (1996), Joseph Roach outlines one exemplary strategy for interrogating the trialectic of remembering, forgetting, and historical bodies. He examines circum-Atlantic performances deeply enmeshed in colonialism, the slave trade, and other violent local encounters across multiple dimensions of difference. Roach then uses these events to explore

> how culture reproduces and re-creates itself by a process that can best be described by the word *surrogation*. In the life of a community, the process of surrogation does not begin or end but continues as actual or perceived vacancies occur in the networks of relations that constitute the social fabric. Into the cavities created by loss through death or other forms of departure, I hypothesize, survivors attempt to fit satisfactory alternatives. Because collective memory works selectively, imaginatively, and often perversely, surrogation rarely if ever succeeds. (p. 2)

Performance is the ideal lens through which to view cultural (re)production in/as history because "specific performances so often carry with them the memory of otherwise forgotten substitutions—those that were rejected and, even more invisibly, those that have succeeded" (Roach, 1996, p. 5). For performance-based critical historians like Roach, as for Faulkner, the past is not dead. It is not even past. It presents itself to the contemporary researcher as pockmarked by ellipses. It gets rerouted in new directions or sent down blind alleys, or it is taken up by the next generation of actors in borrowed clothes, sometimes ill-fitting, sometimes tailored too well. It never simply disappears.

In a related vein, performance-based approaches to history explore relationships between here and now, there and then, through both textual and corporeal micropractices. The performance studies scholar Diana Taylor (2003) uses the formulations "the archive" and "the repertoire" to describe the critical historian's objects of analysis. She writes:

> "Archival" memory exists as documents, maps, literary texts, letters, archeological remains, bones, videos, films, CDs, all those items supposedly resistant to change. . . . There are several myths attending the archive. One is that it is unmediated, that objects located there might mean something outside the framing of the archival impetus itself. What makes an object archival is the process whereby it is selected, classified, and presented for analysis. Another myth is that the archive resists change, corruptibility, and political manipulation. (p. 19)

The archive continually interacts with the "repertoire," which

> . . . enacts embodied memory: performances, gestures, orality, dance, singing— in short, all those acts usually thought of as ephemeral, nonreproducible

knowledge.... Performances also replicate themselves through their own structures and codes. This means that the repertoire, like the archive, is mediated.... Embodied and performed acts generate, record, and transmit knowledge. (pp. 20–21)

Taylor argues for a methodology that both uses and expands conventional understandings of the archive, one that focuses on "scenarios" rather than simply on texts: "The *scenario* includes features well theorized in literary analysis, such as narrative and plot, but demands ... attention to milieux and corporeal behaviors such as gestures, attitudes, and tones not reducible to language" (p. 28).

This is precisely what D. Soyini Madison (1998) does in her analysis of the oral narratives of Mrs. Alma Kapper. Madison uses "poetic transcription" to preserve the rhythms and cadences that animate Mrs. Kapper's oral history and connect her personally, culturally, and historically to the melodious forms of African American speech (p. 322). Along with her sensitivity to what Barthes (1985) would call "the grain of the voice," Madison brings a keen awareness of the relationship between these embodied practices and the realities they represent in Mrs. Kapper's narrative ("the told") and in her performance of it ("the telling"). In one narrative, Mrs. Kapper describes confronting a crooked white landowner who cheated his workers by misrepresenting cotton prices and paying them far less than what they were entitled to. Madison gently uplifts the social, political exigencies that undergirded the complex relationships between the textual told and the corporeal telling, here and now, there and then, in her informant's story.

> Mrs. Kapper's performance in the told presented the brave woman who stood up for herself and others against the oppressive landowner. It was the boast within the told that strained against the years of fear and resentment manifested in the whispered telling. The two performances are evident in Mrs. Kapper's narrative: she tells off the landowner, "sho' did!" and at the same time—after more than sixty years, from a distance of thousands of miles, in the safety of a public day care program and in the privacy of our little room behind closed doors—she still felt she had to whisper. (p. 331)

For critical performance scholars, this sensitivity to embodiment in the multiple interactions between archive and repertoire is not one-way only. Critical performance scholars recognize and acknowledge that they too are enabled and constrained as bodies in history. Consider Lisa Merrill's (1999) precise, situated engagement with the intersections of archive and repertoire in the case of the 19th-century American actress, Charlotte Cushman. Merrill begins her examination of Cushman's remarkable life by reflecting on the "passions embodied and remembered" in an entry in her diary:

> Every time I request the diary, I wait a few impatient minutes while the librarians retrieve it. The diary is fragile, guarded, filed away. . . . The pencil marks are faded and smudged. I hold the diary carefully in my hand and note how Cushman, a lesbian in an era before some claim the word—or the self-identification—existed, wrote about the woman she was leaving behind. Others have seen this diary—certainly the partner who survived Charlotte and the few twentieth century researchers who wrote or attempted to write biographies. What do I see that they have not? How has the shared referentiality of lesbian experience and recent work in gay and lesbian history allowed me to see and understand the apprehensions and the longing Charlotte felt as she sat on shipboard, more than a century and a half ago, summoning up the memory of her lover? (pp. 1–2)

Shannon Jackson (2000) reminds us that "[c]allused fingers, numb limbs, and swollen feet are all quite literal reminders of the bodily basis of research" (p. 3), whether in the field or in the archive. In the opening paragraphs of her essay in this section, Ruth Bowman reminds us of this too.

The essays that follow interrogate history by reading and expanding the frame of the archive in light of specific embodied repertoires. Both Bowman and Dwight Conquergood capture the grains of bodies and voices as they ask: What has been expelled from or ignored by the archive? What tropes and traces can the critical historian follow to observe the complex genealogical processes of surrogation at work in a Louisiana plantation/museum, and in the history of speech communication itself? Both essays make history go by offering and modeling methods of critical analysis, of "doing" history, that include but move beyond explicating their particular sites. Further, these essays interrogate the processes by which archival histories are themselves made and authorized and show us how, using the tools of performance-based scholarship, they can be remade.

References

Barthes, R. (1985). The grain of the voice. In *The responsibility of forms: Critical essays on music, art, and representation* (R. Howard, Trans.; pp. 267–277). New York: Hill & Wang.

Jackson, S. (2000). *Lines of activity: Performance, historiography, Hull-House domesticity.* Ann Arbor: University of Michigan Press.

Madison, D. S. (1998). That was my occupation: Oral narrative, performance, and black feminist thought. In D. Pollock (Ed.), *Exceptional spaces: Essays in performance and history* (pp. 319–342). Chapel Hill: University of North Carolina Press.

Merrill, L. (1999). *When Romeo was a woman: Charlotte Cushman and her circle of female spectators.* Ann Arbor: University of Michigan Press.

Phelan, P. (1995). Thirteen ways of looking at *Choreographing Writing.* In S. L. Foster (Ed.), *Choreographing history* (pp. 200–210). Bloomington: Indiana University Press.

Pollock, D. (1998). Introduction: Making history go. In D. Pollock (Ed.), *Exceptional spaces: Essays in performance and history* (pp. 1–45). Chapel Hill: University of North Carolina Press.

Roach, J. (1996). *Cities of the dead: Circum-Atlantic performance.* New York: Columbia University Press.

Taylor, D. (2003). *The archive and the repertoire: Performing cultural memory in the Americas.* Durham, NC: Duke University Press.

5

Rethinking Elocution

The Trope of the Talking Book and Other Figures of Speech

Dwight Conquergood

To read without uttering the words aloud or at least mumbling them is a "modern" experience, unknown for millennia. In earlier times, the reader interiorized the text; he made his voice the body of the other; he was its actor.

Michel de Certeau, *The Practice of Everyday Life*

The performer sits under a spotlight surrounded by books on performance. She touches, smells, and tastes some of the books. She holds one of the books up to her ear. She notices you are there. She looks up to speak.

D. Soyini Madison, "Performing Theory/Embodied Writing"

The intellectual currency of "performance" has stimulated a rediscovery of elocution by literary historians[1] and a resuturing of elocution and oral interpretation into the intertwining disciplinary genealogies of English, speech, theater, and performance studies (Jackson, 1999; Lee, 1999). Earlier historical studies of elocution and oral interpretation were written from a history of ideas perspective: the explication of theories and practices in order to trace a line of ideas, issues, debates, and pedagogies.[2] Perhaps the most influential example of this kind of scholarship is Wallace A. Bacon's 1960 article, "The Dangerous Shores: From Elocution to Interpretation," a metadisciplinary essay in which he named and thereby enacted a watershed moment for the field at midcentury. This signal publication—arguably the flagship essay for the new interpretation of literature movement—charted an historical course from elocution's "just and graceful management of the voice, countenance, and gesture" to a "modern view of interpretation as the study of literature through the medium of oral performance" (p. 149). Bacon (1976) theorized the performance of literature as a site for encountering and developing what he called a profound "sense of the other." Drawing on two strands of Bacon's scholarship—his landmark historical research on elocution and his theoretical research on "a sense of the other"—I attempt to rethink and revive interest in elocution by investigating it from the perspectives of those "others" against whom it erected its protocols of taste, civility, and gentility.

Because the major theorists and exemplary practitioners written into the extant history of elocution are overwhelmingly white and privileged, I want to relocate elocution within a wider sociohistorical context of racial tension and class struggle. I approach the elocutionary movement from "below," from the angle of working-class and enslaved people who were excluded from this bourgeois tradition and disciplined by it but who nonetheless raided and redeployed it for their own subversive ends.[3] Drawing on slave narratives, working-class histories, and other historical documents, this essay excavates a hidden history and radical tradition of elocution and oral interpretation.

Voices That Matter

To reach the higher rungs of class respectability, voices had to be "legible," assessed in elocutionary terms of "clarity" and "purity of tone." Anna Russell's *The Young Ladies' Elocutionary Reader* (1853) described an uncultivated voice as smudged like a printer's error: "It resembles, in its effect to the ear, that presented to the eye, when the sheet has been accidentally disturbed in the press, and there comes forth, instead of the clear, dark, well-defined letter, executed distinctly on the fair white page, a blur of half-shade" (p. 15). Elocution was tinctured with printer's ink. It would do for platform and social performance what printer's type did for scribal culture: systematize, standardize, and reproduce exemplary models in which the idiosyncrasy and excess of the oral could be repressed, regulated, and recirculated. Elocution developed and flourished in the 18th and 19th centuries during the crucial period of the rise of industrial capitalism and advance of science, reason, engineering, and commitment to progress and improvement. E. P. Thompson (1963) argued that the industrial "pressures towards discipline and order extended from the factory . . . into every aspect of life: leisure, personal relationships, speech, manners" (p. 401). As part of the same historical and cultural milieu, elocution drew from the same vocabulary: One of its early formations was called the "mechanical school" of elocution (Mattingly, 1972; Roach, 1985). Elocution expressed in another key the body discipline so characteristic of industrial capitalism, but this was a discipline imposed on the bourgeoisie, a way for them to mark "distinction" from the masses (Bourdieu, 1984). Punning on the title of Walter Benjamin's (1969) well-known essay, we can think of elocution as the management of voice in the age of mechanical reproduction.

Elocution was designed to recuperate the vitality of the spoken word from rural and rough working-class contexts by regulating and refining its "performative excess" through principles, science, systematic study, and standards of taste and criticism (Butler, 1997, p. 152). Textual enclosure was the technology of control; thus elocution, an art of the spoken word, was circumscribed by literacy. Ambivalently related to orality, elocution sought to tap the power of popular speech but curb its unruly embodiments and refine its coarse and uncouth features. It was the verbal counterpart, in the domain of speech, of the enclosure acts that confiscated the open commons so crucial to the hardscrabble livelihood and recreation of the poor and privatized them for the privileged classes. Elocution seized the spoken word, the common currency to which the illiterate poor had open access, and made it uncommon, fencing it off with studied rules, regulations, and refinements. An art of linguistic enclosure, elocution's historical rise and development corresponded roughly with the legislative acts of enclosure and displacement, the "clearances," that produced "surplus populations" and cheap labor for urban factories (Marx, 1867/1930, pp. 803–807). The pulpit and the lectern were the loci classici, exemplary sites of demonstration, but these capital sites extended to everyday speech and presentation of self. Elocution was practiced by professional public speakers and readers but was also embodied as a general social sign of gentility as the bourgeoisie conversed, read aloud, and entertained in their parlors. The hegemony of the pulpit and lectern extended into the habitus of the class-conscious home. Coextensive with sartorial codes, like dress it was a way of displaying social status and class background.

Elocution promoted a sizing up of bodies and auditing of voices, a critical scrutiny of "the grain of the voice" (Barthes, 1985). There was a political economy of the voice: How one spoke was part of a circuit of comparison and exchange that produced social value, "the 'sonorous materiality' of words exchanged" (Certeau, 1997, p. 102). Voices were "cultivated" and traded up. The thriving business of elocutionary lectures, training manuals, exercises, lessons, handbooks, workshops, and demonstrations pivoted on this trading up of voices and acquisition of "vocal superiority," vocal capital (Rush, 1879, p. 578). According to James Rush (1879), author of a key elocutionary text, *The Philosophy of the Human Voice*, "Intonation and other modes of the voice" betray class pretenders to "a cultivated ear" (p. 480), to "the ear of a refined and educated taste" (p. 518). Rush reveals that elocutionary proprieties were staked in overlapping class and racial tension with his choice of negative examples: "Hence with a Slavery agitator" and "an abolition preacher about the streets, there is equally an ignorant disregard to the proper, and certainly to the elegant uses of the voice" (p. 480).

The opening scene of Harriet Beecher Stowe's best-selling novel *Uncle Tom's Cabin* (1852/1994) dramatizes the elocutionary surveillance and auditing of other bodies and voices. Stowe introduces one of her most contemptible characters, the slave trader Haley, by immediately subjecting him to a close critical examination of body, voice, and demeanor: "He was a short, thick-set man, with coarse, commonplace features, and that swaggering air of pretension which marks a low man who is trying to elbow his way upward in the world" (p. 1). *Air* was a key word grounded in the dramaturgy of social relations; it referred to a style of personal presentation, demeanor, that registered class tension, as in "putting on airs." Stowe encourages the cultivated reader to "catch" this slave catcher in the act of class pretension. She first tells us that his speech was "in free and easy defiance of Murray's Grammar" (p. 1) and then dramatizes his slips and class-marked dialect: "Yes, I consider religion a valeyable thing in a nigger, when it's the genuine article, and no mistake" (p. 2). Later, she describes him as someone who "slowly recited" texts: "He was not a remarkably fluent reader, and was in the habit of reading in a sort of recitative half-aloud" (p. 101). Haley's labored oral reading skills are in marked contrast to the elocutionary ability of light-skinned blacks, particularly Cassy: "She then read aloud, in a soft voice, and with a beauty of intonation" (p. 313).

Haley's "gentleman" interlocutor, Mr. Shelby, escapes critical inspection; the narrator keeps at a respectful remove and quickly merges him into the class habitus of his "well-furnished dining parlor": "Mr. Shelby . . . had the appearance of a gentleman, and the arrangements of the house, and the general air of the housekeeping indicated easy, and even opulent circumstances" (p. 1). Genteel bodies pass as unmarked norms of decorum, whereas "low-bred" and "vulgar" bodies are marked by their deviancy from bourgeois standards of taste.

Throughout the novel, Stowe articulates racial and class identity and moral character against norms of elocution in complex and troubling ways. The imbrication of colorism and elocution is particularly disturbing. The "full blacks" speak in thick dialect with "barbarous, guttural, half-brute intonation" (p. 300), whereas the light-skinned "mulatto" George Harris "talked so fluently, held himself so erect" (p. 10) and had a self-possessed "attitude, eye, voice, manner" of speaking (p. 172). Stowe's class animosity is expressed in grotesque descriptions of "low-bred" whites whose coarse features and elocutionary shortcomings correspond with moral flaws. These characters— Haley, Loker, and Legree—speak in dialect and are not quite white (Jacobson, 1998). Stowe's detailed, head-to-toe inspections of working-class white bodies ironically mirrors the scene of invasive physical examination of black bodies for sale at auction (p. 289).[4]

Elocutionary protocols anticipated Judith Butler's (1993) theory of performativity as the reiteration, "citation," of a set of norms, but elocution would rework performativity as disembodied citationality into a re-embodied *recitationality* (p. 14). The normative would become naturalized through habitual performance, and the hegemonic force is captured in Rush's (1879) description of elocutionary discipline as "frequent repetition" becoming "an eficacious [sic] habit" until "atention [sic] fading into habit" enables "the shore to be reached, and the life to be saved" (p. 479). But the metaphor of swimming, "sucesfully [sic] employed in danger," reminds us that elocution was part of a punitive regime of body discipline and vocal discrimination (p. 479).

The "natural school" of elocution demonstrates how hegemony works: that is, what is really cultured and acquired masquerades as "nature," thereby concealing its invention and artifice (Vandraegan, 1949). The artistic bedrock of "natural" expression is revealed in Rush's (1879) observation that "the world of Taste goes to the Theater to hear the purest style of Elocution" (478). Although every inch a studied disciplining and remaking of body and voice to accrue class distinction, elocution was ideologically masked as "natural language" (Fliegelman, 1993, pp. 79–94). The uncultivated were then marked as aberrant and unnatural, corruptions of nature. Elocution wielded the double-edged sword of "nature" against the poor and untutored. Too little cultivation of taste and manners branded one as coarse and uncouth, a transgressor of "universal" laws of "truth, propriety, and taste" that were "drawn from nature" (Rush, 1879, p. 477). On the other hand, too self-conscious a presentation of refinement led to charges of "affectation [sic]" (p. 477). The upwardly mobile classes had to run an elocutionary gauntlet between "awkwardness" and "afectation," too little or too much art (p. 477).

But it was the rerouting of literacy through oral communication, however refined and regulated, that rendered elocution vulnerable to penetration and pilfering from the very classes it was erected against. The spoken-word dimension of elocution provided for the "spillage" from the enclosed written word that the unlettered poor swept up and made their own (Linebaugh, 1992, p. 168). According to John Brewer (1997), the elocutionary practice of public readings mediated the divide between literate elite and illiterate laborers:

> Reading aloud, both in public and in private, was a universal practice that enabled non-readers to share in the pleasures of the literate. In homes, taverns, coffee houses, in fields and on the street, oral and literate cultures were married through the ministrations of the public reader. (p. 187)

Thompson's monumental history *The Making of the English Working Class* (1963) is replete with examples of "radical reading rooms" where "the custom of reading aloud the Radical periodicals, for the benefit of the illiterate" nurtured "the values of intellectual inquiry and of mutuality" (p. 743). Thompson includes the description of a remarkable, subversive oral reading at a meeting of an underground insurrectionary movement in a field near Sheffield in 1800:

> "[A]t 10 o'clock in the Evening—an orator in a Mask harangues the people— reads [aloud] letters from distant societies by the light of a candle and immediately burns them" (p. 474).

Henry Mayhew (1861/1968) amply documented "street elocution" and "street recitations" in his first volume of *London Labour and the London Poor*, thus making clear that the laboring classes and lumpenproletariat "pitched" and repackaged an elite performance form to their own subaltern needs and recycled it within the scrappy survival economy of the streets (pp. 232–238). They developed their own ethno-aesthetics and standards of evaluation; with a wink to his middle-class reader, Mayhew refers to the discriminating judgment of "a critical professor of street elocution" (p. 236).[5]

The Trope of the Talking Book Reconsidered

In his pathfinding scholarship on the African American literary tradition, Henry Louis Gates (1988) identifies the "trope of the Talking Book" as "the central trope" (p. 152), "the ur-trope," "the fundamental repeated trope" of the Anglo-African tradition that symbolized the tensions between the spoken word and the written word, the African's journey from orality to literacy (pp. 131, 198). He cites Olaudah Equiano's rendering of this trope in *The Interesting Narrative of Olaudah Equiano . . . The African: Written by Himself* (1789/1967) and a prototype for the genre of slave narrative:

> I had often seen my master and Dick employed in reading, and I had a great curiosity to talk to the books, as I thought they did, and so to learn how all things had a beginning: for that purpose I have often taken up a book alone, in hopes it would answer me, and I have been very much concerned when it remained silent. (p. 40)

Gates discusses this passage as an allegory for the struggle of blacks to insert their voice into white texts, to register a black presence in Western literature. The text does not speak to Equiano, according to Gates, because his black countenance and speech stand in Western texts as signs of absence. Gates either ignores or is unaware of the elocutionary milieu within which printed texts were generated, received, interpreted, and *performed*. Voice is not just a metaphor, as Gates would have it, and the vocal performance of texts is not just an allegory but a concrete material practice that suffused literacy in 18th- and 19th-century Anglo-American culture. Elocution illustrates Ngũgĩ wa Thiongo's (1998) concept of "orature," that liminal space between speech and writing, performance and print, where these channels of communication constantly overlap, penetrate, and mutually produce one another. Although Gates has many insightful things to say about the trope of the talking book, he misses the obvious fact that Equiano was signifyin(g) on the widespread elocutionary practice of reading books aloud.

Black people in bondage had an ambivalent relationship with the elocutionary movement of white America. On the one hand, it provided them access to written and printed texts from which they were excluded by draconian legislation that outlawed literacy for enslaved people. One enslaved man had his eyes burned out for learning to read (Berlin, Favreau, & Miller, 1998, p. 280). Much valuable information was leaked through public readings and the practice of reading aloud in the domestic sphere. Although Sojourner Truth never learned to read, she was a great admirer of Walt Whitman's *Leaves of Grass* after first hearing it publicly read (Reynolds, 1996, p. 148). And during the time of her enslavement, she engaged in insurgent eavesdropping, pressing her ear to the door of her mistress's room when confidential letters were read aloud (Truth, 1850/1993, p. 41).

At the same time, white middle class voice, gesture, and countenance were constructed against the black voice and body, the "savage" and "barbarous" (Rush, 1879, pp. 578, 579). Thomas Jefferson (1781/1993), well schooled in elocution, believed that racial "difference is fixed in nature" and contrasted the communicatively flexible and richly expressive blushing white countenance against the illegible opacity and blank unresponsiveness of the black face:

> Are not the fine mixtures of red and white, the expressions of every passion by greater or less suffusions of color in the one, preferable to that eternal monotony, which reigns in the countenances, that immoveable veil of black which covers the emotions of the other race? (p. 238)

He equated blackness with impediment and incommunicability, the antithesis to elocutionary ideals of clarity, contrast, precision, emphasis, variety, fluency, distinction, and balance on vocal as well as visual registers. And, of course, Jefferson misread a complex, deliberate, embodied survival art of protective cover and veiling of feelings as an absence. Enslaved and other vulnerable people do not have the luxury of transparent, clear, direct, and open communication when interpersonal encounters are framed and reverberate with power (Scott, 1990).

In an article in the *Chautauquan,* a journal connected with the 19th-century elocutionary lecture circuit, Sojourner Truth was described as a "grotesque figure" (Carter, 1887, p. 479). In an *Atlantic Monthly* article titled "Sojourner Truth: The Libyan Sibyl," Stowe (1863) described Truth's vocal quality in terms of "the strong barbaric accent of the native African." For Stowe, Truth seemed "to impersonate the fervor of Ethiopia, wild, savage, the hunted of all nations." Mixing racial and class condescension with romanticism, she compared Truth's performance style to that of the French Jewish actress from an impoverished background, Rachel Felix, who "was wont to chant the 'Marseillaise' in a manner that made her seem the very spirit and impersonation of the gaunt, wild, hungry, avenging mob" (p. 477).[6] And Stowe actually performed Truth in dialect for the amusement of her Boston Brahmin social circle (Painter, 1996, p. 154).

If we reconsider the trope of the talking book in early slave narratives as a sign of kidnapped Africans' initial encounter with the elocutionary practice of reading books aloud, then the racially charged tone of the first recorded example—*A Narrative of the Most Remarkable Particulars in the Life of James Albert Ukawsaw Gronniosaw, an African Prince, as Related by Himself* (1770/1996)—makes more sense. Gronniosaw's most painful and defining experience of racial difference was his exclusion from elocution, the refusal of the master's book to speak to him when he put his "ear down close upon it." Recently sold into slavery and new to the culture of "white folks," he was a keen observer of embodied signs who "watched every look" of his new master, a ship captain, so that he could adapt and survive within this new world. His master's custom of reading aloud to the ship's crew both startled and delighted him. "I saw the book talk to my master; for I thought it did, as I observed him to look upon it, and move his lips" (p. 38). Admiration led to imitation, but when he tried to engage the book in dialogue, "open'd it . . . in great hope that it would say something to me," he was deeply disappointed that "it would not speak." He experienced this silence as a culminating moment of exile and excommunication and as a profound rejection of his humanity. Despondent, he concluded "that every body and every thing despis'd me *because I was black*" (p. 38; italics added). His dawning racial consciousness and deep alienation emerged from the jarring encounter with elocution, the preeminent performance of whiteness.

Elocution existed in dialectical tension with minstrelsy, the most popular entertainment form of the 19th century (Lott, 1993, p. 4). Elocution had its framed events—public lectures, readings, recitations, orations, lyceum debates and declamations—but they were marketed as instruction more than entertainment. Unlike minstrelsy, the whole idea and motive for attending an elocutionary performance was to identify with, imitate, and extend the platform model of performance into social performance and the everyday performativity of whiteness. Whereas blackface minstrelsy was a theatrically framed mimicry and parody of blackness, elocution can be thought of as the performativity of whiteness naturalized. Exceeding the bounded performance event, elocution was an all-encompassing style of speaking and deportment that extended from the public sphere into the habitus of the home; hence the elocutionary training for "ladies," who otherwise were not encouraged to speak in public (Ryan, 1994). Because of its hegemonic reach and penetration—"the just and graceful management of the voice, countenance, and gesture"—elocution was more "popular," in the sense of pervasive, even than minstrelsy.

Antithetical in style, elocution and minstrelsy opposed and played off one another in striking and complex ways. Both performance traditions were enormously invested in voice, demeanor, and class difference. Elocution represented the high end, a respectable interest in vocal quality, dignified presence, and improvement for the rising classes. Minstrelsy expressed the low end, a disreputable fascination with vocal difference, burlesque bodies, and vulgar entertainment. Although their connection is seldom discussed, there was mutual acknowledgment, crossover, and some slippage between these contemporary performance formations. Popular elocutionary readers included "dialect pieces," such as Beecher's *Recitations and Readings: Humorous, Serious, Dramatic, Including Prose and Poetical Selections in Dutch, French, Yankee, Irish, Backwoods, Negro, and Other Dialects* (1874). The abolitionist lecture circuit, enfolded within elocutionary lecture circuit, titillated staid middle-class audiences by featuring speeches from fugitive and former slaves. Citing an antislavery newspaper account, John Blassingame (1977) documented that, during one of these speeches, the audience "cheered, clapped, stamped, laughed and wept, by turns" (p. 123). After hearing the lecture of a fugitive slave, Lydia Maria Child observed that she had "seldom been more entertained" and that his "obvious want of education" and "the uncouth awkwardness of his language had a sort of charm" (quoted in Blassingame, 1977, p. 151). John Collins, an agent of the American Anti-Slavery Society, noted in 1842 that "the public have itching ears to hear a colored man speak" (quoted in Blassingame, 1977, p. 123).[7] Coincidentally, the Virginia Minstrels troupe, credited with developing the standard format for the full-fledged minstrel show, formed in the winter of 1842–43 (Lott, 1993, p. 136).

At the opposite pole, minstrel shows included "lectures," along with songs and dances, in their repertory. These "lectures" were caricatures of elocutionary decorum. Black speech and bodies were made to look all the more ridiculous and degraded within the heightened frame of white bourgeois elocution. But these "lectures," along with the stock character of the well-spoken "interlocutor" who was "genteel in comportment" (Lott, 1993, p. 140), were also send-ups of elocutionary propriety. W. T. Lhamon (1998) argues provocatively that in the early years of minstrelsy white lumpen youths identified with blackface as a way of defiantly signaling their disdain and distance from the bourgeois society that excluded and harassed them.[8]

A striking example that brings into sharp focus the dialectical relationship between elocution and minstrelsy is Stowe's strategic response to the minstrelization of *Uncle Tom's Cabin* in the hugely popular Tom shows (Bowman, 2000). As a rebuttal to the sensationalized theatrical adaptations, she dramatized the novel as an elocutionary platform reading for the antislavery lecture circuit. Without recourse to copyright laws, Stowe pitted her own adaptation for dignified solo lectern performance against the minstrelized stage adaptations that were proliferating to her dismay. To further exercise authorial control, she designed her adaptation expressly as a virtuoso vehicle for a designated elocutionary reader whom she had befriended. The title page of the 1855 adaptation reads, *The Christian Slave, a Drama, Founded on a Portion of Uncle Tom's Cabin. Dramatized by Harriet Beecher Stowe, Expressly for the Readings of Mrs. Mary E. Webb.* Trained by the Philadelphia professor of elocution, A. A. Apthorp, Webb drew large and enthusiastic audiences to her dramatic readings of Stowe's text. In Boston's Fremont Temple, she performed *The Christian Slave* to a packed house of

3,500 people, one of the largest audiences ever assembled in that place (Clark, 1997, p. 342).

To complicate further the racialized class politics of *The Christian Slave* readings, Stowe's designated elocutionist, Mary E. Webb, was a woman of color, the daughter of an escaped slave and a "wealthy Spanish gentleman," and was dubbed the "Black Siddons" (Clark, 1997, p. 342). One can only imagine how Webb was "read" as she publicly read from Stowe's lectern-mounted text, doing all the voices (27 characters), including white women and men, as well as black men and women, with some of the blacks and the low-class whites, such as Haley, speaking in thick dialect and the middle-class whites and some of the blacks, such as the light-skinned Cassy, speaking in elevated diction. Refracted through Webb's cultivated voice but racially marked body, Stowe's heteroglossic text must have taken on even more levels of mimicry and layers of "multiaccentuality" (Volosinov, 1986, p. 23). The discreetly channeled thrill of cross-racial impersonation, imposture, and gender play that energized Webb's elocutionary readings needs to be read with and against the contemporary minstrel stage productions. In what ways were Webb's elocutionary readings of *The Christian Slave* a counterperformance to minstrelsy, and in what ways were they complicit with minstrelsy? How did the shadow of minstrelsy intensify the interplay of pleasure and subversion that simultaneously consolidated and unsettled the norms of elocution underpinning Webb's readings? Deliberately produced to trump minstrelsy, Webb's staged readings may have tapped its transgressive charge (Stowe interspersed scenes with songs, including "Way Down Upon the Swanee River"). But whatever else one can say about this politically complicated production, a black woman entered the public sphere as the literal embodiment of the trope of the talking book. The text did speak to and through a black voice and body, and Webb made enough money from her highly successful transatlantic reading tours to support her family, providing her husband with the economic security to leave his business and devote time to completing a novel (Clark, 1997, p. 343).

If Webb's enactment of the trope of the talking book was constrained by white patronage and the protocols of elocution, then Sella Martin's signifyin(g) on this trope provides a remarkable example of black counterpublic reading that Gates does not consider. Martin recounts that, after being sold separately from his beloved mother at the age of 10, he worked as an errand boy in a hotel, where he learned all manner of things by eavesdropping on the guests: "I learned, too, from seeing them reading and writing, that they could make paper and the little black marks on it talk" (Blassingame, 1977, p. 709). He made up his mind that he would learn this skill and set about cajoling and tricking the white boys to teach him the alphabet and how to read. He saw the liberatory potential of literacy, and after his first underground spelling lesson, "with the A B C ringing in my memory, I saw myself already writing a free-pass" (p. 711). He practiced on found texts, "spelling signs and trying to read placard advertisements for runaway slaves" (p. 710). Hearing him spelling out words all the time, the other slaves believed that he could read. One Sunday, three older slaves took him to the woods under the pretence of gathering wild grapes but, once there, pulled out a newspaper filched from the master and demanded that the young Sella read aloud a passage about abolitionists. Overwhelmed because he had only rudimentary spelling skills and had never attempted to read a newspaper before, but afraid of angering his companions by protesting lack of proficiency, he decided to fake it:

> This would be my excuse for looking over the paper with determination to read what I felt they would be pleased to hear, no matter though it should not be in the paper. I handled the paper with a trembling hand, and . . . to my great surprise, I made out this heading of a leading article: "Henry Clay an Abolitionist." I read on a little further. . . . Of course I did not make out fully all the long words . . . but I made a new discovery about my being able to read at all. . . . What I read, or pretended to read, gave the most intense satisfaction, and awakened the wildest hopes about freedom among my hearers. (p. 711)

He becomes self-consciously literate in the transformative moment of reading aloud for a keenly listening audience. This scene is a rite of passage, a "breakthrough into performance": He accomplishes what he mimes and pretends (Hymes, 1981, p. 79). Away from overseers, in the runaway space of the woods where his black compatriots are controlling the scene, the stolen text does talk to and through the young slave. This extraordinary example of the trope of the talking text gives new meaning to Certeau's (1984) subversive analogy of "reading as poaching" (p. 165).

Word spread rapidly, and the same night the hotel kitchen where Martin worked was crowded with slaves from all around, petitioning him to read aloud "some book or newspaper which they had filched from their masters' libraries" (Blassingame, 1977, pp. 711–712). Thus was launched his underground career, his "regular task," of counterpublic "reading to the slaves": He became "an oracle among the slaves" who paid him to perform their poached texts.[9] These ongoing "clandestine" oral readings forged a fellowship of resistance, created "ties which bound" him "in a confederacy of . . . wrong-doing." And the solidarity forged in this insurgent performance space overrode even the master's authority. When his master discovered his illicit elocutionary activity and threatened him with flogging and the auction block—"Don't let me hear of your reading to the slaves again"—he disobeyed because of the reading-forged "ties that . . . it seemed safer to run the risk of being crushed by, than to attempt to break" (p. 712).

While still enslaved, Frederick Douglass (1855/1969) also galvanized a secret slave counterpublic reading group that attracted as many as 40 members. "[H]olding it in the woods, behind the barn, and in the shade of trees," he read to them from *The Columbian Orator*, a popular elocutionary handbook of the day. Inside this subaltern performance space, "an attachment, deep and lasting," developed among the participants. In his autobiographical *My Bondage and My Freedom*, he says that when looking back on the experiences of his life, he recalled "*none* with more satisfaction" than this secret reading circle that constituted an empowering affective homosocial community: "the ardent friendship of my brother slaves. They were, every one of them, manly, generous and brave, yes; I say they were brave, and I will add, fine-looking" (pp. 267–268).

By far the most inventive and radical example of signifyin(g) on literacy and refiguring the trope of the talking book comes from the obscure biographical sketch of Bartley Townsley (Gates, 1988, does not include Townsley in his landmark study of the trope as key to how "the white written text" was made to "speak with a black voice" [p. 131]). Worth quoting at length, Townsley's story is a dramatically compelling example of how enslaved people raided, short-circuited, and rerouted white texts, re-citing them for their own subversive, liberatory ends:

> One night, when he had gone to bed and had fallen to sleep, he dreamed that he was in a white room, and its walls were the whitest he ever saw. He dreamed that some one came in and wrote the alphabet on the wall in large printed letters, and began to teach him every letter, and when he awoke he had learned every letter, and as early as he could get a book, he obtained one and went hard to work. One night very late, when he had come from his coal-kiln, he gathered his books as usual and began to try to spell, but it was not long before he came to a word that he could not pronounce. Now, thought he, what must I do? Then, remembering an old man who was on the farm, about fifty yards away, in a little old cabin, who could read a little, he thought he would go and ask him what the word spelt. The word was i-n-k. So he went quietly through the yard, for it was a very late hour of the night to be moving around, and reaching the cabin, he called him softly, Uncle Jesse! Uncle Jesse! Uncle Jesse! He said (the old man) who is that? Bartley. What do you want this time of the night? I want to know what i-n-k spells! The old man hallooed out, ink! He then returned to his cabin saying ink, ink, ink. After that night he never had any more trouble with ink. In 1852 he began to learn how to write well enough to write his own passes [to steal away]. (Carter, 1888/1969, pp. 112–113)

It is difficult not to read this account as an allegory: the overwhelming whiteness of the enclosed room where he first encountered the alphabet, the symbolic significance of the word he found in the book but could not speak—i-n-k. In the dream where he first saw the writing on the wall, the pages of a book loomed as white walls of a room—the "whitest" he had ever seen—that engulfed him in whiteness. "Ink!" was the revelatory pronouncement that emptied literacy of whiteness and reinvested it with a distinctive black presence as it signified on the colloquialism, "black as ink." A strong black voice calling out "ink!" to him in the dark of night revealed the blackness that was inside texts all the time and that he had not been able to recognize in the blinding whiteness of the room. I-n-k performatively coalesced into "ink!" through transposition from the visual medium of the white page to the auditory register of Uncle Jesse's black voice. Through the synesthesia of recalling printed letters to vocality, first through his oral spelling, i-n-k, and then Uncle Jesse's robust calling, "hallooing out," he was able to hear/see the blackness that was inextricable from the material substance of printed letters. "Ink!" became the signifyin(g) password that liberated literacy from the "white room" and set it loose on the open road in the form of counterfeit freedom passes: "After that he never had any more trouble with ink."

Forgery, both literal and metaphorical, was the key operation and driving force behind slave literacy, and the source of slaveholders' anxiety about slaves learning to read and write. The counterfeit pass was the copy that was both a surrogation and theft of the master's textual power and a depletion of his capital investment. Elocution provided other opportunities for filching the master's texts in order to raid knowledge, reroute authority, and undermine power. We know from Sella Martin's narrative that slaves stole books and newspapers, but they also filched the spoken word. Thomas Johnson (1909) remembered: "While in slavery I would catch at every word that I heard the slave master use, and would repeat it over and over again until I had fixed it on my memory" (p. 40). They also closely studied demeanor and diction and filched elocutionary style. Johnson practiced speaking "with dignity of manner and with much dignity of diction" (p. 40). The acclaimed biographer William S. McFeely (1991) imaginatively reconstructs the young enslaved Frederick Douglass's elocutionary rehearsals:

> If he could say words—say them correctly, say them beautifully—Frederick could act; he could matter in the world. . . . Alone, behind the shipyard wall, Frederick Bailey [Douglass] read aloud. Laboriously, studiously, at first, then fluently, melodically, he recited great speeches. With *The Columbian Orator* in his hand, with the words of the great speakers of the past coming from his mouth, he was rehearsing. He was readying the sounds—and meanings—of words of his own that he would one day speak. (pp. 34–35)

The secret always seeps, enclosures are poached, and hoarded knowledges escape the forms of those who would encrypt them.

Continuities

Recent work in black cultural studies calls for a "black 'performance studies'" that puts performance at the center of black cultural politics and resistance (Diawara, 1996, p. 304; Gilroy, 1995). Black radical scholars are reclaiming oral interpretation of literature as an emancipatory pedagogy and performative cultural politics. bell hooks (1995) situates the performance of literature at the center of the "live arts" tradition that flourished within black working-class communities and historically links it to elocution: "The roots of black performance arts emerge from an early nineteenth century emphasis on oration and the recitation of poetry" (p. 212). She grew up in that tradition and provides an insider view:

> As young black children raised in the post-slavery southern culture of apartheid, we were taught to appreciate and participate in "live arts." Organized stage shows were one of the primary places where we were encouraged to display talent. Dramatic readings of poetry, monologues, or plays were all central to these shows. Whether we performed in church or school, these displays of talent were seen as both expressions of artistic creativity and as political challenges to racist assumptions about the creative abilities of black folks. . . . In my household we staged performances in my living room, reciting poetry and acting in written or improvised drama. . . . I grew up in a working class family, where the particular skills of black art expressed in writing poetry were honored through the act of performance. We were encouraged to learn the works of black poets, to recite them to one another. In daily life, this was both a means of sharing our cultural legacy and of resisting indoctrination from Eurocentric biases within educational institutions that devalued black expressive culture. (pp. 211, 213)

Significantly, hooks turns to ethnography for the project of reclaiming and revaluing African American traditions of performed literature: "It is useful to think in terms of ethnographic performance when charting a cultural history of African-American participation in the performing arts" (p. 213).

Autobiographies provide rich corroborative evidence for hooks's claims about the importance and pervasiveness of oral interpretation of literature in black working-class culture. One thinks immediately of Mrs. Bertha Flowers in Maya Angelou's (1970) *I Know Why the Caged Bird Sings,* who initiated the young Maya into the pleasures of literature. She loaned her books and instructed her to "read them aloud." Oral interpretation was mandatory, she insisted, because "words mean more than what is set down on paper. It takes the human voice to infuse them with the shades of deeper meaning" (p. 82). And when Mrs. Flowers performed literature, Angelou remembers the impact: "I heard poetry for the first time in my life" (p. 84).

In his autobiography *Voices and Silences*, James Earl Jones (1994) recounts his glorious experiences of reading Edgar Allen Poe aloud on an improvised stage in his high school gymnasium in Depression-era Michigan. Even more revealing is the passage in which he remembers his Uncle Bob Walker who loved to recite Shakespeare:

> He was a fine man, not endowed by society or economy with the chance to be highly educated. He worked in the foundry after his discharge from the army. He was unpretentious in his speech but he read Shakespeare with a full appreciation of the English language. I witnessed the joy he took in the words, and found it contagious. (p. 66)

Jones dedicated his autobiography to his high school teacher of literature and oral interpretation.[10]

It is important to take an-*other* look at elocution and oral interpretation and to write revisionist histories that include the encounters and experiences of excluded others for at least three reasons: (1) it is long overdue; (2) it complicates in productive ways our understanding of disciplinary genealogies of performance studies; and (3) it provides compelling evidence and inspiring examples of how dispossessed people, in the word of Marta Savigliano (1995), "trick-back" on an apparatus of oppression, how they trip up and turn its overwhelming force and massive weight against itself and thereby leverage an alternative, provisional space of liberatory struggle (p. 17).[11]

Notes

1. See Fliegelman (1993), Looby (1996), and Portelli (1994). Gerald Graff's (1987) institutional history of English is also helpful, particularly chap. 3, "Oratorical Culture and the Teaching of English" (pp. 36–51). David Reynolds's (1996) cultural biography of Walt Whitman is also useful, especially chap. 6, "American Performances: Theatre, Oratory, Music" (pp. 154–193). Garry Wills's award-winning *Lincoln at Gettysburg* (1992) is a very accessible introduction to the elocutionary milieu of 19-century America. See Cmiel (1990) for more detailed coverage of the same elocutionary ground.

2. See Bacon (1964), Bahn and Bahn (1970), Gray (1960), Howell (1959), Robb (1941), Thompson (1983), and Wallace (1954). For a notable exception from the intellectual history approach, see Mary Strine's (1983) important cultural study of Rush's *Philosophy of the Human Voice* (1879).

---

3. I am particularly indebted to Hobsbawm (1997), Thompson (1963), and Chauncey (1994). Methodologically, I have been influenced by recent work in historical ethnography, notably Comaroff and Comaroff (1991, 1992, 1997), Dening (1996), di Leonardo (1998), Poole (1997), and Savigliano (1995). See also the splendid new performance historiography work of Fuoss (1999), Jackson (1999, 2000), Merrill (1999), Pollock (1998), and Roach (1985, 1996).

4. This essay is not the place, but Stowe's *Uncle Tom's Cabin* begs for a critical rereading from the perspective of the elocutionary milieu that engendered and permeated the novel. Stowe often uses voice, as well as hands—e.g., "delicately formed hand" (p. 4), "a peculiar scowling expression of countenance, and a sullen, grumbling voice" (p. 186)—as metonyms for character. She devotes extraordinary attention to vocal quality, countenance, and hands in both narrative summary and scenic description. And the novel is filled with scenes of characters reading aloud.

5. Cuban cigar makers hired lectors to read aloud literary and sociopolitical texts in the factory to stimulate their minds and provide relief from the mind-numbing labor of cigar rolling. The workers agreed on the reading materials in advance and paid the public reader out of their own pockets. This proletarian elocutionary tradition gained a reputation for being subversive, and in 1866 Cuba passed a law forbidding this practice in all factories. Cuban immigrants brought the tradition of the factory floor lector to America, where it continued until the 1920s. See Manguel (1996, pp. 110–114).

6. Stowe (1863) refers to the actress only as "Rachel." I thank Lisa Merrill for identifying "Rachel" and pointing me to background materials.

7. This is the same John Collins who immediately recruited the fugitive Frederick Douglass to the abolitionist lecture circuit after hearing him speak spontaneously at the first antislavery convention he attended, barely three years after his escape from slavery. Douglass (1855/1969) recalled how Collins would introduce him on the circuit as a "graduate" from "the peculiar institution" of slavery, "*with my diploma written on my back!*" (p. 359; emphasis in original).

8. In addition to the important scholarship on minstrelsy of Lott (1993) and Lhamon (1998), see that of Cockrell (1997), and Bean, Hatch, and McNamara (1996).

9. I am drawing on Nancy Fraser's important work on "counterpublics" in "Rethinking the Public Sphere" (1990). I connected Fraser's work on subaltern counterpublics with performance ethnography in "Rethinking Ethnography" (Conquergood, 1991, p. 189).

10. See also Rogers's (2000) biography of Barbara Jordan for detailed evidence of the persistence and importance of elocutionary activities in 20th-century black working-class communities. See especially chap. 4, "The Gift of the Voice" (pp. 35–59).

11. See also Lowe and Lloyd (1997) for a vigorous analysis of the "alternative" spaces that crack open or can be pried apart within the contradictions of late capitalism (pp. 1–32).

References

Angelou, M. (1970). *I know why the caged bird sings*. New York: Bantam.

Bacon, W. A. (1960). The dangerous shores: From elocution to interpretation. *Quarterly Journal of Speech, 46*, 148–152.

Bacon, W. A. (1964). The elocutionary career of Thomas Sheridan (1719–1788). *Speech Monographs, 31*, 1–53.

Bacon, W. A. (1976). Sense of being: Interpretation and the humanities. *Southern Speech Communication Journal, 41*, 135–141.

Bahn, E., & Bahn, M. (1970). *A history of oral interpretation*. Minneapolis: Burgess.

Barthes, Roland. (1985). *The grain of the voice*. New York: Hill & Wang.

Bean, A., Hatch, J. V., & McNamara, B. (Eds.). (1996). *Inside the minstrel mask: Readings in nineteenth-century blackface minstrelsy*. Hanover, NH: Wesleyan University Press.

Beecher, A. C. (Ed.). (1874). *Beecher's recitations and readings: Humorous, serious, dramatic, including prose and poetical selections in Dutch, French, Yankee, Irish, backwoods, Negro, and other dialects*. New York: Dick & Fitzgerald.

Benjamin, W. (1969). The work of art in the age of mechanical reproduction. In H. Arendt (Ed.), *Illuminations* (Trans. Harry Zohn) (pp. 217–251). New York: Schocken.

Berlin, I., Favreau, M., & Miller, S. F. (Eds.). (1998). *Remembering slavery: African Americans talk about their personal experiences of slavery and freedom*. New York: New Press.

Blassingame, J. W. (Ed.). (1977). *Slave testimony: Two centuries of letters, speeches, interviews, and autobiographies*. Baton Rouge: Louisiana State University Press.

Bourdieu, P. (1984). *Distinction: A social critique of the judgement of taste* (R. Nice, Trans.). Cambridge, MA: Harvard University Press.

Bowman, R. L. (2000). Domestic(ating) excess: Women's roles in *Uncle Tom's Cabin* and its adaptations. *Text and Performance Quarterly, 20*, 113–129.

Brewer, J. (1997). *The pleasures of the imagination: English culture in the eighteenth century*. New York: Farrar, Straus, Giroux.

Butler, J. (1993). *Bodies that matter: On the discursive limits of sex*. New York: Routledge.

Butler, J. (1997). *Excitable speech: A politics of the performative*. New York: Routledge.

Carter, E. R. (1969). *Our pulpit illustrated: Biographical sketches*. Chicago: Afro-Am Press. (Original work published 1888)

Carter, H. (1887). Sojourner Truth. *The Chautauquan, 7*, 477–480.

Certeau, M. de. (1984). *The practice of everyday life* (S. Rendall, Trans.). Berkeley: University of California Press.

Certeau, M. de. (1997) *The capture of speech and other political writings* (L. Giard, Ed.; T. Conley, Trans.). Minneapolis: University of Minnesota Press.

Chauncey, G. (1994). *Gay New York: Gender, urban culture, and the making of the gay male world, 1891–1940*. New York: Basic Books.

Clark, S. R. (1997). Solo black performance before the Civil War: Mrs. Stowe, Mrs. Webb, and 'The Christian Slave.' *New Theatre Quarterly, 13,* 339–348.

Cmiel, K. (1990). *Democratic eloquence: The fight over popular speech in nineteenth-century America.* New York: William Morrow.

Cockrell, D. (1997). *Demons of disorder: Early blackface minstrels and their world.* Cambridge, UK: Cambridge University Press.

Comaroff, J., & Comaroff, J. L. (1991). *Of revelation and revolution: Christianity, colonialism, and consciousness in South Africa* (Vol. 1). Chicago: University of Chicago Press.

Comaroff, J. L., & Comaroff, J. (1992). *Ethnography and the historical imagination.* Boulder, CO: Westview.

Comaroff, J. L., & Comaroff, J. (1997). *Of revelation and revolution: The dialectics of modernity on a South African frontier* (Vol. 2). Chicago: University of Chicago Press.

Conquergood, D. (1991). Rethinking ethnography: Towards a critical cultural politics. *Communication Monographs, 58,* 179–194.

Dening, G. (1996). *Performances.* Chicago: University of Chicago Press.

Diawara, M. (1996). Black studies, cultural studies: Performative acts. In J. Storey (Ed.), *What is cultural studies?* (pp. 300–306). London: Arnold.

di Leonardo, M. (1998). *Exotics at home: Anthropologies, others, American modernity.* Chicago: University of Chicago Press.

Douglass, F. (1969). *My bondage and my freedom.* New York: Dover. (Original work published 1855)

Equiano, O. (1967). *Equiano's travels: The interesting narrative of the life of Olaudah Equiano or Gustavus Vassa the African* (P. Edwards, Ed.). London: Heinemann. (Original work published 1789)

Fliegelman, J. (1993). *Declaring independence: Jefferson, natural language, and the culture of performance.* Stanford, CA: Stanford University Press.

Fraser, N. (1990). Rethinking the public sphere: A contribution to the critique of actually existing democracy. *Social Text, 25/26,* 56–80.

Fuoss, K. W. (1999). Lynching performances, theatres of violence. *Text and Performance Quarterly, 19,* 1–37.

Gates, H. L., Jr. (1988). *The signifying monkey: A theory of Afro-American literary criticism.* New York: Oxford University Press.

Gilroy, P. (1995). ". . . To be real": The dissident forms of black expressive culture. In C. Ugwu (Ed.), *Let's get it on: The politics of black performance* (pp. 12–33). Seattle, WA: Bay.

Graff, G. (1987). *Professing literature: An institutional history.* Chicago: University of Chicago Press.

Gray, G. W. (1960). What was elocution? *Quarterly Journal of Speech, 46,* 1–7.

Gronniosaw, J. A. (1996). A narrative of the most remarkable particulars in the life of James Albert Ukawsaw Gronniosaw, an African prince, as related by himself. In V. Carretta (Ed.), *Unchained voices: An anthology of black authors in the English-speaking world of the eighteenth century* (pp. 32–58). Lexington: University of Kentucky Press. (Original work published 1770)

Hobsbawm, E. (1997). On history from below. In *On history* (pp. 201–216). New York: New Press.

hooks, b. (1995). Performance practice as a site of opposition. In C. Ugwu (Ed.), *Let's get it on: The politics of black performance* (pp. 210–221). Seattle, WA: Bay.

Howell, W. S. (1959). Sources of the elocutionary movement in England, 1700–1748. *Quarterly Journal of Speech, 45*, 1–18.

Hymes, D. (1981). Breakthrough into performance. In *In vain I tried to tell you: Essays in Native American ethnopoetics* (pp. 79–141). Philadelphia: University of Pennsylvania Press.

Jackson, S. (1999). *Disciplinary genealogies.* Paper presented at the annual conference of Performance Studies international, University of Wales, Aberystwyth.

Jackson, S. (2000). *Lines of activity: Performance, historiography, Hull-House domesticity.* Ann Arbor: University of Michigan Press.

Jacobson, M. F. (1998). *Whiteness of a different color: European immigrants and the alchemy of race.* Cambridge, MA: Harvard University Press.

Jefferson, T. (1993). Notes on Virginia. In A. Koch & W. Peden (Eds.), *The life and selected writings of Thomas Jefferson* (pp. 173–267). New York: Random House. (Original work published 1781)

Johnson, T. L. (1909). *Twenty-eight years a slave.* Bournemouth, UK: W. Math & Sons.

Jones, J. E. (1994). *Voices and silences.* New York: Simon & Schuster.

Lee, J. (1999). Disciplining theater and drama in the English department: Some reflections on "performance" and institutional history. *Text and Performance Quarterly, 19*, 145–158.

Lhamon, W. T., Jr. (1998). *Raising Cain: Blackface performance from Jim Crow to hip hop.* Cambridge, MA: Harvard University Press.

Linebaugh, P. (1992). *The London hanged: Crime and civil society in the eighteenth century.* Cambridge, UK: Cambridge University Press.

Looby, C. (1996). *Voicing America: Language, literary form, and the origins of the United States.* Chicago: University of Chicago Press.

Lott, E. (1993). *Love and theft: Blackface minstrelsy and the American working class.* New York: Oxford University Press.

Lowe, L., & Lloyd, D. (Eds.). (1997). *The politics of culture in the shadow of capital.* Durham, NC: Duke University Press.

Madison, D. S. (1999). Performing theory/embodied writing. *Text and Performance Quarterly, 19*, 107–124.

Manguel, A. (1996). *A history of reading.* New York: Viking.

Marx, K. (1930). *Capital* (vol. 1; E. Paul & C. Paul, Trans.). New York: Dutton. (Original work published 1867)

Mattingly, A. (1972). Art and nature: The mechanical school in England, 1761–1806. In E. M. Doyle & V. H. Floyd (Eds.), *Studies in interpretation* (pp. 255–272). Amsterdam: Rodopi.

Mayhew, H. (1968). *London labour and the London poor* (Vol. 1). New York: Dover. (Original work published 1861)

McFeely, W. S. (1991). *Frederick Douglass.* New York: Norton.

Merrill, L. (1999). *When Romeo was a woman: Charlotte Cushman and her circle of female spectators*. Ann Arbor: University of Michigan Press.

Painter, N. I. (1996). *Sojourner Truth: A life, a symbol*. New York: Norton.

Pollock, D. (1998). *Exceptional spaces: Essays in performance and history*. Chapel Hill: University of North Carolina Press.

Poole, D. (1997). *Vision, race, and modernity: A visual economy of the Andean image world*. Princeton, NJ: Princeton University Press.

Portelli, A. (1994). *The text and the voice: Writing, speaking, and democracy in American literature*. New York: Columbia University Press.

Reynolds, D. (1996). *Walt Whitman's America: A cultural biography*. New York: Vintage.

Roach, J. (1985). Nature still, but nature mechanized. In *The player's passion: Studies in the science of acting* (pp. 58–92). Newark, NJ: University of Delaware Press.

Roach, J. (1996). *Cities of the dead: Circum-Atlantic performance*. New York: Columbia University Press.

Robb, M. M. (1941). *Oral interpretation of literature in American college and universities: A historical study of teaching methods*. New York: Johnson Reprint, 1969.

Rogers, M. B. (2000). *Barbara Jordan: American hero*. New York: Doubleday Bantam.

Rush, J. (1879). *The philosophy of the human voice: Embracing its physiological history; Together with a system of principles, by which criticism in the art of elocution may be rendered inteligible, and instruction, definite and comprehensive* (7th ed.). Philadelphia: J. B. Lippincott.

Russell, A. (1853). *The young ladies' elocutionary reader*. Boston: James Munroe.

Ryan, M. P. (1994). *Women in public: Between banners and ballots, 1825–1880*. Baltimore: Johns Hopkins University Press.

Savigliano, M. (1995). *Tango and the political economy of passion*. Boulder, CO: Westview.

Scott, J. C. (1990). *Domination and the arts of resistance*. New Haven, CT: Yale University Press.

Stowe, H. B. (1855). *The Christian slave, a drama, founded on a portion of "Uncle Tom's Cabin," dramatized by Harriet Beecher Stowe, expressly for the readings of Mrs. Mary E. Webb*. Boston: Phillips, Sampson.

Stowe, H. B. (1863). Sojourner Truth, the Libyan sibyl. *Atlantic Monthly, 11*, 473–481.

Stowe, H. B. (1994). *Uncle Tom's cabin* (E. Ammons, Ed.). New York: Norton. (Original work published 1852)

Strine, M. (1983). Performance theory as science: The formative impact of Dr. James Rush's *The philosophy of the human voice*. In E. Thompson (Ed.), *Performance of literature in historical perspectives* (pp. 509–527). Lanham, MD: University Press of America.

Thompson, D. (Ed.). (1983). *The performance of literature in historical perspectives*. Lanham, MD: University Press of America.

Thompson, E. P. (1963). *The making of the English working class.* New York: Vintage.

Truth, S. (1993). *Narrative of Sojourner Truth* (M. Washington, Ed.). New York: Vintage. (Original work published 1850)

Vandraegan, D. E. (1949). *The natural school of oral reading in England, 1748–1828.* Unpublished doctoral dissertation, Northwestern University.

Volosinov, V. N. (1986). *Marxism and the philosophy of language* (L. Matejka & I. R. Titunik, Trans.). Cambridge, MA: Harvard University Press.

wa Thiong'o, N. (1998). Oral power and Europhone glory: Orature, literature, and stolen legacies. In *Penpoints, gunpoints, and dreams: Towards a critical theory of the arts and the state in Africa* (pp. 103–128). Oxford: Clarendon.

Wallace, K. R. (Ed.). (1954). *History of speech education in America.* New York: Appleton-Century-Crofts.

Wills, G. (1992). *Lincoln at Gettysburg: The words that remade America.* New York: Simon & Schuster.

6

Diverging Paths in Performance Genealogies

Ruth Laurion Bowman

Plato suggests somewhere that memory is like an aviary inside your head, with all these birds flying around, such that you might reach in for a ringdove and accidentally pull out a turtledove.

Lawrence Weschler, *Mr. Wilson's Cabinet of Wonder*

Genealogy is history in the form of a concerted carnival.

Michel Foucault, "Nietzsche, Genealogy, History"

An expanse of cleanly mown grass stretches before me, between where I sit in the shade of the "Sugar House" and the "Overseer's House" that rests comfortably enough behind a rough-hewn fence and within the cool embrace of the crape myrtles, palms, holly, and yucca that surround it. A small well rests in the middle of the green, cooled too by a spread of palmettos, the whole preventing a clear view of the house, a variegated green blur in the heat rising from the shorn expanse in one slow wave of indifference. It's hot. A frog burps behind me and the cicadas whirl. My leg itches.

As I turn to focus on the buildings that line either side of the green, always in my periphery then and as I write now, I long to be haunted by an image, any sense will do, of the past represented here. I have a "desire to speak with the dead," it seems (Greenblatt, 1988, p. 1), or, like Roach (1996), to know that "the voices of the dead may speak freely now only through the bodies of the living" (p. xiii). Or . . . how did the romantics put it?

My imagination runs thin, however, as the present tense smacks me square on with the indifference of four stout lime-washed cabins on my left and, on my right, two more with a barn of sorts in between. The buildings are pretty: compact and tidy, material tied back at the open doorways, one, two, three, down the line, the white structures gaining contrast from the green they frame in symmetry. For all I know, they could be bungalows in an artists' community by the sea.

I shake free of that image, scratch my leg, and yawn back at the buildings, recalling what I do know. All but two of the buildings were one- and two-pen slave cabins, circa the 1830–40s, and many were occupied well into the 1960s, mostly by sharecroppers. Among this group is the barnlike structure, outfitted now to serve as a working "Blacksmith Shop." The other two buildings, the overseer's house and the cabin to its left, now a "School House," date from the same antebellum period. My friend Jim Flanagan tells me that a raised walkway once connected the latter to the back porch (now gone) of the former, serving as a kitchen for the overseer and then, just prior to the 20th century and well into the 1920s, as a school for his children and those of the yeoman farmers who lived nearby (Flanagan, 2000, p. 32).

All the buildings save one of the slave/sharecropper cabins were original to Welham, a large sugar plantation located near the town of Hestor on LA 44. Known regionally as the River Road, the two-laner snakes along the Mississippi between Baton Rouge and New Orleans through an area commonly referred to as "Cancer Alley" due to the high percentage of illness and death among those who live in the communities that service the petrochemical plants lining the river now. Massive, well-fortified compounds nestled oddly (at first sight) among the cane fields, the two industries are fronted here and there by antebellum plantation homes that various individuals and a good number of oil companies have purchased and restored as tourist attractions (Pezzullo, 2003).

The front-stage prominence of the Big Houses on the River Road is a result of the French *arpent* survey system and the largely linear organization of plantations along southern Louisiana waterways. On rivers and bayous, the *arpent* system was used to divide the land into long narrow strips measuring 2 to 20 *arpents* in width (an *arpent* is just less than an acre, says Jim) and

40 *arpents* in depth, thus ensuring that each of the early settlers had access to the social-economic mainstream of transportation. There too, close to the river and on the elevated rise of the natural levee, settlers built their homesteads, which, as farmers merged their holdings into larger plantations, were replaced by the Big Houses (Flanagan, 2000, pp. 19–20). Catching the cool of the river breezes, surrounded by gardens and fortified with fence, the resplendent mansions displayed their prosperity to the traffic on the river while, in the linear depth of the tract, backstage if you will, lay "the Quarters," most of which were organized in the "French Creole linear" pattern derived from the plantations in the French colonies of the West Indies (Flanagan, 2000, p. 25).

First in line in the Quarters was the house of the overseer, his status demarcated by a clump of shade trees and a fence. The dwellings and workshops of the blacksmith and carpenter, the sick house, and the commissary followed, and thereafter the two rows of slave cabins. The whole was divided down the middle by a dirt road that ran to the sugar-processing houses located just adjacent to or within the cane fields and back again, past the rows of slave cabins, past the commissary and blacksmith shop, past the house of the overseer, and past the Big House to the landing on the river, where the hogsheads of sugar and barrels of molasses were loaded on steam- or keel- or flatboats and shipped up or down the river, thereby "supplying half the sugar consumed in the United States" in antebellum times and supporting the boast of the Big Houses as representing the most prosperous group in Louisiana of the period (Flanagan, 2000, pp. 26–29, 21).

While today many of the Big Houses still stand and, at plantation sites such as Evergreen and Lara, the Quarters too, the antebellum plantation that was Welham is gone. In 1975, the Marathon Oil Company of Ohio purchased the plot for a reported $5.5 million from Leon Keller and John Poche, who were farming it for cane. Despite local efforts to save the Welham mansion, the company demolished it in the predawn hours of May 3, 1979 ("The Rape of Welham,"1979, p. 2). Prior to the Marathon purchase, Keller and Poche donated some of the outlying buildings to Ione and Steele Burden, a sister and brother who lived in their own (smallish) Big House on a 450-acre plot just outside of Baton Rouge. As the museum director, David Floyd, told me, the farmers, "wanting to extend their fields, were about to bulldoze 'em anyway. You know, farmers hate anything in the way of plowing. They don't like trees, they don't like buildings, so why not?"[1] Between the late 1960s and early 1990s, Ione and Steele would entrust their property to the Burden Research Foundation of Louisiana State University (LSU), a part of which would become the LSU Rural Life Museum and Windrush Gardens.

Relaxing behind his desk in the overflow of his office, Floyd explains:

[T]he museum started kind of obscure. Steele had an idea which Miss Ione supported financially. . . . It was his idea, his concept, that he wanted to preserve one slave cabin and, if you look at the early documentation, that they set aside an acre in this area so he could put a little farmstead and he didn't want it to have a little Anglo-Saxon cabin-type thing. He was really wanting, his idea was, nobody was really talking about, much less preserving, the elements of dealing with slavery and the working force of the plantations, and he had had an interest in it practically all his life. And so he went up and down the river looking for one cabin . . . and he found the whole complex of Welham. . . . They gave it to him to move here, and he set it up to where it is now—[on acreage traced back through the Burden line to 1856, when John Charles Burden,] born and raised in England, married a local girl, name of Emma Gertrude Barbee, who received [the property] as a wedding gift by family tradition—that's what the family says, but we're finding out that, yeah, while that may have been true, they actually had to buy it. [The couple named the property] Windrush because Burden came from the Windrush River area of England, [and he thought] this worn creek [Floyd smiles] looked like Windrush River, you know, the romanticism of the time period.

A frog burps and the cicadas whirl, and the emigrant structures stand in the rising heat of more memories than their own.

In this essay, I take a few walks through the LSU Rural Life Museum and Windrush Gardens in an effort to understand the poetics of the place. I am intrigued by how the museum performs the histories it represents and how I perform the history I write here. Both performances are predetermined to the extent that genealogical methods of historiography, particularly performance genealogies, inform my perspective on how histories are made. Here, I compare, contrast, and draw on two specific methods: Joseph Roach's method of "genealogies of performance" as he articulates and practices it in *Cities of the Dead: Circum-Atlantic Performance* (1996) and the genealogical history W. G. Sebald writes in *The Rings of Saturn* (1998). As I treat them here, these two histories complement each other. Roach provides guidelines for doing a performance genealogy, whereas Sebald offers creative alternatives within those guidelines. In the parlance of contemporary performance studies, we might understand Sebald's history as an example of performance or performative writing (see Pollock, 1998b). He draws on conventions typical of creative fiction to activate historical agency in his writing and in our reading of his history.

Arising from this complement is the key difference I pursue in the two genealogies. At work in the cultural exchanges of the academy, academic press, and disciplines currently guided by the politics of poststructuralism, Roach displays critical command of the subjects and manifest theories in the positivist style of an analytical essay. Significance is made, and its meaning is clear in Roach's history. Although Sebald's text is praised as "an extraordinary palimpsest of natural, human and literary history" (Richard Eder, quoted in Sebald, 1998, back flyleaf), its key marketing genre is "fiction" (Sebald, 1998, back flyleaf). This genre fusion, or gap, enables Sebald to write against "the much-vaunted historical overview" where "we . . . see everything from above, see everything at once, and still we do not know how it was" (Sebald, 1998, p. 125). Instead, Sebald leaves such productive history making to the reader to pursue or not.

In the following chapter, I summarize the key components of Roach's method, as informed by Foucault, and then take a look at the genealogy Sebald writes. In my analysis of the LSU Rural Life Museum that follows, I draw on both models as discursive perspectives from which to view the museum and to inform how I write about it here. Understanding that "museums are sites in which socially and culturally embedded theories [and practices] are performed" (Macdonald, 1996, p. 3), it would be a stretch for me to say that the LSU Rural Life Museum enacts a genealogical history, although by chance or accident it seems to drift in that direction at times. The politics of my poetics, then—the "stories" I "tell . . . to make sense of [the] museum" (Macdonald, 1996, p. 3)— are not aligned with those of the museum, although, given the genealogical instructions I use, they may drift in that direction at times.

Genealogies of Performance

It is precisely the politics of communicating with the dead that concern me generally.

Joseph Roach, *Cities of the Dead: Circum-Atlantic Performance*

But the truth is that we do not know what the herring feels.

W. G. Sebald, *The Rings of Saturn*

In *Cities of the Dead,* Roach acknowledges that his method, genealogies of performance, is indebted to Michel Foucault and the critical or effective genealogy he advances in "Nietzsche, Genealogy, History" (1977). In that essay, Foucault reiterates Nietzsche's disparaging view of origin as an ideological construct of essences or truths, a myth about the good old days from which we have digressed and hence take measures to restore. While the interpretive spin on the origin may change, the "meta-historical deployment of ideal significations," teleological movements, "immobile forms," continuity over time, totality, and objectivity operate to legitimize the atemporal truth of the origin and, thereby too, the sovereignty of those who benefit from its conservation or reclamation (Foucault, 1977, pp. 142, 146, 152). "Rather," Foucault argues, "if [the genealogist] listens to history"—if he views events as unique rather than unified by a devolutionary ideal—"he finds that . . . the historical beginning of things is not the inviolable identity of their origin; it is the dissentions of other things. It is disparity," discontinuity, division, and difference within individuals, as well as within and between contesting parties and events (p. 142). History then is antistructure. It is a "profusion of entangled events . . . fabricated in a piecemeal fashion" that emerge in response to random conflicts (pp. 155, 142, 152). History as genealogy is a discursive method, activated by the historian and the critical tools she uses to liberate divergence from the backwater of traditional histories and make some sense of it (p. 153). In so doing, she also masters the disabling myth of history and identity as rooted in essential origins.

To exercise the method, the genealogist enters a vast "field of entangled and confused parchments . . . that have been scratched over and recopied many times" (Foucault, 1977, p. 139). There, she isolates the accounts in time, as context- and culture-specific "events on the stage of historical processes," seeking to engage the different as well as recurring scenes, roles, and interpretations that emerge, prevail, are residual, or are absented altogether in the events she undertakes (pp. 152, 140). Not unlike the practice of "thick description" used by cultural anthropologist Clifford Geertz (1973), and not unlike the close readings that "gave old fashioned literary study its immense interpretive authority" (Veeser, 1989, p. xii), a genealogy focuses on the physical rather than the metaphysical event. It then reads the physical event meticulously so as to reveal the various and divergent particulars that show the culture(s) in action and cultural histories as enacted. For Nietzsche and Foucault, close reading of events is directed toward the body as materially and discursively inscribed by history and (though we may pretend otherwise) as the locus of an unstable identity and disintegrating substance—that is, an imprint of historical processes (Foucault, 1977, pp. 155, 148). As a material site of change, the body verifies historical events and serves the critical imperative of genealogy: to deconstruct the metaphysical hocus-pocus of origins and those who have and have not profited from them. Hence, Foucault assigns genealogy the "task . . . to expose a body totally imprinted by history and the process of history's destruction of the body" (p. 148).

Such exhortations have led a number of critics to contend that, in his attempt to expose the fallacy of origins (i.e., as hegemonic constructs), Foucault produces his own totalizing myth: an implacable code of dominance where man is never subject of but always *"subjecting to"* manifest systems of power (Montrose, 1989, p. 33; italics in original). Further, as Edward Said (1986) writes,

> Foucault's imagination of power is largely within rather than against it. . . . His interest in domination was critical but not finally as . . . oppositional as on the surface it seems to be. This translates into the paradox that Foucault's imagination of power was by his analysis . . . to reveal its injustice and cruelty, but by his theorization to let it go on more or less unchecked. (p. 152)

In support of Said's comments, we might observe that, like Michel de Certeau, the later Foucault of *Discipline and Punish* and *The History of Sexuality* views power as "positive and productive," as not so much "repressing dissent" as "organizing and channeling" it (Graff, 1989, p. 169). However, we also might rethink the troublesome "paradox" Said notices as a rhetoric of dissociation in Foucault's treatment of power, how he sees it operating in a past event, and his use of it in the present. The different tacks suggest Foucault's attempt "to leave things [e.g., past events] undisturbed in their own dimensions and intensity" (Foucault, 1977, p. 156)—an attempt well illustrated, I think, by John Berger's understanding of how a photograph (particularly an uncaptioned photograph) highlights the discontinuity in time between the depicted event and our own (cf. Barthes, 1981; Berger & Mohr, 1982). In other words, a "genealogy does not pretend to go back in time to restore an unbroken continuity" or "to demonstrate that the past actively exists in the present" (Foucault, 1977, p. 146). For Foucault, the representation of the historical event is not aimed toward pragmatic ends, although, by one's active critique (one's theorization for instance), a genealogist can "liberate . . . man by presenting him with other origins than those in which he prefers to see himself" (p. 164). In Foucault's work, an origin of dominance, which effects a dissociated, shifting, and ironic I/eye, replaces the origin of individuality. In this way, too, Foucault abides by his axiom that genealogists "reveal their grounding in a particular time and place," acknowledge their "slanted" perspective, and offer "a deliberate appraisal, affirmation, or negation" of a controversy (pp. 156–157).

In his introduction to *Cities of the Dead* (1996), Roach specifies Foucault's tenets of genealogy in terms of performance, as both a legitimate means of historiography and the subject of his study. In the latter case, Roach focuses on circum-Atlantic performance as constituted by events that occurred in the port cities of London and New Orleans in the 18th through the late 20th centuries. Like Foucault, Roach rejects objectivist, diachronic models of historiography, exercising instead a "comparative approach" (Roach, 1996, p. 4), where events are viewed as synchronic and specific to time and place. Also like Foucault, Roach parries the homeostatic view of social relations as practiced in structural/functionalist histories. Particularly cogent in Roach's analyses is James Clifford's (1988) claim that "[g]roups negotiating their identity in contexts of domination and exchange persist, patch themselves together in ways different from a living organism" (p. 338; quoted in Roach, 1996, p. 191). As Roach shows us, the disparate cultures he entertains are porous, resilient and, in most cases, inventive in their maintenance, adaptation, plundering, and transformation of cultural practices in light of changing circumstances. In this way, Roach makes "visible the play of difference" and deferral (in Derrida's sense) within and between the cultural groups and events he undertakes (p. 4).[2] Thus he refuses the myth of a Euro-colonial monoculture, heeding instead Gwendolyn Hall's call that "national history . . . be transcended, and colonial history treated within a global context" (quoted in Roach, 1996, p. 10).

To gain access to the intercultural patchwork, Roach (1996) investigates a wealth of resources from diversified media that "attend not only to 'the body,' as Foucault suggests, but also to bodies" in performance (p. 25). Drawing on Ngũgĩ wa Thiong'o's concept of orature, Roach reinstates the presence and pressure of bodies *in* text, of orality *in* print, as well as observes this same interplay in reverse (p. 11). The spectacle of the scaffold, in Foucault's *Discipline and Punish*, becomes a spectacle of sweat in Roach's text. Bodies "do" things and, in Roach's concentration on theatrical, cultural, and everyday performance practices as enciphered in print, oral, visual, and live representations, they do a lot of things, differently and in excess. Roach's resource base and corporeal sensitivity gird his theoretical project, which is to locate performance as central to historical processes and politics of remembering and forgetting.

To activate the link between performance and history, Roach draws most directly on Richard Schechner's definition of performance as restored behavior, a mnemonic activity in which people recall and enact preexisting signs and codes of culture[s] to articulate who they are, often in adherence to or deviation from the sources they draw upon. Based as it is on memory, the restoration of behavior is never exact, although there may be a "constancy of transmission across many generations" that is "astonishing" (Schechner, quoted in Roach, 1996, p. 3). To activate the critical imperative of genealogy, Roach highlights the illusive constancy as well as the partiality of restored behavior and reconceives it as a process of "surrogation." For Roach (1996), performance as surrogation "best describe[s]" how a culture "reproduces and re-creates itself" by "trying out various . . . stand-ins" (i.e., restored behaviors/memories) to fill the vacancies of loss or imposed lack that have emerged over time (pp. 2–3). While at first Roach appears to totalize the aim of surrogation as a "doomed search for originals" that all groups enact (p. 3), his application differentiates between those who attempt to reproduce the original so as to gain from its reiteration and those who do not. Here, they re-present with a difference, in order to counter disabling origins through the play of *différance*. The role of the genealogist is to investigate the diverse memories and counter-memories she finds so as to perform an "intricate unraveling of the putative seamlessness of origins." Thus she enacts "a strategy of empowering the living through the performance of memory" (pp. 30, 34).

Typically, Roach introduces his analyses with a specific manifestation of orature, a performance expression or practice cited/sited in the historical record, which he details in terms of its kinesthetic or spatial particularities.[3] Roach proceeds to interpret the practice as an instantiation of a wider cultural code and tracks it in other cites/sites of orature. For example, at the top of Chapter 5, "One Blood," a character from Dion Boucicault's melo-drama *The Octoroon: or, Life in Louisiana* (1859) situates the audience in Louisiana on "the selvage of civilization" (quoted in Roach, 1996, p. 179). Roach reads the thickly woven space as a frontier where, over the course of the drama, Anglo-American culture will displace the creolized interculture through the ideological practices of manifest destiny, or "one blood" (p. 181). Roach tracks this code to other transmissions, such as the antebellum slave market, "fancy-girl" auctions, and Storyville brothels of New Orleans, fine art depictions of female octoroons and quadroons, and sentimental fictions that depict the death of the "noble savage." He also tracks the code to instances in other time periods, such as the 1896 *Plessy v. Ferguson* case, which gave rise to "separate but equal" laws across the country. Interwoven with these memories are resistant or countermemories, such as the ghost dances and intertribal pow-wows of Native Americans, the format of the latter influ-enced by Anglo-American Wild West shows like those toured by Buffalo Bill in the late 19th century.

Roach also returns to the present to observe acts of orature that variously replicate, adapt, or transform the memories he has tracked in the past. In Chapter 5, he finds that the sex circus of Bourbon Street, NFL football in the Louisiana Superdome, and Madonna's "material girl" practices perpetuate the code of "one blood" through their segregation, marketing, and appro-priation of black bodies. In fierce resistance to the constancy of this mem-ory/loss is the "invented . . . tradition" of the "working class black people of New Orleans": that is, the subversive and spectacular performances of the Mardi Gras Indians (Hobsbawm & Ranger, quoted in Roach, 1996, p. 194).

To document the living memory of history as it is publicly enacted by people in the present, Roach (1996) follows Michel de Certeau's lead and takes a "walk in the city" of his subject. Roach's professed aim is "to gain an experience of the cityscape that is conducive to mapping the emphases and contradictions," the continuities and ruptures, "of its special memory" (p. 13). Although Certeau suggests that "to walk is to lack a place" (quoted in Roach, 1996, p. 13), Roach appears to have a pretty good idea of where he's headed and what he wants to map: The living memory of white culture in New Orleans is limited to those practices that appear to reproduce the origin of white supremacist entitlement that Roach observed operating in the past, while the living memory of nonwhite cultures is shown to be inventive and regenerative. For instance, on his walks, Roach finds that the "Afrocentric form" of "Second Line parades" is "less like forgetting than replenishment" (pp. 14–15); the trickster performance of the black King Zulu atop his Mardi Gras float is "much more complicated" than that of the "Eurocentric" King Rex atop his Mardi Gras float (pp. 20–21); and, "through the disguise of masking Indian," the Mardi Gras Indians enact an "imaginative re-creation and repossession of Africa" (p. 207).

My concern here is to query not the performances but rather the discursive aim and strategies Roach uses to restore them. In order "to excavate the past that is necessary to account for how we got here and the past that is useful for conceiving alternatives to our present condition" (Arac, quoted in Roach, 1996, p. 25), Roach structures a seamless line of descent, a devolutionary history within his genealogy, that shows the constancy of racist, reproductive behavior on the part of "white culture" in New Orleans. To hold the line intact, the ethnic, gender, sex, class, and generational disparities and inconsistencies in "white culture," the piecemeal assemblage of multiple cultures, are elided. "White culture" becomes an immobile form, its surrogates King Rex, white krewes, and David Duke. In striking contrast, the alternatives to our present condition emerge, as manifested in "black culture" and its inventive restoration of Afrocentric and Native American practices. To uphold the significance of the regenerative alternatives, Roach drains them of their disparities too. The in/visibility of women in "black" as well as "white" Mardi Gras spectacle and the appropriation of Native American practices by the Mardi Gras Indians—as if the former culture(s) is but a handmaid to the latter—go unchallenged by Roach. As a result, the "special memory" of contemporary performance in New Orleans becomes a surrogate for a fairly predictable binary-based critique of race relations and politics, a memory that tells us more about the cultural exchange and expectations of our academic discipline(s) in 1996 than it does about the "living memories" of the multiple cultures at work within, upon, and against the black/white culture of opposition in New Orleans.

Roach's study then articulates a challenge to the genealogist. As we move to "master history so as to turn it to genealogical uses" (Foucault, 1977, p. 160), for instance, by offering alternatives to our present condition, how do we do so without draining genealogy of history, of the very "accidents," "deviations," "errors," "false appraisals," and "faulty calculations" that are the basis of genealogy and that "continue to exist and have value for us" today (Foucault, 1977, p. 146)? Foucault urges us to use parody, systematic dissociation and, as subjects, to resist the "deployment of the will to knowledge" (p. 164). It seems to me that Roach offers a similar answer, but it emerges in the performance practices he writes about rather than through his discursive agency as writer/genealogist.

In *The Rings of Saturn,* W. G. Sebald (1998) writes a genealogy that addresses this same challenge through conventions we commonly associate with fiction and, more recently, performance or performative writing. By means of first-person subjectivity, a polyglot of narratives, body metaphors, metonymic lists, and surreal juxtapositions, Sebald claims historical and performative agency. The conventions signal to the reader that the history is furnished forth, it emerges, through his writing. However, due to the double-voiced poetics of many of the conventions, they also indicate that the meaning and significance of the history are ambiguous and multiple. The reader then must participate in producing the history Sebald offers. While Sebald does imply a critical appraisal of the events he recounts, the conventions he uses (as well as the content) refuse a pose of exhortation or decree (i.e., a will to knowledge). Indeed, they often operate to suggest deviations or errors in the implied appraisal, thereby provoking the reader to form her own opinion. As Foucault (1977) says of "genealogy," Sebald's poetics construct "history in the form of a concerted carnival" (p. 161). They allow him to master history through his orchestration of it while simultaneously retaining the politics of disparity.

The instigating context of Sebald's history is a walk he takes in August 1992 along the coast and in the countryside of Suffolk County in eastern England. Unlike Roach, Sebald seems less sure of where he is going and why, and frequently he becomes sidetracked or even lost—for instance, on a treeless heath or in a labyrinth of hedges. Like Walter Benjamin's *flâneur,* Sebald walks in an unpremeditated or distracted state (Urry, 1996, p. 51), open to the influence of the landscape he passes through—the sea, cliffs, towns, resorts, old estates, hamlets, homes, and people—and what it might have to tell him. The result is a maze, at times a flood, of memories. Spurred by a particular site in the present, Sebald recalls and connects disparate natural, cultural, social, and individual histories. He also includes the first-person accounts of people he remembers or visits on his walk.

Once a popular seaside destination, now economically depressed and thinly populated, the county of Suffolk bears memories that reflect and ignite the history Sebald recounts. Generally, this concerns British and European imperialism, its height in the 19th century and its decline in the 20th. As with the profusion of events and the vast field of sources Roach tangles within his genealogy, Sebald's account offers a rich, in-depth rendering of events in time and place. Also like Roach, Sebald takes care to investigate incidents in terms of their global context and ramifications. For instance, in Chapter 4, he recalls "the fact" that "in the entire history of colonialism . . . there is scarcely a darker chapter than the one termed *The Opening of the Congo*" (p. 118), propagated under the imperial might of King Leopold of Belgium in the late 19th century. Sebald views the "sordid farce" (p. 117) through the life story and perspective of Joseph Conrad, who, while commanding a Belgian steamer in the Congo, meets Roger Casement, British consul at Boma. Upon returning to Britain, Casement lobbies protests, first against the oppression of the Congolese and then against "the white Indians of Ireland" (p. 129). Casement's support of "Home Rule" and the Irish liberation army results in his imprisonment and execution at the hands of the British government. Between the two individual histories, Sebald recalls a visit he made to the memorial site of the Battle of Waterloo, located just outside Brussels. There, from atop a raised platform, he viewed an "authentic" representation of the battle in a huge panorama. The experience prompts Sebald to ruminate on the relationship between the imperialist mentality and "the much-vaunted historical overview" used to represent it (pp. 124–125).

Sebald's rumination operates in a reflexive manner of course, directing attention to his own representational strategies. Aware of how, in content and in the discursive claim to content, "no document of civilization" is "free of barbarism" (Benjamin, 1969, p. 256), Sebald crafts language to acknowledge and interrogate his possession of it and its purported meaning. Sebald is particularly incisive in this regard when he makes appeals to our sense of sight and crafts body imagery and metaphors. His comprehension of the politics of the body and visual/sight-based representations is demonstrated in his analysis of Rembrandt's *The Anatomy Lesson*, which he offers in the first chapter. Situated as it is, Sebald's analysis serves as an introductory lesson of its own, seeming to anticipate the visual "tricks" he will play in subsequent chapters (cf. Pollock, 1998a, pp. 5–9).

In Sebald's account, *The Anatomy Lesson* depicts a Guild of Surgeons standing over the corpse of Aris Kindt, a petty thief. The main surgeon, Dr. Nicolaas Tulp, is explaining his dissection of Kindt's arm to the others, who have their gaze directed toward an "open anatomical atlas in which the appalling physical facts [of the body] are reduced to a diagram . . . such as envisaged by . . . René Descartes" (p. 13). Sebald continues:

> Though the body is open to contemplation, it is, in a sense, excluded, and in the same way the much-admired verisimilitude of Rembrandt's picture proves

on closer examination to be more apparent than real. Contrary to normal practice, the anatomist . . . has not begun his dissection by opening the abdomen and removing the intestines . . . but has started . . . by dissecting the offending hand. Now, this hand is most peculiar. It is not only grotesquely out of proportion compared with the hand closer to us, but it is also anatomically the wrong way round. . . . In other words, what we are faced with is a trans-position taken from the anatomical atlas . . . that turns this otherwise true-to-life painting (if one may so express it) into a crass misrepresentation at the exact centre point of its meaning, where the incisions are made. . . . I believe there was deliberate intent behind this flaw in the composition. That unshapely hand signifies the violence that has been done to Aris Kindt. It is with . . . the victim . . . the painter identifies. His gaze alone is free of Cartesian rigidity. He alone sees that greenish annihilated body, and he alone sees the shadow in the half-open mouth and over the dead man's eyes. (pp. 16–17)

Having disseminated his lesson (and seen/written the body too), Sebald, like Rembrandt, proceeds to subvert the Cartesian claims of objectivity, fac-ticity, and wholeness in various ways. For one, he interjects photographs throughout his text that are fuzzy, ill-composed, obscure, or seemingly irrel-evant in content or that in their reproduction testify to their partiality. He also embeds within descriptive evocations queries regarding the material facts. On "a bizarre, elongated carriage," for instance, "the shafts protrude much too far forward, and the coachman's box seems a long way from the rear." The writer's ability to capture, recontextualize, and fictionalize visual materials is implied in the same passage when Sebald observes the young Joseph Conrad sitting inside the carriage, "watching from the dark the scene he will later describe" (p. 106).

Sebald also crafts potent body metaphors that relate the dissolution of the body to the like dissolution of the Empire that compelled its decay. In most cases, the imagery insists on making visible a body that typically is unseen, such as the bodies of laborers or the interior of the body and its threatening excesses. In the concluding chapter, for instance, Sebald interweaves the var-ious threads of the silk industry he has traced throughout the text into the laboring-decaying body of the silkworm, which in turn serves as a metaphor for the bodies of the Norwich silk weavers, the labor history of Britain gen-erally, and the "scholars and writers with whom they had much in common . . . [all] straining to keep their eye on the complex patterns they created" and "pursued, into their dreams, by the feeling that they have got hold of the wrong thread" (p. 283).

To play many of his visual tricks, Sebald relies on literary language and its similar inability to fully capture its subject. Sebald often highlights the par-tiality or lack in language by making use of metonymic lists. In the tradition of historical chronologies and timelines, itineraries and agendas, and our daily scrawl of "Things to do," the lists simultaneously evoke the subject and imply the gaps in the representation. The latent power of the metonym surfaces, particularly when used to represent subjects that are about, or that evoke, an experience of loss or absence, such as leave-takings, death, memory, history. The haunting of what is/not present is provoked in Sebald's description of the once lavish, now decrepit estate of Somerleyton. He recalls:

> The velvet curtains and crimson blinds are faded, the settees and armchairs sag, the stairways and corridors . . . are full of bygone paraphernalia. A camphorwood chest which may once have accompanied a former occupant of the house on a tour of duty to Nigeria or Singapore now contains old croquet mallets and wooden balls, golf clubs, billiard cues and tennis racquets, most of them so small they might have been intended for children, or have shrunk in the course of the years. (p. 35)

While Sebald consistently implies that the past is resistant to our possession of it, when he engages other people and listens to their stories, he allows ample if not full voice to them. Whether positioned in the past or present, this other storyteller may speak for pages, offering a personal memory, appraisal, or rumination that in some way extends and provides a new perspective on the broad social history Sebald traces in his text. Due to the length, the lack of quotation marks, scanty dialogue tags, stories within stories, and Sebald's occasional interjections, the common effect is one of confusion regarding who "owns" the memories being recounted. Is history, as conceived by Sebald, a polyglot of people who, through voice, emerge into our presence? Or, once again, is history resistant to such claims, indifferent finally to the heteroglot of disparate memories within and haunting the surface of our own?

Questions such as these are embedded throughout *The Rings of Saturn*. The extreme manifestations are figured forth in surreal dreams, experiences of isolation, and moments when the narrating subject disappears into the shadows of another voice, memory, or reality he has created. Sebald's sense of the transient subject in and of history tempts nihilism, a view of reality where "on every new thing there lies already the shadow of annihilation" (cf. Anderson, 2003; Sebald, 1998). However, within our very movement forward, within our transient walks in the city or countryside, it appears that a chance "trifle" can give rise to "slumbering . . . memories" (Sebald, 1998, p. 255), which in their recall backward counter the movement forward. As Sebald offers,

> What would we be without memory? We would not be capable of ordering even the simplest thoughts, the most sensitive heart would lose the ability to show affection, our existence would be a mere never-ending chain of meaningless moments, and there would not be the faintest trace of a past. (p. 255)

The LSU Rural Life
Museum and Windrush Gardens

Initially, this museum was kind of a second thought.

David Floyd, personal communication

The LSU Rural Life Museum and Windrush Gardens are folded within the 450-acre Burden Research Plantation, a "green space" donated in small tracts to LSU by Ione and Steele Burden between the late 1960s and the early 1990s. Situated, as it is, in wealthy south Baton Rouge at the intersection of I-10 and the commercial sprawl of Essen Lane, the property is prime real estate, aching, say some, to be developed. The land is protected, however, under the strict covenants of the Burden Research Foundation. It must be used for "agricultural and horticultural research and the Rural Life Museum only," says David Floyd. "In other words, a politician can't build his house out here; they can't sell a square inch or less . . . without losing it." To ensure compliance, the Burdens thought it "better to have three watchdogs": the foundation itself, the chancellor of the LSU Agricultural Center, and the provost and chancellor of the university. "Counter and counterbalances," says Floyd. "If one chancellor goes running amok, the other chancellor has legal means to counter his actions or whatever."

The job of the watchdogs, then, is to keep the commercial vortex at bay. The metaphoric dogs, alert or sleepy as the case may be, patrol the entrance to the museum, a one-lane road that turns aside from the jerk of traffic on Essen Lane to twist a winding path through the property, past dirt lanes that disappear into old growth bottomland and hardwood forests, past cultivated fields of sugar, vegetables, and roses, past a cow or two, over a creek bed and around a bend to the LSU Rural Life Museum and Windrush Gardens.

The entrance to the museum is through "the Barn": A large, low building of sheet metal—a Butler building, I guess it's called—with multiple additions protruding here and there, some painted inside or out to create the effect of worn wooden planks. Framed by foliage and a few crude benches, a broad open-air entrance welcomes visitors to the main gallery just inside, cement floor below and, in the exposed height above, 20 or so ceiling fans in a slow, steady spin. The hush of air mingles with the hum of the fluorescent lights and stirs the must from the jumble of artifacts that overflows the room. The general impression is a lack of urgency, as if I might as well sit on the bench out front for awhile before I pay the modest fee, retrieve a guide, and wander through the main gallery to the rear entrance where, just outside under shade, I find another bench to sit on.

The visitor's guide brochure tells me that the purpose of the museum is for the visitor "to learn and to enjoy the lifestyles and life-ways of the rural people of Louisiana" (LSU Rural Life Museum, n.d., n.p.). The museum boasts the "largest collection of material culture of 19th century Louisiana" and is the state's "oldest museum to interpret slavery." Two maps constitute the bulk of the brochure. The smaller locates the artifacts collected in the Barn under headings such as "Bathing," "Textiles," "Cotton," and "Slavery." The larger map shows the buildings located out the back door of the Barn. They extend over five acres and are divided into two main sections. "The Working Plantation" consists of the buildings I mentioned at the beginning of this chapter, plus a kitchen, post office, commissary, pigeon cote, smokehouse, a few chicken coops, and a handful of outhouses, crescent moons cut high in the doors for light, ventilation, and décor. The brochure assures me that the buildings are "authentically furnished to reconstruct all the major activities of life on a typical 19th century working plantation."

"The Folk Architecture section consists of buildings with divergent forms of construction illustrating the various cultures of Louisiana," such as a pioneer cabin, a corn crib, and a potato house; shotgun, dog-trot, log, and Acadian houses; and a grist mill, jail, church, and cemetery. The guide does not specify the "various cultures" the structures represent, and I find that only an inkling of the diversity can be gathered from the title plates attached to the front of the buildings. The least fuzzy in this regard is the caption on the log house, or "Stoner-Athens Cabin." Built in 1840, it is the "type of construction favored by yeoman farmers of British descent [usually Scots or Irish] who moved west from Virginia and the Carolinas and settled throughout the Upland South." The plate on the "Pioneer House" over-looks the cultural context in favor of detailing when the structure was built, where, and of what and stating that between 1810 and 1960 it housed five generations of the same family. The plates on the "Dog-Trot" and the "Acadian" houses offer the title only. Perhaps the curators assume that vis-itors will access the various cultures by decoding the architectural signs or, in the case of the Acadian House, that they know the history of *Le Grande Derangement* or recall Longfellow's romantic transmission "Evangeline, a Tale of Acadie." At the very least, they might connect *Acadian* to its cor-rupted form, *Cajun,* and thereby recall the "trademarks" of Cajun culture, such as "jambalaya . . . Cajun music . . . piroques, Spanish moss, alligators, swamps, bayous, and Cajun cabins just like this one" (LSU Rural Life Museum, 1998b, p. 39)—common in the lowland areas of south central and west Louisiana, where, today, one is just as likely to find oil workers in pickups, a burger and beer, popular country, rock and rap, a Wal-Mart or two, and low-slung ranch-style homes.

A small dirt path separates the Folk Architecture section from the Working Plantation. Here, the title plates take care to distinguish between ante- and postbellum periods and the cultures of the slave, sharecropper, and overseer. Most of the captions on the cabins refer to the life of the antebellum slave, one detailing the sparse furnishings, handmade implements, and crude lighting devices crafted by the slaves or "handed down to them by the plantation's owner or overseer." Others reference the postbellum culture of the tenant farmer or sharecropper, who "was at least able to make, purchase, or barter for basic items such as beds, mattresses, [and] lanterns." However, due to the uniform look of the cabins and their continued use as residences through the mid-1960s, it would appear that the material conditions, if not the culture, of the African American sharecropper were similar to those of the antebellum slave. I asked David Floyd about this, and he observed that the plantation section "covers a gamut, since it's both free and slave. . . . In postbellum times, the inhabitants of those houses were still workers on the plantation but, by law anyway, legally free. Now, whether their life was changed by any means is up to debate. Of course, in many cases, at many times, it didn't change, it didn't change much."

While the title plates and buildings imply little change in the living conditions of the slave and sharecropper, the responsible agents and agencies (e.g., of racism and classism, to start) in the diverse periods that stretch from Reconstruction through to the 1960s and beyond are not described here. One result of the oversight is that a monolithic Slave-Sharecropper emerges, a kind of pasteboard figure, who, caught in the conflated space and time and lacking all correspondence, appears liable for his or her condition. Likewise, the counterhistories of slaves and then sharecroppers piecing together articulate, resilient, and diverse cultures from the resources at hand are not remembered in the title plates or buildings—unless the visitor veers in her thinking toward irony or cynicism. That is, in the exterior ordering of the two sections (i.e., in the appearance, arrangement, and relationship of the buildings), a single pastoral universe emerges, a safe if not pleasing microcosm of rural life in Louisiana. Due to the ambiguous title plates, the conflation of time, the close proximity of the buildings within and between sections, and the tidy homes and well-cut lawns—water lilies afloat in upturned sugar kettles—it would appear that while the slave-sharecroppers have dwellings a tad smaller than those of their Acadian-Scots-Irish neighbors just across the street, they're "making do" pretty well.

The pretty pastoral *geist* of rural life extends into and is an extension of the Windrush Gardens that directly adjoin the plantation section. The guide tells me that the gardens "expand over twenty-five acres" and include "winding paths, lakes, and open areas." There's also a goat and two antebellum structures that are original to the property: the Burden Big House and the house of the hostler, who cared for the mules and horses. The buildings date from 1856, when John and Emma Burden took up residency on the property, which was given to them—according to "family tradition" anyway—by Emma's uncle, William S. Pike, a pioneer settler and prominent businessman of Baton Rouge. The Burdens vacated the house in 1870 when old John Burden died, and it remained empty until the 1920s, when his grandson, William Pike, his wife, Ollie Steele, and their children, Ione, Pike Jr., and Steele, returned to live permanently at Windrush (LSU Rural Life Museum, 1998a, pp. 21–22).

Now, Steele Burden was an accomplished landscape architect, "probably Louisiana's best-known landscape designer during his life," says Floyd. Drawing on his expertise and the "renaissance of interest in plantation life during the thirties—which was due in part to the popularity of southern writers such as Margaret Mitchell and Francis Parkinson Keyes (she and Steele were big buddies, you know, in Louisiana, everybody's connected to everybody else)—Steele began to restore the gardens of antebellum plantation homes, including those at Windrush." Apparently, in the last quarter of the previous century, the tenant farmers on Windrush had raised livestock and the land had become a "cattle run." To reclaim it, Steele researched and then reproduced the gardens of antebellum designers who in their time had reproduced the European and romantic fad of intermixing wild and formal areas, thereby creating pastoral hideaways (from the evils of industry or what have you), replete with faux if not antique classical statuary, flowing fountains, and ornately patterned beds of flowers.

Once a forest cleared and tilled for profit, then after Reconstruction a cattle run that Steele reclaimed in the height of the Depression as a nostalgic bit of bygone for city folks on their Sunday drives into the country, the gardens are 75 years old now ("old like me," Steele remarked in 1995 shortly before his death), and too overgrown for the fancy flowers to grow. However, due to the height of the trees and the density of the foliage (and a few stubborn statues that continue to gurgle up water into ponds), the gardens seem to highlight—they *gest* toward—their original function.[4] As with the gardens of the Big Houses on the River Road, the lush surround isolates the Burden Big House from the labor and industry in the Quarters. Indicative of romance as discharged through the domestic setting, they tempt amnesia regarding one's complicity in the industrial enterprise, always ongoing elsewhere.

The gardens also isolate the Burden home from the work of the museum, which, as I explain later, is directed toward not only rural life but also the rural life of the working classes. In these terms, the Burden Big House and its legacy—imprinted on Steele at work in his post-antebellum garden—are best forgotten or, at least, elided. The museum does not disseminate the family history in its displays, directions to the house are few, and, should by chance the visitor happen upon the home, she finds it sealed up tight, the windows fogged with dust, its memories reduced to a single title plate that recalls Ione's donation of the building to the museum. The Burden Big House, then, is assigned a backstage part at the museum, as if the curators or perhaps Steele himself (I don't know) were reluctant to have the house perform its memories. It is the pastoral *geist* that is voiced back and forth between the gardens and the museum proper.

A similar message pervades the six-minute video *Whispers of the Past* (LSU Office of Public Relations, 1993), which visitors can view in a small room just off the main gallery. The content of the video runs along the lines of the museum guide. In a voiceover of enthused authority, a male narrator addresses the general purpose of the museum, its different sections, building details, and the broader significance of the museum. A montage of soft-focus images that correspond to the voiced content is shown as the narrator speaks.

While, to start, the narrator references the "antebellum homes" featured in other tourist sites, he quickly reminds us that such "grandeur . . . was shared by only a few. Most Louisianans, both before and after the Civil War, were common folk," and "the Rural Life Museum is a tribute to these Louisianans." By means of class distinction and quantity claims, the narrator separates the world of the rich from that of the poor and legitimates focus on the latter, as if it can represent rural life on its own. Just as the Burden Big House is swept aside in the representation of rural life outside, so too the narrator makes no direct mention of it or Welham or, from this point on, Big Houses and their occupants generally. The narrator's amnesia functions to create an inbred vortex, where the "life . . . of the laboring classes" is a result of the laboring classes—that is, those who occupy the represented world. To deflect the countermemories implicit in such a move, the narrator directs our attention to the broader significance of the micro world when, in conclusion, he asserts that the museum "vividly captures 19th-century rural life, preserving this important part of our nation's rural heritage." In this way, Louisiana rural life is made to correspond to rural life generally and the micro/macro whole to an image of a nation-state where the wealthy have no impact on the poor and vice versa—in short, to a nation where there is no class conflict.

Safely circumscribed within the boundaries of the imagined world, the diverse cultures that constitute rural life are reduced further by the categorical references the narrator makes to "the laboring classes during the plantation era" or "the working-class sector of a Louisiana plantation." Although, a third of the way through the video, the narrator devotes a sentence to the "slave cabins" that "attest to the harsh reality of life in the slave quarters," the general impression is that life was pretty much the same for all rural people, and, given the watercolor images of pretty buildings and objects basking in gentle sunlight (imagine Vermeer), it appears that life wasn't half bad for rural folks. At least, the sun was soft and it never rained . . . in Louisiana.

The video is successful in reproducing the history that is recalled (and forgotten) in the microcosm of rural life represented outside. Thus the museum and video address a key epistemological aim of museums, namely, to create "a space in which the *world is ordered,* in which, with the assistance of material objects, the 'world' is realized, understood and mediated" (Prosler, 1996, p. 22; italics in original). To order the world in this case, the poetics of reproductive surrogation come into play, specifically the reproduction of a pastoral ideal through veris-materiality, isolation, and conflation.

The problematic politics of the aforementioned conventions are compounded during Harvest Days, which is a two-day "living history" event the museum holds every October. The aim of the program is to demonstrate and "interpret activities that took place on Louisiana plantations and farms during harvest time in the 1800s" (LSU Rural Life Museum, 2004a). Clad in 19th-century garb, the "artisans" enact and, in some cases, invite the audience to enact the different activities, such as spinning and weaving, grinding corn, shoeing a horse, cooking on an open hearth, and making soap, bricks, shingles, and fence pickets. A band plays festive Cajun music, folks dance, kids take wagon rides, and, all in all, the event is "fun and educational for children and adults alike" ("Join in the Fun," 1998, p. 1).

I have fun anyway, and, each year, I learn at least one humble fact I actually retain, such as the popularity of an antebellum dish in which a turkey was stuffed with a duck, the duck with a quail, the quail with a songbird, and the songbird with an oyster or two. According to the demonstrator in the kitchen—a pleasant, middle-aged white woman—*turducken,* a turkey stuffed with a chicken stuffed with a duck, is a popular dish in Louisiana today. What I cannot recount are specifics regarding who, for instance, raised the duck, shot the quail, harvested the oyster, prepared the dish, and enjoyed what seems to me to be an extravagant delectable. In other words, the social-cultural matrix of those who "did" the dish—made history "go" in this case (Pollock, 1998a)—is missing from my education. Amend that: The demonstrator and I made history go in this case.

While there is little doubt in my mind that Harvest Days creates a cheery monolith of 19th-century harvest, disregarding the impact of social-cultural factors, shifting technologies, times, and places, the point that intrigues me here is how the live enactment of 19th-century harvest skills, a quite deliberate restoration of behavior, tells me so little about the past. Instead, it seems to me that "the bodies of the living . . . speak [too] freely" for "the voices of the dead" (Roach, 1996, p. xiii). History is mastered by the participants at Harvest Days, not through genealogy (of course), but through simulation (see Baudrillard, 1983). Specifically, the participants' veris-realistic reproduction of activities, in the present time and space of the event, claims precedence over the history or histories of its production. There is no there here. As with reality TV, it is the value of present-ness—of seeming to be present for a "real-life" doing—that attracts us; it empowers us with agency because, due to the insinuation of the present tense, we become part of the act. Unlike reality TV, in which we are cast as judges of those involved in a game of chance, at Harvest Days we are the novices to whom the skilled enactors disseminate their knowledge through simulation. Their possession of history (and/as veracity) is strengthened further by their enactment of subjects I know little to nothing about, such as *turducken* or making bricks. Since prior contexts are elided, the only context I have for understanding *turducken* or brick making is the "doing" context of Harvest Days.

To pursue the same point from a slightly different angle, none of the activities performed at Harvest Days occur in or around the slave/share-cropper cabins or on the green they frame, except the smithy's use of the blacksmith's shop. The planners' seeming avoidance of the space suggests to me that it represents a history that we (planners and participants alike) know of and can recount. When we see or walk through the space, we recall prior people in prior contexts, we recall slavery to start. Such recall resists—it counters and, potentially, defamiliarizes—the present event, the cheery monolith of Harvest Days. The planners' avoidance, then, can be understood as a strategy to minimize the ruptures (e.g., between past and present) that the space incites, or as a subtle tactic to prompt reflexivity, now and then, on the part of the celebrants, or as a sign of recognition and respect toward signifiers that do not float easily into our possession.

Reflexive strategies and tactics are commonplace if not expected in genealogical histories and poststructural practices generally. They provide historians with ways to highlight and deconstruct the politics of production within the events they study, within the discourses they use, and within the exchanges they work. In her essay "Into the Heart of Irony," Henrietta Riegel (1996) discusses how irony, as a reflexive prompt, might be used in museum displays to deconstruct "traditional exhibit practices" (p. 83). Riegel details two cases. In the first, the curator relied on a subtle use of irony, embedding it in the title plates that accompanied the artifacts. According to Riegel, the choice reinforced, rather than interrogated, the typical mode of museum production and reception because, in order to access the irony, the visitor needed to be literate, astute, and intellectually detached from the subject (p. 94). In Riegel's second case, the curator crafted overt ironic markers, intermixing highbrow modes of representation, such as a chronology of authentic items displayed behind glass and accessed through sight, with open displays of popular, mass-produced "junk," temporal and spatial disorder, and hands-on, participant interaction (p. 95). For Riegel, the curator's tactics of "contamination" created "an interpretive space" where (Riegel calls on Bakhtin at this point) "counter voices" or "backtalk" regarding the subject, the exhibit, and the museum context were activated by the visitors, as well as the exhibit (p. 99).

The poetics of contamination Riegel advocates in her essay are used, to different effects, by Roach and Sebald in their respective genealogies. Common in all three cases is the presence of a savvy curator who constructs the discursive space of memories and countermemories with which we interact. Whereas in Riegel's example and Roach's practice the construction and enactment of poststructural irony are coded and claimed as purposeful and ethically sound, Sebald writes to counter that very assumption. In his text, backtalk becomes the constant in history, possessed and used by everyone and hence, as a practice, ethically unstable or relative.

Poetics of contamination are at work at the LSU Rural Life Museum as well; it might be said that they operate to counter my analysis of the museum as a site that represents rural life as a pastoral monolith, if not pleasing to us certainly not challenging, and certainly not indicative of a genealogical approach to history. In my analysis, I have concentrated on the exterior signs for the most part: those material and discursive transmissions that the museum places front stage, as most illustrative and supportive of their aims as expressed in the same materials. The contaminants, or counterviews, lie backstage (like the Burden Big House) or *within* the promoted materials. They are the innards, if you will, of the bodies—the buildings, title plates, and narratives—I have looked at. So, too, they bear similarities to components we find at work inside a genealogy or a genealogist's view of history, such as discontinuity and difference, excessive and entangled subjects and sources, piecemeal forms, partiality, and alternative epistemologies. A key difference, however, is that, at the museum, the contaminating innards seem to arise by accident or chance. Unlike the practices of Roach and Sebald or Riegel's curator of choice, there does not appear to be a savvy curator who arranges the parts, much less directs them toward Deconstructing the Master Plan as I have analyzed it. It happens. However, it happens by chance, by a chance contaminant that gives rise to an episteme of the child, madman, and amateur.

Inside the Barn, there are six public rooms or galleries that at first glance a visitor might mistake as a junk shop, filled to the brim as it is with items that it seems folks found in their barns or their attics or in a box of a loved one now gone and, not wanted or needed, they gave the bits and pieces to Steele and, after he'd passed, to the museum, I guess because they seemed old or odd or of enough value to warrant some keeping, for example, in the section called "Bathing," there is a haphazard row of old privy seats (one and two, square and round, wood and metal) from where at what time whose behind it's not mentioned though scrawled on the wall right next to the seats and over the tub by the bits of old china dug up from the dirt in a New Orleans privy there's a joke "we are told that the bathtub was invented in the 1850s, the telephone in 1876, just think if you had been living in 1850, you would have sat in the bathtub for 26 years without the phone ringing once" and, unlabeled uncaptioned, the items of bathing become those of laundering and lighting and medical and baskets and bridles and someone's stuffed ducks and a river shrimp trap from the twenties it says just beside a pirogue in a pile of 10 that in '52 Bud Oliver built a sausage-shaped item of Perique Tobacco and cutters and canisters, a case of men's hats, a Gibson Girl godawful sculpture of Mary I guess from the sixties it seems and a sampler wreath of curlicue flowers that Edna L. Bailey made with her hands from her relatives' hair, a log water pipe from the combs in a case some quilts and three working a spinning wheel sculpture of why don't you speak for yourself, John? and washing the sacred heart Mr. Steele drew right on the wall (an immortelle) his comic sketches and mingled in weeds that make colorful dyes Chitimacha a basket a charivari noise rolling machine and the toys and the typewriter used on the road as well as your Civil War relic a log behind glass with buttons francais and anglais and two funeral coaches, some buggies and wagons, an ornate peanut cart AND LIKEWISE UNCLEAR is the pile of cotton amassed in a wagon and whether it is, as sworn to at length in a letter and three affidavits, the "Oldest Bale of American Grown Cotton."

I stand in wonderment.

The letter, addressed to no one at all, was written, it says, on December 12, 1905, by a Mr. P. B. Dugan, president of the First National Bank of West Point, Maryland. In it, Mr. Dugan claims an authentic history of this bale of cotton . . . as follows. John Peden, a rather eccentric farmer of northern Oktibeha County of Maryland, owning a number of slaves, had, in about 1860, a disagreeable experience in lending money and declared his intention not to have any more money to lend. Thereafter he sold such part of each cotton crop as was necessary to buy his yearly supplies. The remainder of the crop was placed on the long, spacious veranda in front of his residence. In the course of time, the veranda was fully occupied except an opening for entrance to the house. This was the situation when the writer saw it in about 1867. After Mr. Peden's death, the cotton was gradually sold off, the last of it in the latter 1880s, which was the lot this bank came into possession of. We have documents to establish the foregoing.

On the one hand, we might say the collection in the Barn is a mess. As Floyd confirms, "Steele meant [for it] to look like grandpa's barn. Grandpa, you know, when he got tired of something or he finished with it, he just stuck it in the barn and forgot about it, and that's exactly kind of the scheme of things." Lacking, in grandpa's scheme, is a system of classification and presentation that would instill in the disparate artifacts the network of correspondences and meanings we expect to derive from museums, histories generally, and genealogies certainly. Even the broad thematic aim of the museum, 19th-century rural life in Louisiana, is bypassed in the random mix of urban and rural items, from diverse states, that date from the mid–20th century on back. (Who is "Bud Oliver" after all? And why is his 1952 pirogue on display here?) All the "traditional signs of a museum's institutional authority" are absent in grandpa's barn, including "meticulous presentation, exhaustive captions, hushed lighting, and state-of-the-art technical armature" (Weschler, 1995, p. 40).[5]

On the other hand, the nonchalant display of diverse artifacts in incongruous (dis)order activates a history and historiography that counters the tidy idyll of rural life as represented in the museum's headline materials and my prior account. It is not that this other history is not guilty of conflation. Just as Cajun culture is reduced to the sacred totem of the Acadian House outside, so too the Chitimacha Indians of south central Louisiana are reduced to a bunch of baskets inside. However, the disparate poetics of the context contaminate the tokens similarly, as metonymic bits that highlight absence in the present representation. A comprehensive rendering of Chitimacha culture and, in the broader frame, Louisiana rural life is not assumed here. Rather, the Barn boasts a few found or hand-me-down remnants that, in their assemblage, offer fragments from a world that is multiple. It is not a fragmented view or "vision of multiple worlds" (Mauries, 2002, p. 43). These are just fragments that, in finding their way here, suggest that urban and rural life may have something to do with each other; that diverse people carried diverse things across the street, across the parish, state, and national lines, and into this Barn, where time shows itself as something we make and therefore divergent in what we make of it. Bud's boat might testify to the evolution of the pirogue over time or his devolutionary attempt to restore the origin or, in 1952, Bud's leisure or working-class status; or, like a photograph, the boat might be an image of the subject (Bud) that is impervious to time, that resists anything that has happened to or is discursively imposed upon him (Berger & Mohr, 1982, p. 106).

The stuff in the Barn is history as viewed by genealogy, but before the genealogist gets hold of it. This is not to say that the museum does not own or possess the artifacts, rather that its curatorial management of them is weak. There are no signs of a curator "mapping emphases and contradictions" so as to "unravel the punitive seamlessness of origins" that "continue to influence values and practices . . . today" (Roach, 1996, pp. 13, 30). Rather, as in surreal poetics, the entanglement of random items, or "systematic disorder" (Mauries, 2002, p. 218), reconfigures the production of meaning or of history making in this case, dispersing it across the various items and, in the end, leaving it to the visitor to figure out for herself, or not. While the jumble may incite the visitor toward ironic detachment, it also provokes wonder, irrational connections, and multiple made-up narratives because, as with the work of the surrealists, the collection seems to be inspired by the art of the child, madman, and amateur or *naïf* (Hughes, 1991, p. 227). The bathtub joke, scrawled across the wall of the museum (by Steele Burden, I learned), encourages me to think in such directions anyway. So too do the wagon of corroded cotton and, in a frame perched precariously atop it, P. B. Dugan's letter about the eccentric John Peden. Since the relationship between the two is ambiguous, the visitor is left to wonder whether the cotton on display is part of the "Oldest Bale of American Grown Cotton" or just a bunch of "kind of" old cotton. She also is left with the haunting memory of an old man sitting on his veranda, year after year, amidst a growing heap of useless cotton.

As I discussed in the second section of this chapter, Sebald crafts language to a similar though certainly more deliberate effect in his history. By means of metonymic lists, polyglot narratives, obscure connections, and the recall of dreams and nightmare realities, Sebald disperses the possession and production of history across the various sources, the author, and the reader. He also reminds us that the praxis of defamilarization need not only be evaluative, as in deconstructing reproductive origins; it can also urge us to look afresh, in unfamiliar ways, at things we take for granted, such as how we write our histories.

As it turns out, the chance contaminants at work inside the Barn are due to contingent factors. First, the displayed artifacts were not pursued as much as offered to Steele and, now, the museum by individuals who, as Floyd puts it, "finally found a place for grandma's blanket or whatever." Second, the Barn (and its collection) "was never meant to be a public facility. . . . It was meant to be a repository, an archive for the university and for the university classrooms." Steele, then, was not obliged to concern himself with traditional display practices of museums. Upon receipt of an item, he would catalog it and stick it in the barn, "like grandpa." In lieu of print captions to classify artifacts, he would sketch cartoon scenes or write quotes on the wall more or less analogous to the referred class of items. As Floyd offers, "Steele did everything wrong from a museum point of view." Due, however, to budgetary and staff constraints, there are neither the funds nor the personnel to correct Steele's mistakes today, to reorder the disorder.

The poetics internal to the Barn bleed over, in various ways, to the display of artifacts inside the buildings on the grounds. The hemorrhage is due to the items being drawn from the same random collection and submitted to display practices similar to those of the Barn artifacts. For instance, the School House is filled with such a madcap jumble of items, both rural and urban, from diverse periods and places that it makes history silly, seeming to mock the guide's claim of "authentically furnished" buildings and the goal of authentic surrogation generally. The memory gaps collected here are best illustrated by the "Dictation" sentences found in the teacher's book that lies in a muddle of dust on top of the lectern at the front of the room. Magritte might well have written "Lesson 143," which runs: "A random shot may do great damage. The lambs gambol in the meadow. The stranger met with a fatal accident on the railroad. A rascal stole a scythe from the farmer. What is the breadth of the vessel? Flannel is made of wool. Wagner, the great musician, died recently. The maiden bought some thread and lace. We had a steak for breakfast." This is not a pipe.

Across the way from the School House, inside one of the Slave Cabins, there are ghosts but no bodies. A pallet of rotted straw with a dirty threadbare cloth lies in one corner and, before the empty hearth, a crude chair with gashed webbing. The few cooking implements are dirty and the pots unused. The room is dim, dusty, and sad. I am reminded of the image of crazy John Peden sitting on his front porch with his heap of cotton while those who picked it are absent from the picture. Embedded in this memory is a myth of white supremacy, enacted by whites through the practice of chattel slavery and through Eurocentric perspectives that view slavery as a one-sided act of cultural genocide, whites seeming to eradicate the culture(s) of their victims (Roach, 1996, pp. 6–7, 191–192). Involved in either case is denying visibility to the bodies and actions of slaves except as commodity objects of labor, a pile of cotton, a pallet on the floor. The room is haunted by this myth and the practices we enact to perpetuate it.

The unused aspect of the room also suggests that whoever lived here has left. They have packed up their valuables and moved on. I wonder if the implied leave-taking is meant to serve as a surrogate, a reassuring Uncle Tom, for our collective emancipation, as if the history of slavery is but dust now without repercussions. On the other hand, do the bare-bones leavings quote and thereby redirect the aim of in/visibility and its politics? That is, as staged memory, the room beckons us inside with the promise of showing us those once made invisible and then refuses to show us anything at all. No bodies here, except the ghosts of ideas we find in the dust on the floor.

However, on another walk on a different day, I discover that someone has returned to one of the Slave Cabins and covered the pallet with a small, very pretty, handmade crazy quilt. The new item in the old context tricks the eye, and it tricks with history, contaminating the interior of the cabin and the memories I have and have made of it. The quilt testifies to someone being here; to someone furnishing forth a creative expression drawing on and piecing together remnants of the past. It is a resilient performance: One quilt maker stands in, but not quite, for another (disparity marked by the new in the old); by means of her quilt, she recounts the analogous craft of the museum, both its pretty pastoral and crazy quilt barn, and restores to it, to its memory, a prior performance of patchwork resilience, always not her own.

The trick of the quilt tricked me again when, on that same day, I happened upon two more new quilts on beds in two other buildings. In a single forward rush of time, the surreal ambiguity of the quilt maker and the tenuous gap her performance had contracted between past and present collapsed. In their place was an industrious and creative individual who had volunteered her (or, perhaps, it was his) skills to the museum with the aim of making the sad little shacks more pretty and, as I saw it, making my neat little narrative a mess. People show up and they change things.

Likewise, it appears that Steele drifted from his desired intent due to the unexpected offerings of others. According to Floyd, Steele's initial vision of the museum did not include the Folk Architecture section. He was interested in slavery and at a time when few people were. However, as Floyd tells it, "One of the individuals on [Burden's] committee, name of Jones, his wife had a house in Washington Parish and they didn't know what to do with it. It was the pioneer cabin that is on site now, and [Jones] asked Steele if he wanted it. Now, Steele was a southern gentleman, and Steele, in many cases, could not say no. Or, in many cases if he said no he would never tell you no right off the bat and, many times, never tell you no personally and have somebody else tell you no. So, it's not clear whether he couldn't tell the Jones family no or he actually went and looked at the cabin and said, well, it's interesting, so why not. Anyway, that was the first building that was moved onto the property that had no sense of what [Steele] was trying to do, that kind of veered off in a different direction." Once Steele adopted the cabin, he continued to veer, both accepting offers of and pursuing rural house types on his own.

In this light, the museum is a history of people showing up with their memories and of Steele, unable to say no, accepting them and thereby altering his original plan. Floyd seems to perform a similar agency or surrogacy. While he struggles with some of Steele's choices, such as the green space in the Quarters, he chooses to add to rather than excise what Steele did in the past. The performance of memory as chance aggregations is parceled throughout the museum, imprinted here and there at the bottom of the title plates attached to the buildings and some of the artifacts. "Given in memory of Mary Richardson Carter (1868–1955) by her heirs," "in memory of Mr. & Mrs. Francis Henderson James, Sr. by their children," "by Patricia Curry Bagwell in honor of the Curry family," "by James and Rebecca Stoker Kyle in honor of R. J. and Bernice Stoker," "by Helen L. Athens and family in memory of Edwin P. Athens," "by Mr. Dennis Murrell" and "Mrs. Emily Murphy" and "L. Keller" and "the College Grove Baptist Association" and from Welham and Bagatelle and Petit Versailles and Mount Place and Tyron and Bonne Esperance and Augusta and Longwood plantations and the parishes of St. James and Rapides and Sabine and Washington and Iberville and Tensas and East Baton Rouge, the items bear the memories of these and others and, by virtue of the metonym, all those they don't or can't recall in their movement from one place to another. Like the individuals they remember and the cultures they represent, the seeming permanence of the buildings or artifacts is countered by their transient histories, by their movement through space and time whereby they remake and are remade by those they encounter.

Conclusion: Who Owns This Gesture?

Just prior to the entrance of the museum, in the green space of a roundabout, is a large bronze statue of a slightly stooped, elderly African American man tipping his hat. Titled *Uncle Jack*, the statue was commissioned in the 1920s by Jack Bryan, a white man and resident of Natchitoches, Louisiana. Bryan wanted to honor the hard work and friendship of the African American servants, companions, and fellow workmen he had known as a child and adult. Despite fears that the white community "would not tolerate dedicating the only statue in [Natchitoches] to a Negro," the statue was erected in 1927 in a small park at the foot of Front Street.[6] The original plaque read, "Dedicated to the arduous and faithful service of the good darkies of Louisiana." The statue was "generally accepted and later beloved by the white community in Natchitoches and throughout the United States." Across the country, newspapers, such as the *New York Times*, praised its display.

In 1968, the sculpture emerged as a subject of controversy when a local group of African Americans actively protested its public presence. As a result of adverse publicity and the changing times of the 1960s, city officials had the sculpture removed. It was stored in a hangar at the Natchitoches airport for six years and, upon fielding offers from numerous institutions, including the Smithsonian, Jo Bryan Dourneau, the daughter of the late Jack Bryan, decided to donate *Uncle Jack* to the LSU Rural Life Museum.

The mother of a dear friend of mine passed away a few years ago. After the funeral service, we drove to the cemetery. I was situated just a few cars behind the hearse. As we emerged from an underpass, I noticed an elderly African American man, in a gray sweater and tie, walking on the sidewalk toward us, in the opposite direction we were traveling. As the hearse neared him, the man stopped walking and turned to face the street. Then, he removed his hat and held it over his heart as the hearse and the other cars passed by. He did not know us.

Notes

1. D. Floyd, interview, July 23, 2004, Baton Rouge, LA.

2. *Difference* and *deferral* are combined in Derrida's neologism *différance*, which references the two meanings of the French verb *différer*, "to differ" and "to defer or postpone." The unstable neologism conveys Derrida's view of language (identity and history): namely, a word has disparate, "distinct," and "unequal" meanings that confound a single, determinate meaning and interpose a delay in sense making. Rather than immediately present, meanings move in "the interval of a *spacing* and temporalizing" of language (Derrida, 1973, p. 129; italics in original).

3. For Roach (1996), "three principles govern the practices of memory." "Kinesthetic imagination" refers to bodily practices of restored behavior enacted in the present, residing in the historical record, and imagined (e.g., in anticipation of future action). "Vortices of behavior" are spaces of social contact that, through use, make manifest prevailing values of the day. As sites of potential gain and loss, they draw and encourage people to perform, in support of or opposition to the manifest values. "Displaced transmissions" refer to the adaptation or transformation of historic practices, within or over time, due to the changing needs, conditions, and contexts of the users (pp. 26–30).

4. *Gest* is used here in Brecht's terms, as the signified "gist" or "attitude" of a material gesture, or signifier. Due to how the *gest* is composed, the "social historical laws," norms, or origins from which it is enacted "spring into sight" (Brecht, 1964, pp. 42, 104, 86). *Gest,* then, is a sign of a genealogical moment.

5. The one exception is the "Slavery in Louisiana" exhibit, which was relocated to a separate and more prominent gallery a few years ago and had its artifacts reordered. The exhibit displays select items, carefully arranged and captioned, that provide a chronology of the slave trade as practiced in the Kasai region of Zaire, in the key markets of Charleston and New Orleans, and on southern Louisiana plantations. A DVD entitled *Steal Away: Black Slave Life in Northern America* (LSU Rural Life Museum 2004b) interweaves images of items on display with photographs of slaves. The introductory caption supplants "Eurocentric interpretations" of slavery with the recognition that slaves had "complex social, political, and religious systems of their own," significant traces of which are prevalent in African American and Creole cultures and Louisiana culture generally. In contrast to the rest of the

Barn, the well-ordered exhibit suggests that in light of the topic, the politics of representation and race, and Louisiana demographics, curatorial care was deemed paramount in this case.

6. All quotations in this section are drawn from the *Uncle Jack* title plates.

References

Anderson, M. (2003). The edge of darkness: On W. G. Sebald. *October*, *106*, 102–121.
Barthes, R. (1981). *Camera lucida: Reflections on photography* (R. Howard, Trans.). New York: Hill & Wang.
Baudrillard, J. (1983). *Simulations*. New York: Semiotext(e).
Benjamin, W. (1969). Theses on the philosophy of history (H. Zohn, Trans.). In H. Arendt (Ed.), *Illuminations* (pp. 253–264). New York: Schocken.
Berger J., & Mohr, J. (1982). *Another way of telling*. New York: Vintage.
Brecht, B. (1964). *Brecht on theatre: The development of an aesthetic* (J. Willett, Ed. & Trans.). New York: Hill & Wang.
Clifford, J. (1988). *The predicament of culture: Twentieth-century ethnography, literature, and art*. Cambridge, MA: Harvard University Press.
Derrida, J. (1973). *Speech and phenomena, and other essays on Husserl's theory of signs* (D. Allison, Trans.). Evanston, IL: Northwestern University Press.
Flanagan, J. (2000). *The overseer's house: An historic house report*. Unpublished senior thesis, Baton Rouge, Louisiana State University.
Foucault, M. (1977). Nietzsche, genealogy, history. In D. Bouchard (Ed.), *Language, counter-memory, practice: Selected essays and interviews* (pp. 139–164). Ithaca, NY: Cornell University Press.
Geertz, C. (1973). Thick description: Toward an interpretive theory of culture. In C. Geertz, *The interpretation of cultures: Selected essays* (pp. 3-30). New York: Basic.
Graff, G. (1989). Co-optation. In H. A. Veeser (Ed.), *The new historicism* (pp. 168–181). New York: Routledge.
Greenblatt, S. (1988). *Shakespearean negotiations: The circulation of social energy in Renaissance England*. Berkeley: University of California Press.
Hughes, R. (1991). *The shock of the new* (2nd ed.). New York: McGraw-Hill.
Join in the fun of Rural Life's Harvest Days. (1998, September). *Whispers of the Past* [Louisiana State University Rural Life Museum newsletter], *4*, 1–4.
Louisiana State University Office of Public Relations. (Producer). (1993). *Whispers of the past* [Video]. Available from Louisiana State University, Office of University Relations, 3960 West Lakeshore Drive, Baton Rouge, LA 70808. E-mail: urelat1@lsu.edu.
Louisiana State University Rural Life Museum. (1998a). *Rural Life Museum docent training manual*. Baton Rouge: Author.
Louisiana State University Rural Life Museum. (1998b). *Rural Life Museum folk life*. Baton Rouge: Author.

Louisiana State University Rural Life Museum. (2004a). *Interpretive programs 2004*. Baton Rouge: Author.

Louisiana State University Rural Life Museum. (Producer). (2004b). *Steal away: Black slave life in Northern America* [DVD]. Available from the Louisiana State University Rural Life Museum, P.O Box 80498, Baton Rouge, LA 70898, rulife1@lsu.edu.

Louisiana State University Rural Life Museum. (n.d.). *Louisiana State University Rural Life Museum and Windrush Gardens, Baton Rouge, Louisiana*. [Brochure]. Baton Rouge: Author.

Macdonald, S. (1996). Theorizing museums: An introduction. In S. Macdonald & G. Fyfe (Eds.), *Theorizing museums: Representing identity and diversity in a changing world* (pp. 1–18). Oxford: Blackwell.

Mauries, P. (2002). *Cabinets of curiosities*. London: Thames & Hudson.

Montrose, L. (1989). Professing the Renaissance: The poetics and politics of culture. In H. A. Veeser (Ed.), *The new historicism* (pp. 15–36). New York: Routledge.

Pezzullo, P. C. (2003). Touring "Cancer Alley," Louisiana: Performances of community and memory for environmental justice. *Text and Performance Quarterly*, 23, 226–252.

Pollock, D. (1998a). Introduction: Making history go. In D. Pollock (Ed.), *Exceptional spaces: Essays in performance and history* (pp. 1–45). Chapel Hill: University of North Carolina Press.

Pollock, D. (1998b). Performing writing. In P. Phelan & J. Lane (Eds.), *The ends of performance* (pp. 73–103). New York: New York University Press.

Prosler, M. (1996). Museums and globalization. In S. Macdonald & G. Fyfe (Eds.), *Theorizing museums: Representing identity and diversity in a changing world* (pp. 21–44). Oxford, UK: Blackwell.

Riegel, H. (1996). Into the heart of irony: Ethnographic exhibitions and the politics of difference. In S. Macdonald & G. Fyfe (Eds.), *Theorizing museums: Representing identity and diversity in a changing world* (pp. 83–104). Oxford, UK: Blackwell.

Roach, J. (1996). *Cities of the dead: Circum-Atlantic performance*. New York: Columbia University Press.

Said, E. (1986). Foucault and the imagination of power. In D. Hoy (Ed.), *Foucault: A critical reader* (pp. 149–155). Oxford, UK: Basil Blackwell.

Sebald, W. G. (1998). *The rings of Saturn* (M. Hulse, Trans.). New York: New Directions.

The rape of Welham. (1979, May 10). *News-Examiner* [Lutcher, LA], p. 2.

Urry, J. (1996). How societies remember the past. In S. Macdonald & G. Fyfe (Eds.), *Theorizing museums: Representing identity and diversity in a changing world*. (pp. 45–65). Oxford, UK: Blackwell.

Weschler, L. (1995). *Mr. Wilson's cabinet of wonder*. New York: Vintage.

Veeser, H. A. (1989). Introduction. In H. A. Veeser (Ed.), *The new historicism* (pp. ix–xvi). New York: Routledge.

IV

Synthesizing Scholarship

Introduction

Judith Hamera

B y this point in *Opening Acts*, you have become familiar with a number of key elements of, and commitments in, performance-based approaches to critical communication and cultural studies, and seen these reinforced across multiple essays. These points and presumptions are:

- Performance-based analysis privileges embodied, material experience as a site of research, with all the cohesive and contestory political and historical valences this implies.
- Performance-based research is highly attuned to multiple dimensions of difference, and to how these dimensions play out in the world.
- Performance-based scholarship presumes, from the outset, that both the researcher and the research enterprise are enmeshed in specific, daily, corporeal social and historical circumstances for which both must be response-able and accountable.
- Performance-based critique resonates with, and extends, the foundational theories of critical communication and cultural studies, as well as the works of their contemporary practitioners.

And, finally,

- In performance-based scholarship, divisions between everyday life, space/place, and history may serve specific organizational and logistical purposes, but in the close work of critical analysis these categories overlap, bleed into, and cross-fertilize each other.

Paul Edwards's essay shares these commitments, but he takes the synthesizing dimensions of performance-based critique as his special task. Here history, "real" or "fictional," is mapped onto space/place, "real" and "fictive." This mapping in turn rewrites possibilities for intersections of fact and fiction generally, and for oscillations between Gustave Flaubert's classic *Madame Bovary* and what can only be called "the Bovary-esque" in particular.

You might think that a canonical text would offer a respite to the performance scholar. Unlike bodies in the repertoire, one might assume that the archival *Bovary* would at least sit still. It doesn't, as Edwards amply demonstrates. On the contrary, it seems to spawn performances that then inspire yet more performances, other turns in a genealogical conversation that is both as canonical as a masterpiece and as casual as a walking tour. In performance-based research, even texts are in motion. Edwards demonstrates how the capacitating frame of performance enables the rigorous critic to manage multiple analytical sites and vocabularies and ultimately weave them into a clear, coherent reading that opens up a textual landmark to a world it birthed but might only barely recognize.

7

The Mechanical Bride of Yonville-l'Abbaye (Batteries Not Included)

Remapping the Canonical Landmark

Paul Edwards

After Flaubert, Ry will have won its trial.

René Vérard, *Ry, pays de Madame Bovary*

Emma half closed her eyes to pick out her house, and never had this poor village where she lived appeared so small.

Gustave Flaubert, *Madame Bovary*, 2.9
(de Man edition)

Concerning maps: I lost my cartographic innocence on a November morning in 1991, shortly after taking my seat in the dining room of a bed-and-breakfast in Porthmadog. My wife and I were on a driving tour of

Wales, and I had urged that we come to this town to search for signs of ancestors. But our trip thus far had a split focus. Across the country, several of our hosts had been educators, mostly language teachers, and friends of friends. A few had spoken at length of their involvement in protests demanding such things as bilingual broadcasting and dual-language signage, even of brief stints in jail. For the two of us, this was heady stuff. At this stage in our re-education, even well-known names like "Plaid Cymru" and the "Welsh Language Society" were still subjects for further research.

We were prattling cheerfully about our new friends' adventures to the other couple in the dining room (who had asked us, innocently enough, how we'd been spending our holiday) when we noticed that the emotional temperature in the room had begun to drop. Our neighbors were not Welsh, it turned out, but on holiday from Chester, across the English border, and their concern with Welsh nationalism was—how do I say this?—shaped by different interests. One of them observed tartly, "Well, they were probably just trying to attract attention." Suddenly the room was transformed: from two bourgeois couples, making pleasantries across their plates of inedible fried breakfast, to a pair of dismissive Brits and a pair of upstart, uncomprehending Yanks. Then we all felt a little foolish, and made our timid exits.

We had arrived here, not merely by different routes, but by different maps. The territory was visible to us in different ways. A third map, guiding the movement of our bilingual hosts—who spoke English to the guests and another language "offstage"—would have been hard for any of us to read.

"Doubtless" the fascination with Welsh signage—as Mike Pearson (2001) suggests—possesses "an exotic appeal for the visitor." The sign *names* differently for different readers. More than this: Multiple "small signs" of lived experience "have inscribed the landscape," but the act of mapping reinscribes these signs (not to mention the pieces of "real world" they name) very selectively (p. 37). Different interests (tourism, colonialism, nationalism) drive different selections, and make different maps. Pearson, collaborating with photographer William Yang, constructs his own narrative "map" as part of the "Mapping Wales" project for the Centre for Performance Research. His is one of 13 contributions (some in the form of minimally textualized "artists' pages") to a special edition of *Performance Research,* "On Maps and Mapping" (Gough, 2001), which arose from themes of the 1999 conference of Performance Studies international (PSi).

"On Maps and Mapping" demonstrates both the appeal and the limits of mapping-as-metaphor. The lead essay by the Stanislavski scholar Susan Melrose (2001) is symptomatic. Critiquing the dominance of a "scriptural" and "writerly economy" in performance scholarship, Melrose relates various kinds of visual perception and representation to the activity of mapping. "Looking *maps* what we see—or is what we see *mapped by* what holds the eye, in the field of vision?" (p. 6). The very act of looking is an act of mapping, which we can fix technologically (even if the technology is crude). Not only the old photograph, but even the *mise-en-scène* sketched on a napkin during rehearsal, maps the "signposts" of a "complex intentionality" (p. 15). Throughout Gough's volume, *map* designates many practices, objects, and scenes. Two contributors (Meyer, 2001; Nelson, 2001) relate the rehearsed movements of culturally "traditional" dance to maps of empire. Three others (Clarke, 2001; Kelleher, 2001; Rosenbaum, 2001) relate mapping to spectators' and actors' reductive negotiations of unfamiliar (sometimes ludically organized) physical space. Another essay (Finkelstein & Lynch, 2001) compares the "reassuring" comfort of the hotel room in a foreign country to the surprise-minimizing comforts of the "mapped" world found in guidebooks (p. 63). Yet another (Margolies, 2001) maps a city according to its smells.

No one says much about the distinctiveness of the cartographer's art. Sarah Rosenbaum (2001) touches a nerve when she talks about the "scripted spaces" of maps, a term she borrows from Norman Klein. Our presence on maps within "scripted spaces"—the results of "becoming a sign"—gives us power over the anxiety produced by the "phenomenological complexity" of our continual "placement into the landscape." Yet Rosenbaum suggests that just about any metaphor, other than mapping, might serve the taming of anxious experience: The "data map" of one's movement through the unwritten world "could as well be a novel, a painting or a play" (pp. 54–56).

A professor of performance theory is lost in Skokie, Illinois. He walks into the mini-mart of a gas station and asks, "Do you have any maps?" The clerk behind the counter, an alert poststructuralist, waves a hand toward everything in the shop. (There is no "off the map.") But this answer will not do. Where is the *map*—the piece of paper that shows the *monument?* (Otherwise, how can one turn right?)

What keeps *map,* stretched to its limits, from becoming an exhausted term? Does *map* give us a critical lever not supplied by related terms, other synecdoches for "representational act" like *photograph, archival relic, annal, biography, stage set, production record*?

The present essay examines *map* in the quotidian sense shared by theorist and non-nontheorist when searching for a street address. Maps of this sort have shaped two present-day claims made by the tourist industry of Ry, a small French town. The first is that, in his novel *Madame Bovary,* Gustave Flaubert figuratively and literally remapped the town. The second is that, a century later, the town achieved a multifaceted "victory" by remapping both itself (as Flaubert's Yonville) and the novel (as a series of miniature scenes). The town's claims might or might not constitute an act of *literary criticism*. But they clearly make late additions to an unfinalized history of utterances and their cultural handlings. Among these utterances are the cartographer's map and its near-relation, the diorama (in the term's more recent sense).

Section 1, "Map as Discourse," examines three key terms—*map, diorama, puppet*—that I will need to limit somewhat before applying them. Section 2, "Books as Maps," addresses the question of whether books can be said to "map" things and suggests how the metaphor might be helpful in a discussion of Ry. Section 3, "A Map in Flaubert's Own Hand," takes a close look at the claims of Ry's tourist industry that Flaubert remapped the town in a variety of ways: through writing as well as more conventional street maps. Section 4, "Specters of Eleanor Marx," studies the acts of remapping that Ry made in response to Flaubert. Since one of these is a large motorized model, I need to raise some questions about how it works. Section 5, "Making Pleasantries," reflects upon the power of a cultural and canonical "landmark" like *Madame Bovary*—surely one of the most handled works in modern literature—to survive its continual remappings.

1. Map as Discourse

> To make a map of your favorite mountain, look at other maps of the mountain. Copy whichever you think is the best. When you copy it, add a number of different colored stars and a key to these colors in the margin. "From here, you can see my house in the village below." "Here is a flat sunny rock to picnic on." . . . And so on.
> You've made the map your own.
> Next, climb the mountain, taking with you a number of large colored-paper stars. . . . [I]f you want your map to be inaccurate, place the stars several yards further up the mountain than you indicated. You've now made the mountain your own. (Maya Sonenberg, *Cartographies*)

My recent thinking about maps, and the interests or ideologies that shape them, owes much to Denis Wood's *The Power of Maps* (1992), a Barthes-inflected study addressed by an academic cartographer to noncartographers. While lively and contentious, the book dutifully revisits many commonplaces of contemporary theory. Maps construct, rather than reproduce, the world. They serve to "naturalize the cultural," as Barthes (1957/1972) suggests in *Mythologies,* and, more than this, culturalize the natural. While masking the interests they serve, nevertheless maps "*are* the interests of their authors in map form" (Wood, 1992, p. 71). Unavoidably, they serve the interests of property and capital: "[T]the *land* is there: it is the *property* the map creates" (p. 9). And they are selective, in ways that throw into question even what constitutes a "permanent" feature of the landscape (pp. 81–84). In the research I present below, I confronted repeatedly the force of Wood's insight: "It is the *isolation* of everything *not* on the map that so potently *naturalizes* what's *on* it (what's not on the map . . . *isn't real)*" (p. 87).

But Wood's performance-oriented approach makes fresh connections between maps and communication theory. Through "its propensity toward myth" in the sense pursued by Barthes (1957/1972)—through the persuasive act that is often masked by its representational act—the map attains "the level of discourse" (p. 141). A clever map knows how to mask the interest it embodies: It "babbles" about "everything" in the landscape, for example, when it wants to feign "innocence about the choice of anything" (p. 73). Wood therefore seeks to make us better map users by making us better interpreters of the map's intention when it speaks to us. Such speech rarely happens by means of the language printed on the map: "In the map image, entire words and arrangements of words" jump codes, from linguistic to iconic, in ways that can resemble "concrete poetry" (p. 123). Rather, the map's discourse is produced by an ensemble of effects: an "interplay" of codes and sign systems engaged in constant "dialogue with one another." The dialogue is "multi-voiced," a matter of "harmonies and dissonances" (pp. 139–140). Over a long life of revisions and updatings—multiple handlings by many authors, each serving a different interest—the remapped map becomes "polyphonic." Above these many voices, however, the map's notorious mask of objectivity and *"disinterested science"* announces a "rhetorically orchestrated denial" of its own rhetoric. "The rigorous dispassion of the survey sheet is seductive precisely in the degree to which no sign of seduction is apparent" (pp. 93–94). And even though the successful map reader learns how to resist seduction, that reader's very handling of the map contributes a new voice to the unending dialogue.

It is surprising, then, to find that Wood does not mention the theory of M. M. Bakhtin—for, clearly, the above-cited comments carry his argument from Barthes toward Bakhtinian metalinguistics.[1] The map, like the grunt or the three-volume novel, becomes another form of the "utterance," a basic unit of communication—"real-life dialogue"—rather than a unit of linguistics or cartography (Bakhtin, 1986, p. 75). Not only does the map bristle with internal dialogues, but, like a work of literature, it also carries the potential to produce dialogues, and thereby accumulate diverse new meanings, over what Bakhtin (1986) calls *"great time"* (p. 5). Wood catches the spirit of this when late in the book he calls for a postmodern world alive with *"dueling maps"* (p. 184).

The Power of Maps enriches performance theory by describing the map as utterance: In soliciting a response, it enables and constrains subsequent performances (including everyday use, remapping, and the creation of new maps). In such ways, "the map can be restored to the *instrumentality* of the body as a whole" (p. 183). Remapping: After the ball at Vaubyessard, Emma Bovary glumly considers the distance from rural Tostes to the capitals of glamour. She promptly buys some equipment for living, a map of Paris, "and with the tip of her finger" she traces her future performances up and down its streets (Flaubert, 1857/1965, p. 41).

Wood examines the productions of professional cartographers: reduced-scale representations of territory on paper or other two-dimensional surfaces. Such maps, masking the interests and intentions that produce them, become key pieces of evidence in the story of the French town of Ry. But I examine as well the three-dimensional map known today as the diorama. In using the term, I refer not to the "diorama paintings" developed in the early 19th century by L. J. M. Daguerre (see Daguerre, 1969; Kamps, 2000, p. 6) but to the "small worlds" familiar to tourists:

> The treasured dollhouse, the elaborate model railroad, the hyperrealistic museum habitat display—most of us are introduced to the diorama form early in life. We later notice them all around us: in churches, amusement parks, theaters, toy stores, and architects' studios. . . .
>
> Today, "diorama" is a multi-purpose label for a variety of simulated environments, from grade-school construction-paper Mayan cities . . . to theme parks such as *Italia in miniatura* in Rimini, which reproduces the entire Italian peninsula in the space of a city block. Certainly . . . the dioramic impulse is innate in humans. Small painted wooden models of environments . . . have been found in Egyptian tombs dating from 2,500 B.C., and the tradition of fabricating elaborate Christmas crèches originated in the Middle Ages. (Kamps, 2000, pp. 6–7)

Contributors to the catalogue for *Small World: Dioramas in Contemporary Art* (at San Diego's Museum of Contemporary Art in 2000) consider both scale and life-size (1:1) models in ways that blur the boundaries between old-fashioned museum dioramas and the self-consciously deconstructive work of installation artists like Robert Smithson (see Kamps, 2000, p. 6; Rugoff, 2000, pp. 14–15). They highlight the diorama's heuristic potential:

> The natural history diorama was traditionally haunted by a sense of loss—not only the lost life of the animals displayed, but also the threatened extinction of their natural homes due to the expansion of human civilization. Today, however, the diorama is more likely to evoke a sense of loss related to our

diminishing belief in the modernist conception of an objectively verifiable (or even a consensus) reality, which has been drastically supplemented, if not supplanted, by the paradigm of multiple "operating systems" and the various speculative realities and parallel universes we daily experience as worlds under glass. . . .

Precisely because its antiquated virtual technology has long since ceased to dazzle us, the diorama easily assumes for viewers a transparently metaphoric status as a model. In the hands of contemporary artists, it can thus serve to remind us that our conceptions of nature and art are likewise packaged entities, representational conceits which revolve around and reproduce a specific set of values, fantasies, and assumptions, rather than offering a neutral and direct depiction of the world we live in. (Rugoff, 2000, p. 16)

Of interest here is the belief that the diorama's subversive potential does not require the quotational, theory-inflected self-reflexivity of certain contemporary artists. The disjunction of signifier and signified appears as well, however innocently, in the "antiquated virtual technology" with which we all grew up: the toy-soldier dioramas at American Civil War battlefields, or the self-proclaimed "largest and most beautiful indoor miniature village" in Shartlesville, Pennsylvania (*Roadside America*, 1963, p. 1). Our "delight" in even the most "realistic representations," as Aristotle understood the matter (*Poetics*, 1448b; trans. 1954), resides in our very recognition that the doll is first and foremost a really well-made doll.

When I began to investigate the elaborate diorama at Ry (an obligatory stop on the tourist's visit), I referred in my notes to its reduced-scale, animated human figures as puppets. Some of the best recent writing on puppets suggests that such usage is mistaken. In *Pinocchio's Progeny,* Harold B. Segel (1995) traces the fascination in modernist drama with puppets and their "kin" (marionettes, automatons, robots) from George Sand's puppet shows at Nohant to the work of Heiner Müller and Tadeusz Kantor. The more wide-ranging and speculative study by Victoria Nelson (2001), *The Secret Life of Puppets,* examines the "mirror worlds" of spirituality and materiality, from heresy in Renaissance Europe to contemporary popular culture, where "high technology" performs "transcendent" functions once assigned to "meditation, prayer, or incantation" (p. 278). As we navigate the *mundus subterraneus,* the Roman grotto, the Freudian unconscious, the Marabar Caves of Forster, or the abysses of cyberspace, we keep running into our not-me, our uncanny likeness—often in the form of the puppet. Both authors invite us (Segel more carefully, Nelson more polemically) to regard our relations with material or digital simulacra, fictions of our own fashioning, as dialogic and reciprocal rather than one-way. We succumb to an old-fashioned binarism whenever we try to separate "spirit" from "body," or "creator" from "created," or "natural" from "mechanical," or "human" from "puppet." Not surprisingly, both writers provide extended commentaries on the most striking passage from the 1810 essay "The Puppet Theatre," by Heinrich von Kleist (1997). Human dancers, maintains Kleist's Herr C., will never rival marionettes. Although not godlike in their consciousness, humans enjoy a measure of reflective self-awareness that simply does not burden the marionette (a perfectly engineered material object). Affectation, therefore, always will mar the grace of self-conscious mortals who attempt to defy gravity:

> We see that in the same measure as reflection in the organic world becomes darker and feebler, grace there emerges in ever greater radiance and supremacy. . . . [G]race will be most purely present in the human frame that has either no consciousness or an infinite amount of it, which is to say either in a marionette or in a god. (pp. 413, 416; see V. Nelson, 2001, pp. 61–64; Segel, 1995, pp. 14–17)

Poised between spirit and matter, humans enjoy the perfection of neither. Like the image of the creating god, the figure of the created puppet presents us with the funhouse mirror of our uncanny double.

I find myself persuaded by such arguments, just as I find myself persuaded by Wood's dialogic understanding of maps. But something about all this rings false with my experience of museum dioramas. Creatures as marvelous as Nelson's puppets or Kleist's marionettes do not populate the diorama's "small world." Like the "antiquated" museum technologies of which Ralph Rugoff speaks, the sometimes crude representations of human figures (off-the-shelf toy soldiers or dolls with rotating limbs) simply refuse to "dazzle." They do not talk back. They have no magic. They are not uncanny; in some museum displays, their presentation falls short even of canny. Something about the diorama form itself—perhaps its close resemblance to the two-dimensional map—drives the small human figure in the direction of pure sign. Figurines on a boxed-in landscape are a kind of scenery, signifying "populated." Or so it has seemed to me, from my earliest days of museum going. My discussion of the diorama at Ry, however, will require me to question this view.

My central concern, then, is with two kinds of map, two- and three-dimensional, and with the nature of the figures who dwell in the second kind. I will be concerned as well with the map's potential for dialogic relations with its readers, and with its capacity for change over "great time." But next I must follow the lead of Gough's contributors, and test the limits of map as metaphor—specifically in relation to language and narrative. For the strange case of Ry requires us to consider the possibility that Flaubert's most famous novel (whatever else it is or does) constructs a map of an actual French town.

2. Books as Maps

> The potential of fiction to refer to the actual world inaccurately is most obvious when unreal localities are placed in real surroundings: when Proust's narrator vacations at a Normandy resort called Balbec, when Emma Bovary takes a postal coach from Yonville to Rouen. . . . [I]maginative manipulations of more or less well-known facts highlight the peculiar way external references do not remain truly external when they enter a fictional world. They are, as it were, contaminated from within. (Dorrit Cohn, 1999, *The Distinction of Fiction*)

Various meanings of *map* have a long history in English. Already by Shakespeare's time, the word is both subject and verb. As a noun, it can mean "a representation of the earth's surface, or a part of it" (OED) as well as analogous forms of representation; or it can mean "the very picture or image" of something, as well as the opposite of this, an "aggregation" or "multitude" (OED). "To map" is to make or bring about most of these things. (I put to one side the really rare or obscure meanings: *map* and *mapkin*, for example, could also mean "rabbit.") When Shakespeare writes Part 1 of *Henry IV,* the word *remap* appears to be far off in the history of the language; but Shakespeare shows us the action, when, in Act 3, Scene 1, Mortimer, Glendower, and Hotspur perform a division of the kingdom by rewriting an old map. (King Lear performs a similar remapping in the first scene of his tragedy.) Conventionally, the face is a map: In the face of good Duke Humphrey, a pious King sees "the map of honor, truth, and loyalty" (*2 Henry VI* 3.1.202–203). My favorite example of this appears in *Coriolanus,* when Menenius invites the Tribunes to read "the map of my microcosm" (2.1.62–63): The face maps the inner man, which on a cosmological scale is a different kind of map. But the meaning is stretched when, for example, Titus reads in the body and behavior of the ravaged Lavinia a whole ensemble of "signs," the very "map of woe" (*Titus Andronicus* 3.2.12) that mirrors his own woe.[2]

These uses of *map* have been reaccentuated in interesting ways. When in 1993 a teacher of American studies documents 19th-century theatrical practices, and suggests that certain genres of stage performance "mapped" the same-sex desire of their spectators (Lott, 1993, p. 166), the author employs an "imaginary" loosening of the face and body metaphors common in Shakespeare's day: A physical performance (a set of facial expressions, bodily behaviors in a stage act) epitomizes, and thereby reduces in scale, something ephemeral and wide-ranging (a common emotion, the circulation of desire). The extent to which *map* has been stretched to include *any* act of representation, as in the *Performance Research* examples, appears again in *Postmodern Cartographies* by Brian Jarvis (1998). A teacher of American literature analyzes selected books of theory and fiction, as well as several films, that reflect America's postindustrial, postmodern, urban, and corporeal "landscapes." The new "cultural geographer," exploring the spaces sought or produced by America's "geographical imagination," must learn to map newly imagined national spaces (dreamscapes, bodyscapes) in newly imagined scales (p. 9). Yet despite his wide range of inquiry, the author's richest "cartographic" examples are books.

The book as map: If books "map" landscapes, then in theory they work like other two-dimensional maps. A dialogue of sign systems (language, plates, graphic layout), printed on some kind of material surface (ink on paper, or electronic dots "under glass" as Rugoff suggests), reduces the scale of something unimaginably huge (America, let's say) so that the desiring subject (the gentle reader) can begin to imagine it, and maybe do something with it. (The lack of organizing desire, in such a subject, would seem to be the godlike vision, the bird's-eye view, the cosmic guarantee that a destination would be there if you just kept walking.) But the construction of the map guides and limits (even seduces, if Denis Wood is correct) the play of the reader's imagination.

What happens when writing "maps" other writing? This introduces the question of scale, one of the "three basic attributes" that cartographer Mark Monmonier (1991, p. 5) sees in any map. An English translation of Flaubert's *Madame Bovary* aspires to represent the terrain of the French text in roughly the same number of words. Its desired ratio scale, in other words, is 1:1. But a plot summary—like the pamphlet series marketed to American grade school students under the name of *Cliffs Notes*—performs a shift in scale. Compare a 50-page, chapter-by-chapter summary of *Madame Bovary*, containing about 20,000 words, with an English translation of well over 200 densely packed pages, reaching somewhere around 140,000 words. The map achieves a ratio scale of 1:7. A three-page, double-column *Masterplots* summary produces a count of less than 2,000 words: a small-scale map with a ratio scale of 1:70.

Then what happens with commentary, of the inflationary sort that we encounter in a variorum edition of a Shakespeare play? Jacques Derrida (1994) gives us a version of just such a text. Setting off from six famous words in a famous play—"The time is out of joint"—he produces a meditation (although this is hard to bracket off from the surrounding argument) of about 5,400 words, which ranges from the problems of *Hamlet*'s French translators to the "problem of Hamlet" in Heidegger's German (pp. 18–29). This produces a map with an impossible ratio scale of 900:1, an example of what a fluent French speaker might call *la parole soufflée*. I say "impossible," not because the map doesn't exist, but merely out of respect for convention:

"By convention, the part of the ratio to the left of the colon is always 1" (Monmonier, 1991, p. 5).

Can Flaubert's novel itself be viewed as a map? Flaubert studies abound in suggestions that the novelist produced his character of Emma by remapping other personages, fictional (Mazza in Flaubert's early *Passion and Virtue*) as well as real (Louise Colet, Louise Pradier, or the wife of an *officier de santé* in an actual small town). Against all of his strenuous protests that he was writing an exercise in style, a book about "nothing," we must hold up such comments as this, in a letter of 1853 to Colet, which suggests that he thought of his book as mapping a cultural type: "My poor Bovary, without a doubt, is suffering and weeping at this very hour in twenty villages of France" (quoted in Steegmuller, 1980, p. 195). In other words, his novel has achieved a ratio scale of 1:20. Significantly, *Madame Bovary* strives to achieve one of the major attributes that Wood (1992) identifies in most maps. A clever map erases its author:

> [T]the map is powerful precisely to the extent that [its] author . . . *disappears.* . . . As long as the author—and the interest he or she unfailingly embodies— is in plain view, it is hard to overlook him, hard to see around her, to the world described, hard to see it . . . *as the world.* . . . As author—and interest—become marginalized (or done away with altogether), the represented world is enabled to . . . *fill our vision.* (p. 70)

This calls to mind the host of Flaubert's pronouncements about "eliminating the author" or becoming "like God in the universe, present everywhere and visible nowhere" (quoted in Steegmuller, 1980, p. 173; see pp. 200, 229–230), not to mention the celebrated vanishing act performed by the eyewitness narrator of *Madame Bovary*'s first chapter (see Chambers, 1993, pp. 179–181).[3]

But if the comparison with the desire of cartographers is to have force, it should follow that Flaubert, despite his many denials, must have been trying to represent *something*. And if not a single person or place, as he insisted, then what?

Ross Chambers (1993), in his stimulating *The Writing of Melancholy*, considers the chief object of representation to be social discourse itself. More specifically, Chambers considers the many forms and manifestations of *bêtise*, the stupid or foolish remark (from *bête*, "beast"; a *bêtisier* is a collection of foolish quotations and stupid-sounding received ideas). The complicated device of free indirect style, for example, helps the alert reader to recognize ironic distance in a text that must "repeat conventional discourses of social provenance, that is, discourses that are already stale and hackneyed through endless repetition" (p. 177). But not all readers are alert, and irony is easy to miss. The discourses that the text chooses to map—the endless circulation of banality and cliché from which the text makes its representative selection—"are by definition typical":

> [R]eproducibility is their characteristic. They are easily recognized, which makes them all more or less clichés. Yet the text that reproduces them manages to do it in such a way that the repetition changes signs: *its* repetition is no longer taken as cliché but is considered an original enunciative act. As has often been observed, the problem is to understand the "creative" use of a language that, as the medium of communication, has been made banal and worn out by social use. (p. 181)

As these "typical" discourses invade the text, in which the narrator (like Wood's mapmaker) has strategically relinquished a "distinctive" and "individual" voice, the danger arises that the ironic text will become "difficult to distinguish from the repetitive discourses" that it repeats. "What happens," Chambers muses, "when a text becomes an 'idiot'?" (pp. 177–178).

Our tendency to mistake the map for the territory, encouraged by the pose of "authorlessness" that Wood describes, becomes problematic for the author whose "interest" is irony, and whose feeling for the object of representation is something like contempt. The "melancholic text" of modernism that Chambers describes blurs the boundary "between textual discourse and social discourse," between "the 'intelligent' version" of *bêtise* and *bêtise* itself. For too many readers, "antibourgeois texts" like *Madame Bovary* can "confirm the bourgeois hegemony they oppose" (Chambers, 1993, pp. 184, 195). How often has the novel been read as a kind of cautionary tale for impressionable young women? Such a reading formed part of the defense at Flaubert's own trial (see LaCapra, 1982, pp. 30–52).

Chambers's "melancholic text" is a text that succeeds too well in masking the supposedly coherent subject who authors it. While its "hope" is for the alert reader, capable of catching the irony, its melancholy is for an authorial self who is "master of the communicational act and free to mark it with the seal of its 'originality'" (pp. 178, 184). Such are the dangers for novelist-cartographers who perform their own annihilation. The map so generated is an unstable utterance. Contributing to the instability of *Madame Bovary* (especially for those who perhaps have never read it, but know the gist of the plot when they stumble into a tourist site like Ry) is the Ry tourist industry's insistence that the book is at most a *roman à clef:* a deft masking of a mostly true story about the town's most famous resident, more "documentary" in character than mere fictional realism (see R. Brunon, quoted in Privat, 2004, n. p.).

To speak of representing the clichés and *bêtises* of social discourse as an act of "mapping" is misleading, however, in several important ways. First, the metaphor is strained, as I find it to be in the previously cited comparison by Rosenbaum (2001) of "a novel, a painting or a play" to "a data map" (p. 55). The cartographer's text produces something more than an epitome of a widespread phenomenon (like an overused phrase, or Flaubert's hypothetical Emma prototype "suffering and weeping . . . in twenty villages"). A map's reduction in scale retains a one-to-one relationship between signifier and signified: A streetcorner on a map, unlike "streetcorner" in a dictionary, does not denote streetcorners in general. At stake for the town of Ry in the postwar decades, as I explore below, was the demonstration that Flaubert's novel mapped (with careful distortions) the unique terrain of one particular town, rather than distilling "provincial Norman towns" as a category.

Second, Flaubert's distortions (if we grant Ry's claim) exemplify what Dorrit Cohn (1999), borrowing terms from Benjamin Harshaw, views as "a 'double-decker' model of reference: an internal frame nested within an external frame" (p. 14). The external frame of *Madame Bovary* includes mid-19th-century Rouen, features of which are described by Flaubert's narrator in ways that can be verified for the 21st-century reader by archival records, photographs, nonfiction narratives, and in some cases acts of tourism. Flaubert's description of Rouen—"a real referent if ever there was one"—supplies Barthes (1968/1986) with an example of how "aesthetic function," forever interested in making details meaningful, "halts what we might call the vertigo of notation" and the "narrative *luxury*" of noting the "insignificant": "[I]f it were not subject to an aesthetic or rhetorical choice, any 'view' would be inexhaustible by discourse: there would always be a corner, a detail, an inflection of space or color to report" (pp. 141–142, 144–145).

What Barthes calls the "aesthetic function" is the set of constraints on a vertiginous notation applied by the demands of the internal frame. Cohn insists that an important signpost distinguishing fictional from nonfictional narrative is fiction's "nonreferential" character, which she uses in a qualified way:

[W]hen we speak of the nonreferentiality of fiction, we do not mean that it *can* not refer to the real world outside the text, but that it *need* not refer to it. But beyond this, . . . fiction is subject to two closely interrelated distinguishing features: (1) its references to the world outside the text are not bound to accuracy; and (2) it does not refer *exclusively* to the real world outside the text. (p. 15)

Flaubert is free to create his internal frame or fictional world by remapping an external frame, and is under no obligation to do this accurately or consistently: The real world may be "contaminated from within," Cohn suggests (p. 15), as it may not be (or at least *should* not be) in a work of nonfiction.

Cohn's discomfort with postmodern historiographers like Hayden White (1978, 1987), who diagnose the ubiquity of fiction in narrative generally, provides a helpful approach to the case of Ry. The tourist industry has never denied that Flaubert wrote a work of fiction. In doing so, he performed an interesting spin on the fanciful cartography described by fiction writer Maya Sonenberg (1989), which supplies the epigraph for Section 1: He made the map his own by putting his different-colored stars in deliberately inaccurate places. A century later, the citizens responded—made the town their own once again—by throwing down two sets of large paper-colored stars, with big dotted lines connecting the "real" sites and Flaubert's "contaminations" so that tourists could more easily contemplate the differences.

3. A Map in Flaubert's Own Hand

> To compete with each other, destinations must be distinguishable, which is why the tourism industry requires the production of difference. It is not in the interest of remote destinations that one arrive in a place indistinguishable from the place one left. . . .
> "Sameness" is a problem the industry faces. (Barbara Kirshenblatt Gimblett, *Destination Culture*)

Among Flaubertistes, the story of the allegedly "real" Monsieur and Madame Bovary is too familiar to bear repeating. But for the rest of us, here is "the whole story" (abridged) of Eugène Delamare's "misfortunes" in the small town of Ry, drawn from the "double portrait" of novelist and novel by Francis Steegmuller (1950):

> Delamare, a few years older than Flaubert . . . , had been an impecunious and mediocre medical student at the Rouen hospital under Dr. Flaubert [the novelist's father]. He had never passed all his examinations, and like many another young Frenchman of the time who could not afford to continue his medical studies to the end, had conten[t]ed himself with becoming not a full-fledged doctor, but an *officier de santé*—an inferior category of licensed medical man then in existence. He had become the local health officer in a country town near Rouen, and after the death of his first wife, a widow older than himself, he had married a charming young girl of seventeen . . . , the daughter of a nearby farmer. . . . She quickly came to despise her husband, longed for a more vivid life, began to spend too much money on clothes, . . . took lovers, sank even more deeply into debt, . . . and finally poisoned herself. (pp. 218–219)

So much, apparently, was discussed by Flaubert and his friend Maxime du Camp, as Flaubert struggled to imagine a suitable subject for a novel. Eugène Delamare survived his second wife Delphine (or Adelphine, née Couturier) less than two years: Whether from suicide by slow poisoning, or (like Flaubert's Charles) from excessive grief, he died a week before Christmas, 1849. (Flaubert and du Camp had just set off on their tour of the "Orient," and so the novelist would not hear of this second death for many months.) Steegmuller suggests that Flaubert's mother became a benefactress of the Delamares' orphaned daughter (p. 219), although on what evidence he does not say. But René Vérard (1983, pp. 55–61) cites documents suggesting the Flaubert family's involvement with Eugène's indebtedness. The novelist, on his return from the Near East, might have had fresh reminders of the Delamare business at the time he began work on *Madame Bovary*.

For several decades, Vérard labored to demonstrate that the market town of Ry—18 kilometers due east of downtown Rouen, according to my Michelin of Île-de-France—is in fact the "real" and original setting of Flaubert's novel. His chain of research extends back to the investigations of the Rouen journalist Georges Dubosc, who in 1890 first visited Ry with the intention of uncovering Flaubert's "reality-model" (Vérard, 1983, p. 15) and found there the aging counterparts of three characters.[4] One was Augustine Ménage, who claimed to be the original maid, Félicité, in the Bovary household. Another, François Thérain, described starting the coach service between downtown Ry and downtown Rouen in 1846—thereby identifying himself as the original Hivert, driver of the "Hirondelle," on whose wings Emma flew to her adulteries with Léon. And Alfred-Adolphe Joanne, who would have been helping his father behind the great semi-semicircular counter of the town pharmacy when Delphine first accompanied her new husband to Ry, took over the family business in the year of Delphine's death—thereby becoming a major contender for the title of Monsieur Homais (Vérard, 1983, pp. 72–89). Subsequent visits merely confirmed Dubosc's conviction that "Ry was Yonville-l'Abbaye": "[I]t's there where Emma Bovary lived, loved, suffered and died" (quoted in Vérard, 1983, p. 16).

Although "from then on," Ry became a "place of pilgrimage" for Flaubertistes (Vérard, 1983, p. 16), the authenticity of the shrine did not go unchallenged. There was first the problem of Flaubert's own blanket denial, in the famous letter to Mlle Leroyer de Chantepie of March 18, 1857: "*Madame Bovary* has nothing 'true' in it. It is a totally invented story" (Steegmuller, 1980, p. 229). Vérard deals with this by reminding us that Flaubert and his publishers had been very recently on trial for inflicting upon Second Empire readers an outrage to public morals; he suggests that Flaubert no doubt was anxious to downplay the possible resemblances between the novel's descriptions and the "real" world. One should weigh this, he advises, against the compelling evidence of the less-quoted letter of May 9, 1855, to Flaubert's friend Louis Bouilhet. Laboring away at Book 3, the novelist worries that the ending, "which in reality was more fully filled out," would seem "skimpy [étriquée] in my book" (Flaubert, 1974, p. 497).[5]

But the gauntlet was thrown down in December 1953, when René Herval, then president of the Society of Norman Writers, advanced the dangerous suggestion that Yonville-l'Abbaye might be *any* of the country towns that Flaubert visited. Why not Forges-les-Eaux? This larger town, northeast of Ry and over twice the distance from Rouen, was well-known to Flaubert— and boasted besides a superior candidate for the "real" Homais, a notoriously long-winded pharmacist, free-thinker, and municipal councilor named Mallard. While willing to concede that Homais was the novelist's condensation of several historical personages, Vérard nevertheless locked arms with the citizens of Ry against a full-scale assault: the "crazy endeavor" of Herval and his gang of pedants to deny Ry "the honor of having largely inspired Flaubert." But perhaps Ry had itself to blame. This was, after all, the age of the automobile—yet despite "the approach of a vast movement of tourism," including Bovary tourism, "the 'terrain' had not been 'marked'" with indications of Delphine-Emma's whereabouts. Through its own neglect, the town had left itself open to the malicious ravings of crackpots. Lacking the wiles of a "contemporary Homais" (where *is* Monsieur Homais when we need him?), the citizens of Ry did the next best thing: They created, on November 23, 1954, a "Bovary Committee" to rescue from oblivion the town's "beautiful 'legend,'" which was in danger of being "swiped" (Vérard, 1959, pp. 18–20; Vérard, 1983, pp. 19–20). The "marked terrain" that one finds today in downtown Ry is the result of that committee, guided by Vérard's research.

Vérard's first answer to Herval was the 1959 monograph *The Victory of Ry.* Here he unfolds the evidence assembled, and even tackles the vexing question of whether Delphine Delamare actually killed herself; his antagonist Herval, not surprisingly, supported the theory of death by natural causes (Vérard, 1959, pp. 39–40).[6] Of interest is Vérard's recourse (as countertactic in this war of the Flaubertistes) to maps.

Vérard concludes his monograph by unpacking two passages from the novel with reference to local maps of the mid–19th century (Vérard, 1959, pp. 53–59). Homais's tedious explanation of Yonville's climatological conditions, on the night of Charles and Emma's arrival (2.2; Flaubert, 1857/1965, p. 57), identifies two significant features of Ry's topography: a sheltering rise to the west (called "the Saint Jean hills" in the novel) and to the northeast the Bois de St. Denis (the novel's "forest of Argueil," named after a town some

14 kilometers further off). This in itself is not conclusive. "But let's continue" (Vérard, 1959, p. 53). Did not the Municipal Council of Ry, in 1837, take measures to dissipate just the sort of "poisonous fumes," unique to the neighborhood, of which Homais complains? And did it not begin to take steps, in the late 1820s, to improve the road to Martainville and the national route connecting Rouen and Beauvais? This leads us to the second passage, the famous opening of Book 2: a kind of mock-Baedeker, in which the novel gives us explicit (if deliberately misleading) directions for finding a fictional town on a "real" map (2.1; Flaubert, 1857/1965, pp. 49–51). But the town is not fictional, Vérard maintains, if you know how to read the code. Substitute "Martainville" for "la Boissière," and the valley of the "Crevon" for the valley of Flaubert's "Rieule, a little river that runs into the Andelle after turning three water-mills near its mouth" (Flaubert, 1857/1965, p. 49)—and there you are! Even the novel's date for the completion of a new road, 1835, pretty much squares with municipal records. (But let us grant after all that Flaubert, unlike Vérard, did not want the reader's first desire, immediately upon finishing the novel, to be a visit to the "real" town.) "Map in hand," in any case, "Forges-les-Eaux is eliminated" (Vérard, 1959, p. 54).

And there is more. The cadastral surveys of Ry—especially the one of 1852—are enormously helpful in measuring the precise extent of Flaubert's remapping. Vérard is able to count the number of posts supporting the tile roof of *les halles*: 44 compared to Flaubert's 20 (Vérard, 1959, p. 56) but occupying the same space in relation to the *Grand-Rue,* "a gunshot long and flanked by a few shops on either side" (2.1; Flaubert, 1857/1965, p. 51).[7] Flaubert has exercised fictional license: Ry's church, for example, has been pushed across the street and up the block. As with the cast of characters, however, the novelist "leans constantly on reality" (Vérard, 1959, p. 45). Throughout *The Victory of Ry,* the phrase *la réalité* recurs with the insistence (but without the irony) of *la fatalité* in Flaubert's novel.

"But there is better still. Bovary's house in Yonville-l'Abbaye is clearly situated" (Vérard, 1959, p. 59). One of Eugène Delamare's two residences in Ry supplies the *mise-en-scène,* in most important details, for Emma's escape route through her garden: the steps, the small gate, the proximity to a stream leading down the block to the Crevon.[8] The cadasters of 1827 and 1852 show even the presence, at the time, of the *"Allée"* that Homais points out to his new neighbors: a "convenience for a doctor," since "one can go in and out unseen" (2.2; Flaubert, 1857/1965, p. 59; cf. Flaubert, 1857/1972, p. 121).

What is so moving, finally, about this odd little book is not the "victory" of the title, Vérard's triumphant conviction that he has settled the hash of Herval and company, who "divided the Flaubertistes" with their "violent polemics" (Vérard, 1959, p. 59). It is, rather, the tenderness with which the author recalls the spot in Ry that has always struck him, and that has similarly affected the little guided tours he has led over the years: the bottom of Emma's garden, where he can fantasize watching her (like one of the voyeuristic neighbors Emma fears) depositing her love letters for Rodolphe, or racing off for a morning rendezvous. He dreamily wonders "in what other region a little stream bordered by walls, steps, and gates, can flow not far from the houses, washing up against the gardens." Certainly not Forges-les-Eaux, he hastens to add, "where the river passes a kilometer away from the houses!" (Vérard, 1959, p. 59). Such a restored site in Ry has become, for him, the kind of full-size diorama that Rugoff (2000) suggests is "haunted" for us "by a sense of loss" (p. 16).

The town of Ry, in gratitude for his service, invited Vérard to revise and expand this material for an illustrated tour book, marketed exclusively by the local museum that was established in 1977. To open your personal copy of the handsome 96-page volume *Ry, pays de Madame Bovary* (Vérard, 1983), and gain access to its secrets, you must perform a piece of old-fashioned business: You slice a brown ribbon, sealed in wax stamped with the town's name. Inside you find, along with much that is familiar, some real surprises, including the following reconstruction of Charles's name:

> Why the patronymic "Bovary"? Wouldn't the author have sought to combine the essential trait of the character of his unfortunate hero (who was a clumsy oaf [*lourdaud*]) with the place where he lived his misadventure? Whence the fusion of "bova" (beef [*boeuf*] in Latin) and of ry . . ."*un boeuf à Ry*"? (Vérard, 1983, p. 6)

A shameless piece of touristic self-promotion, perhaps—but at least Ry has a sense of humor about itself. Alongside this, even Flaubert's joke of marrying Léon to "Mlle Léocadie Leboeuf" late in the novel (3.11; Flaubert, 1857/1972, p. 437) seems a little tame.[9]

More surprising, by far, is a piece of advice. The eager pilgrim can save the effort of searching for the remains of Delphine Delamare. Following the interest aroused by Dubosc's first newspaper articles, Delphine's headstone was stolen from the churchyard in 1896. We are lucky at least to have an old photo, taken by a local Flaubertiste and *bovaryste*, which Vérard reproduces: "Here lies the body of Delphine Couturier, wife of M. Delamare physician [*médecin*], deceased 6 March 1848. Pray God for the repose of her soul" (Vérard, 1983, pp. 45–46).[10]

But the biggest surprise—the trump card of the laborious argument in Vérard's previous book—arrives on two facing pages (Vérard, 1983, pp. 38–39). The mirrored images are maps. One, a reproduction of the Ry cadaster of 1827, has been modified to indicate points of interest on a present-day "Literary Pilgrimage," including the route that Delphine-Emma would have taken to the chateau of Louis Campion (Vérard's prototype for Rodolphe). The other is the *"plan graphique"* of downtown Yonville l'Abbaye drawn by Flaubert himself, as reproduced from Flaubert scholar René Dumesnil's volume of "iconographic documents."

Dumesnil (1948) explains:

> The appearance of the market town of Ry hardly changed over a century, and the *grand'rue* is still bordered by the same houses with a single upper floor, sheltering the inn, the pharmacy, the shops of the local tradespeople. Flaubert drew in his own hand a map, the elements of which were taken from the real topography of Ry, but transposed, mixed up by design, to take out of the novel whatever would permit the reader to match up with certainty the imaginary Yonville-l'Abbaye and the very real town of Ry. One sees on the map the placement of the houses inhabited by the major characters. (pp. 230–231)

He goes on to suggest that Flaubert moved the church precisely from fear of bringing the reader a little too close—as Vérard would appreciate—to *"la réalité"* (p. 231). More recently, Dumesnil (1961/1965) has had tart things to say about the "whole archive of exegetic works on the *real* (?) Emma Bovary" and the "disputed and often dubious" anecdotes that have gathered around the Delamare story and has endorsed the theory that Flaubert remapped his own *Passion and Virtue.* Nevertheless, his archival work added some important masonry to Vérard's "cornerstone" (Vérard, 1983, p. 48).

As literary interpretation, of course, biographical "remapping" is limiting and limited. It reaches its reductive depth in a comment by the Flaubert scholar Jean de la Varende: In *Madame Bovary,* "[T]he author operates only by training his mirror on the characters and the situations. He doesn't narrate, he doesn't describe, he doesn't paint: he traces the outlines" (quoted in Vérard, 1983, p. 51). Ultimately Vérard is more generous: He concludes his earlier monograph by acknowledging that a work of astonishing imagination grew out of a story that, as Flaubert first heard it, could be contained "on a single page" (Vérard, 1959, p. 60)—a mere *"historette"* or anecdote, to borrow Jacques Suffel's term (quoted in Vérard, 1983, p. 22), a small-scale map.

But Vérard's efforts illustrate Wood's view of the map as discourse—which I read against Bakhtin's ideas about the utterance's potential to provoke dialogues, beyond the historical author's silence. What has happened is richer and more complicated than a single, closed event: a one-time-only "remapping" of a real town's real event into a famous "masterpiece." The town of Ry at the end of December 1849—the town that preexisted Flaubert's work on his novel—was already a "marked terrain," enabling and constraining Flaubert's subsequent performance, which in turn enabled and constrained future performances. One of these was the remapping of postwar Ry as a tourist attraction. Another was the remapping of Flaubert's celebrated novel itself as a tourist attraction—a kind of inset to the larger map. Over "great time," map answers map answers map.

4. Specters of Eleanor Marx

RAIMONDO
Eccola!   [Here she is!]
CORO
Oh giusto Cielo!   [Good Heaven!]
Par dalla tomba uscita!   [Like something from the grave!] (Salvatore
                           Cammarano, *Lucia di Lammermoor*, 3.1)

Emma keeps dying. The incompleteness—the ongoingness—of her death has always puzzled me. Emma's earliest childhood reading is haunted by martyred or murdered or self-sacrificing women whose lives were cut short: Mary Stuart, Joan of Arc, Agnès Sorel, the Virginie of Bernardin de Saint-Pierre's famous tale, and no doubt (among Scott's historical novels, which Emma devoured) Lucy of *The Bride of Lammermoor*. These literary deaths provoke performances; her "real" mother's death provokes another (2.6; Flaubert, 1857/1965, pp. 24–28). Emma is always already dying, in rehearsal for her own unpredictable death scene, which is reputed one of the greatest in Western literature. And she keeps dying, through force of repetition. Even as Emma began to fade from Charles's memory, "every night he dreamt of her; it was always the same dream. He approached her, but when he was about to embrace her she fell into decay in his arms" (3.11; Flaubert, 1857/1965, p. 252). Flaubert's announcement of Emma's death (3.8) famously employs a negative statement in the imperfect tense: "Elle n'existait plus" (Flaubert, 1857/1972, p. 418), "She had ceased to exist" (Flaubert, 1857/1965, p. 238), she wasn't existing any more. Stylistically, this draws Emma's death away from what Mario Vargas Llosa (1986) has called "singular or specific time" in the novel (often expressed by the *passé simple,* as in the sentences preceding the announcement of Emma's no longer existing) and toward what he calls "circular time or repetition" (pp. 170–177).[11] Emma joins another imaginary sisterhood, as ongoing as the "lyric legion" of "adulterous women" who sing to her after the horseback ride with Rodolphe (2.9;

Flaubert, 1857/1965, p. 117). Its members range from the heroines of Emma's childhood reading to some fictional deaths to come: Edna, the "Creole Bovary" of Chopin's *The Awakening* (Culley, 1976, p. 153), and Ellen, the narrator's Emma-like bride in *Flaubert's Parrot* (Barnes, 1984, pp. 180–192). They include as well Eleanor Marx, daughter of Karl, who in her early 40s committed suicide after the discovery of Edward Aveling's deception; her 1886 translation of *Madame Bovary*, the first to be published in English, was remapped (subsequent to updated topographic surveys) by Paul de Man (Flaubert, 1857/1965) for the "substantially new" version published as a Norton Critical Edition. This raises an ontological question about fictional "life" in Flaubert, as Derrida (1994) suggests in his punning use of "*hauntology*." "A question of repetition: a specter is always a *revenant*. One cannot control its comings and goings because it *begins by coming back*" (pp. 10–11).

Flaubert's mode of presentation is repetition. In *Madame Bovary*, free indirect style "forces the text to 'repeat' the social discourse embedded in the discourse of the characters, and in this novel . . . 'reality' is defined as a degraded domain, because it is subject to a law of repetition" (Chambers, 1993, p. 175). Which is more "degraded," more of a backward step, killing oneself or repeating oneself? What does it mean for the central character to cling, out of habit, to the baseness of a degraded bliss? Emma becomes aware, by the end of the novel, of a specter haunting her relationship with every "real" man: She has the vision of "another man . . . , a phantom fashioned out of her most ardent memories, of her favorite books, her strongest desires" (3.6; Flaubert, 1857/1965, p. 211). We recognize that the "reality" of this phantom, for her, is subject, like language, "to a law of repetition." Chambers (1993) provides this map of the novel:

[I]n her adulterous affairs, Emma undergoes the same passing on from one man to another (but with a repetition in the chain of repetitions itself). Each affair leads her back to the calm monotony of marriage: after six months with Rodolphe, "they were to one another like a married couple, tranquilly keeping up a domestic flame" [2.10] . . . , and with Léon "Emma found again in adultery all the platitudes of marriage" [3.6]. . . . And finally, exploited erotically as she is by men, Emma's desire simultaneously makes her vulnerable to the commercial seductions of Lheureux. (pp. 181–182; cf. Flaubert, 1857/1965, pp. 123, 211)

By so reviewing these features of *Madame Bovary*, we can see somewhat better why attempts to turn it into a play have never been very successful, and why the various feature films have seemed either ludicrously melodramatic or merely drab. For dramatic tragedy and the "classical" Hollywood screenplay are driven by incident, which Emma yearns for but seldom experiences. Imagine that you are a producer, in search of a four-act tragedy about a woman trapped in a boring, repetitive marriage to a good-natured dullard, and yearning for something *truly* done; her frustration with two other men in her life (one a dreamer, the other a well-heeled brute) finally drives her to take her own life. Why go to the trouble of adapting *Madame Bovary?* Stage *Hedda Gabler.*

Flaubert himself was wary of stage adaptations, and discouraged a potentially lucrative proposal from the Théâtre de la Porte-Saint-Martin at the height of the novel's celebrity (see Troyat, 1992, p. 161). Among other things, stage pictures share the drawbacks of all pictures, like book plates. The very idea of an illustrated edition of *Salammbô* makes Flaubert "frantic": "It was hardly worth the trouble using so much art to leave everything vague," he writes in 1862, "if some clod is going to come along and destroy my dream with his stupid precision" (quoted in Troyat, 1992, p. 183). For what kind of theater could represent the "circular time or repetition" that fascinates Vargas Llosa? It would have to be a cruel theatere—not in Artaud's sense but precisely the opposite. In its mode of presentation, it would need to achieve a relentless repetition, a rigorous lack of variation beyond the reach of even the best-rehearsed actors.

I have crossed an ocean to make my first pilgrimage to Ry, and I expect the approach to be a little more challenging. But the tourist office in Rouen is ready for me. Before my carefully worded request is halfway out of my mouth, the clerk hands me a very attractive fold-out map, "Promenade au pays d'Emma Bovary," the complete plan for a day trip in Emma-land. (I won't be needing the Michelin after all—apparently people do this a lot.)

While the 15-stop tour takes you everywhere, from les Bertaux to la Huchette (with clear instructions on where to find the Emma plaques in the surrounding towns), the main event is the visit to Ry. Clearly the Bovary Committee has been hard at work: The rival Forges-les-Eaux, although mentioned in the novel, disappears into an arrow pointing away, a sign for where one of the roads might lead you. A small victory: "It is the *isolation* of everything *not* on the map that so potently *naturalizes* what's *on* it (what's not on the map . . . *isn't real*)" (Wood, 1992, p. 87).

Vérard (1983), by documenting the town in all its palimpsestic richness, saves me the trouble of narrating my "promenade" on a sunny May morning in 1998. Let me note simply that my gaze was impatient. I did not so much stare *at* the surface of the town as *through* it. I attended to signs of present life—like the "Video Bovary" boutique on the *Grand-Rue*, the postmodern lending library—only when they screamed at me.

The highlight of the walking tour is an old *pressoir* on the banks of the Crevon, saved from ruin and brought back to life in 1977 as the Galerie Bovary Musée des Automates. You enter to a splendid reconstruction of the Jouanne Pharmacy shop front (a dazzling evocation of Homais's display of jars) and exit through a "documents" museum, displaying much of the evidence that Vérard discusses as well as press clippings from Ry's first century as a tourist shrine.

But what everyone comes to see is the display of 500 animated puppets, built and arranged in tableaux by one Michel Burgaud (with coiffures contributed by his mother, backdrop frescoes by his sister, and original music by his niece). Upstairs are whimsical arrangements on desultory themes: Eskimos and penguins, cowboys and Indians, a Japanese scene, firemen rescuing someone from a burning building, silver swans causing flowers to appear as they spread their wings. On the ground floor, 300 of the automated puppets "perform the principal scenes from the novel by Gustave Flaubert, 'Madame Bovary.'"

How do I say this? You have to see it. The basic human templates are a pair of inexpensive dolls, male and female. I remember these simulacra being sold in big naked heaps, in bins at what (in American small towns) we used to call the "dime store." Each doll is about 6 inches high, and some of its parts can move: The head rotates on its neck, the arms rise and lower at the shoulders, and the legs move at hip sockets and knee hinges.

Burgaud has not merely costumed them and set them in scenes, he has motorized them. The chief expressive unit of these actors is the "take" (as in "double take"): for human actors, a head or face movement expressive of sudden interest or surprise. The takes in this performance are not subtle: The whole head goes. And they are not double, but abyssal and infinite.

Some of the scenes are sheer spectacles, in which lots of figures do the same thing (such as a dance step) over and over again. But in the many intimate scenes, the chief gestic unit (due to the actors' limited range) is noticing something, being surprised by something, taking an interest in something. (The head action sometimes performs ambiguously what the textual caption clarifies, although in places the text clashes with the *mise-en-scène*.) The first tableau, from Part 1, Chapter 1, combines spectacle and interest taking. "We were in class when the headmaster came in, followed by a new boy" (Flaubert, 1857/1965, p. 1). Male templates, dressed as students, sit at school desks. The door swings open, revealing the headmaster and young Charles. The same clockwork causes all heads in the room to turn. The door closes; the heads turn back. When you enter the theater, Charles is always already arriving. His curious new classmates "take," and still will be doing so when you leave.

Here is Burgaud's map of *Madame Bovary*. (I am standing with my back to the door of the pharmacy exhibit, and reading from left to right.) Charles was arriving at school (1.1). Charles was married to the widow Dubuc (1.1). Emma, in a blue merino dress with three flounces, was opening the door of her father's house, and Charles was turning his head to notice her (1.2). Guests at the wedding of Emma and Charles were looking around (1.4). During the early days of their marriage, Emma was having more trouble falling asleep than Charles (1.7). At Vaubyessard, dancers at the ball were moving back and forth (1.8). Catherine-Nicaise-Elisabeth Leroux was receiving a medal at the *Comices agricoles de la Seine-Inférieure* (2.8). Just before their first lovemaking, Emma and Rodolphe were sitting on a log (2.9). On the way to meet her lover, Emma was crossing the stream (2.9). Returning home from her lover's, a startled Emma was turning her head to see Binet, who was popping up out of a barrel-shaped duck blind (2.10). The stars were shining through the leafless jasmine branches, while Emma and Rodolphe were embracing under a canopy, beneath a sunny blue sky (2.10). Emma was wondering why she was so unhappy, while Lestiboudois was raking close by (2.10). Against the same fresco, Hippolyte was having a corrective box put on his leg, and another Hippolyte was having his leg cut off (2.11). While Emma, rocking, was telling her lover that they could live anywhere, an amazed Rodolphe was shooting her a look (2.12). Little Justin, staying close to Emma's shoes, was watching Félicité at work (2.12). While Rodolphe was driving out of town, Emma was upsetting the table (2.13). In Rouen, Charles, Emma, and Léon were leaving the opera (2.15). In Rouen, Léon and Emma were visiting the Cathedral (3.1). On the coach route between Rouen and Yonville, there was a beggar, a wretched creature (3.5). On the Seine at Rouen, Emma and Léon were riding in a boat (3.3). As Emma was violently opening her corset, a startled Léon was shooting a glance at her naked breasts (3.6). Félicité was running in with news that Emma's furnishings were to be sold (3.7). As Monseiur Guillaumin was reaching out to grope her, Emma was turning her head away in disgust (3.7). Emma was stuffing her mouth with arsenic (3.8). Before the body of his dead wife, Charles, hands to face, was spinning back and forth—while the pharmacist and the priest were sleeping nearby (3.9). Little Berthe was discovering the body of her father, seated upright on a bench (3.11). The end—except it is not the end. After you look at the pharmacy again, you can go around as many times as you wish.

One of Burgaud's "interests" in mapping the book this way is to select passages (do some of them even qualify as incidents?) that show off his actors to their best advantage. What they do superbly well is *repeat* a few things—among them one of the greatest clichés in the language of gesture, the "take." This enables Burgaud's company to represent parts of the novel that have confounded the talents of playwrights and screenwriters. The performance achieves some astonishing successes.

Notable among these is the ability to represent Emma in a nonlinguistic code. LaCapra (1982) describes the "image of Emma in general" as "a magnificent figure for the interplay between determinacy and indeterminacy in the text." Some of her features are "variable": Her eyes change color, for example. "But we do not know precisely what she does look like, and we are tempted to say that, presented with any picture of her"—Jennifer Jones, Isabelle Huppert, the picture on the cover my Gallimard paperback—"we would exclaim: 'That's not quite it'" (p. 157). Burgaud solves the problem of Emma's appearance by exhausting it through repetition: Very quickly we cease to pay attention to it. In performance at the Musée des Automates, Emma ceases to look like anyone in particular because she lives in a world where every woman looks like Madame Bovary. The heroine's chief distinguishing characteristic, aside from her costume changes, is that she looks like herself *more often* than does any other woman. Her identity among other women is conferred not by difference but by statistical density. We know she is Emma through a double semiotic system. Below a given tableau, a strip of text from the novel (often beginning, or breaking off, in midsentence) names an Emma activity, usually being performed with one or more male characters. Within the tableau, we then locate the doll signifying "woman" doing a certain thing among the dolls signifying "man."

Concerning the men, however: Since there are more of them among the major characters, the basic "man" doll body requires additional distinguishing signs. Here the museum's theater achieves a cheerfully startling realization of one of the novel's most elusive effects. Emma's dissatisfied movement through relations with different men, which leads to her desire for the "phantom" of "another man," receives this performance: All of Emma's men are the same doll with different hair. (Rodolphe is dark, Charles red/brown, Léon blond.) Even the blind man, who mocks Emma's quest for "another man" with his musical arrival beneath her deathbed window, is Charles/Léon/Rodolphe with a different surface treatment. (How true. I wish my students could see this.)

The performance carries repetition to a ridiculous degree. Even the painted backdrop for the tableaux, a sign tells us, "reproduces Ry, which
e walking tour. The backdrop painting has a kind of
d the model for the *Comices agricoles,* for example,
but the church we've just seen in Ry, represented in
pt us to say, "Oh, there's the church." But despite
he painted images show no concern for the "stupid
ubert complains.

This is perhaps the only theater that could stage *Madame Bovary*. The museum dioramas are as startling in conception as they are in execution. There is a camp delight in remembering such displays from my American childhood, and the pleasures of the Ry Musée des Automates are campier still. If I read subversive or ironic intent into all this, I must pinch myself with a reminder from Chambers (1993): that irony, like sincerity, is an effect of reading "and therefore cannot be *proved*—by textual analysis, for instance" (p. 187).

Intentionally or not, however, the automated performance manages to send up, however crudely, the book's most forceful device: the "intelligent" repetition of *bêtise*, which serves the representation of repetitive actions. The puppets do this by foregrounding repetition unbearably (as no human actors could do, at least for very long) so that almost nothing else about the book is perceptible. The victory of Ry: The town's diorama room responds to *Madame Bovary* as cruelly as the novel first responded to Ry itself, already "marked" by its "beautiful legend." The labor of this mechanized map has some of the relentlessness that Dacia Maraini (1998) alleges in her feminist critique of Flaubert: Despite its pose of authorlessness, the novel betrays a lethally motivated author who "pursues" the heroine "with a ruthlessness and tenacity that verge on the grotesque" (p. 1).[12] I suspect that the designers of the Galerie Bovary exhibit were unconcerned with the ideological exposure of authorial interest. But the performance, however innocent its intentions, mercilessly alienates a major device in the novel's arsenal of "pursuit."

Much as I would like to dismiss this spectacle as an exercise in kitsch, it seems to be subverting some of my most sacred assumptions about the "art" of *Madame Bovary*, and it will take me a little while to clear my head. (How many times have I gone around?) Standing once again at the door of the Jouanne-Homais pharmacy exhibit, I feel a little like Charles just before his death (3.11; Flaubert, 1857/1965, p. 252). A strange thing is happening: While continually thinking about the novel, I am forgetting it nevertheless, and grow a little desperate at the feeling of my images fading in spite of all efforts to retain them. But some phantom book keeps coming back, like a strange dream that repeats. And I confess to feeling a little like Emma on her first ride with Rodolphe (2.9; Flaubert, 1857/1965, p. 114). Pausing at the top of a hill I've never before ascended, and seeing *Madame Bovary* spread out before me (but through a fog), I squint a little, trying to pick out something I would recognize at close range. Never has my poor little novel appeared so small.

Would I get any closer if I went around again? "A masterpiece always moves, by definition, in the manner of a ghost" (Derrida, 1994, p. 18). Perhaps I should wait until it comes back to me.

5. Making Pleasantries

A huge passivity has settled on industrial society. . . . Professor Norbert Wiener, maker of mechanical brains, asserts that, since all organic characteristics can now be mechanically produced, the old rivalry between mechanism and vitalism is finished. After all, the Greek word "organic" meant "machine" to them. . . . As terrified men once got ritually and psychologically into animal skins, so we already have gone far to assume and to propagate the behavior mechanisms of the machines that frighten and overpower us. (Marshall McLuhan, *The Mechanical Bride*)

Then she turned on her heel all of one piece, like a statue on a pivot, and went homewards. (Gustave Flaubert, *Madame Bovary*, 2.6 (de Man edition))

Ever since its author went to court in 1857 for offenses against public morals and religion, *Madame Bovary* has resisted anything that has been thrown at it: reviews (positive and negative), encomia, hostile reappraisals, adoring elevations to "masterwork" status, critical exegesis, "ideology" and deconstruction, adaptation into other media, Jean-Paul Sartre, Jennifer Jones, and plastic dolls with rotating heads. The book has survived even its admirers (among whom I count myself). It will outlast fallout and cockroaches. It cannot be remapped, even though someone or other is always remapping it. Its utter indestructibility inspires the imp in every reader to shoot first and ask questions later.

Madame Bovary survived its encounter with Mary McCarthy (1964), who passed the book through multiple interpretive frames (including the frame of Ry and the sordid tale of the Delamares).[13] In Emma's bourgeois predicament, the smart McCarthy saw an anticipation of another form of deadly repetition: "mass-produced culture" that "had not yet reached the masses" as it would in the American postwar era. "Emma's 'tragedy' from her own point of view," as McCarthy sees things at the dawn of the age of the credit card, "is her lack of purchasing power" (p. xviii). Even worse, *cultural* capital diminishes in value through circulation, as culture-consuming Americans were beginning to discover:

[A]ll ideas become trite as soon as somebody expresses them. This applies indifferently to good ideas and bad. . . . Ideas and feelings as well get more and more soiled and grubby, like library books, as they pass from hand to hand. (p. xv)

The early publications of Marshall McLuhan had foreseen already how passive humans would grow toward the very machines "that frighten and overpower" them. Had Emma been around in the American 1950s, McCarthy suspects, she would have grown toward the television (p. xvii) and possibly away from the romantic gesture of suicide. (In old European books, women end their lives; people on television, however, keep repeating themselves.) The novel's only true romantic is a "tongue-tied" one. The "docile," "placid miracle" of Charles qualifies him as the "hero" of a book that does not bear his name (pp. xix–xxiii). The self-effacing romanticism of McCarthy's version of Charles had been idealized in the hypothetical rebels against materialist and technological conformity who dot the pages of McLuhan's *Mechanical Bride* (1951)—curiously dated figures, in light of later developments of McLuhan's thought about technology's impact on consciousness.

When I first came across McCarthy's essay, I was already an admirer of her writing, and it struck me that her keen novelist's eye had sized up something very accurately. Repetition in Flaubert degrades or empties out whatever it touches—and it touches everything. This appears to function as a powerful theme of the work, an inescapable condition of life in its fictional world. To give this theme a playfully suggestive jolt, McCarthy briefly imagines how the characters might behave in the decade through which she has just lived. I refer to a "golden age" of mass marketing and mass taste, "one of history's great shopping sprees," which Thomas Hine (1987) has dubbed America's "Populuxe" era. The irony at the heart of "Populuxe" ("a synthetic word" for "popular luxury," with "a thoroughly unnecessary 'e,' to give it class") is the false promise of fashioning individuality in the very act of consuming sameness:

> The essence of Populuxe is not merely having things. It is having things in a way that they'd never been had before, and it is an expression of outright, thoroughly vulgar joy in being able to live so well. "You will have a greater chance to be yourself than any people in the history of civilization," *House Beautiful* told its readers in 1953. (pp. 3–4, 6)

McCarthy understands just how misleading such a promise is for her own age and suggests that Flaubert understood this as well about Norman provincial mores: "The pursuit of originality is as pathetic" for the novel's author "as Emma's decorating efforts." What strikes McCarthy as notably "modern" about the work that "is often called the first modern novel" is its early concern "with what is now called mass culture": the formation of a cultural imaginary through the circulation of such things as advertising images and *idées reçues*. The lending library in Flaubert anticipates media as various as television and comic books. "Rodolphe in his château" is an instant cliché; he "would be a perfect photographic model for whiskey or tobacco" in the pages of *Esquire* or *Playboy* (McCarthy, 1964, pp. xv–xvii). Emma, set loose in Populuxe America, would perform a string of different incidents, but her experience of repetition in such a setting would be intensified, and would lead to a similar disillusionment.

One implication of this line of thinking is that *Madame Bovary* itself cannot escape the fate of its characters' utterances. Any "pursuit of originality," provincial or cosmopolitan, becomes "pathetic"; "all ideas," good and bad alike, "become trite as soon as somebody expresses them" (McCarthy, 1964, p. xv). Recall that the "melancholic text" described by Chambers (1993) must repeat the very discourse that it wants to critique, and thereby runs the risk of becoming the "idiot" that it tries to describe with intelligence (pp. 177, 184). McCarthy seems headed toward such a conclusion—but reverses direction with her almost affectionate reading of Charles, the novel's inarticulate romantic and chief idiot who nevertheless functions as Emma's "redeemer." By this, McCarthy means that he redeems her *for us*, the readers, despite our exasperation with "the moral void" of "her fatuous conversation and actions": His "simple and profound" adoration, finally, "is contagious" (p. xix).

If McCarthy is correct, then Charles redeems more than Emma. He redeems the *bêtise* itself, by reaccentuating it in contexts that increase, rather than exhaust, its power to make meaning. We need to look only at the most famous example of this, the worn-out "grand mot" that measures the depth of Charles's grief and his capacity for forgiveness: "C'est la faute de la fatalité!" (3.11; Flaubert, 1857/1972, p. 445), it's the fault of fate.[14] As Charles utters this for the benefit of a momentarily startled Rodolphe, the novel wants us to remember what Charles surely does not, that *la fatalité* might have lodged in his memory after reading the letters to Emma from her lovers. The word appears as a cynical calculation—"a word that always helps," that never fails to have an effect (2.13; Flaubert, 1857/1965, 146)—in Rodolphe's farewell letter to Emma, and circulates as one of the novel's emptiest "profundities." When Charles reaccentuates this empty word, however, he achieves something quite different than a further emptying and "soiling" of it, of the sort that fascinates McCarthy earlier in her essay (p. xv). His *utterance*—a unique, unrepeatable performance, as Bakhtin suggests—fills the *bêtise* with the kind of extralinguistic elements that we can understand only from the larger speech act described by Flaubert's narrator.

Following Charles's declaration, the brief scene in the market at Argueil ends abruptly: "Rodolphe, who had been the agent of this fate, thought him very meek [*bien débonnaire*] for a man in his situation, comic even and slightly despicable [*un peu vil*]" (3.11; Flaubert, 1857/1965, p. 255; see

Flaubert, 1857/1972, p. 445). Are we to share Rodolphe's contempt at this moment? (The question persists, I suspect, for every reader upon every reading. Despite McCarthy's soft-hearted assessment, it would take a reader with a heart of stone to read the autopsy of Charles—Canivet "opened him and found nothing"[15]—and not burst out laughing.) An early draft of the scene contains fuller indications of the utterance's extralinguistic content:

> Rodolphe, however, who had been somewhat the agent of this fate, was extremely surprised. He found him all too good-natured for a man in his situation, too accommodating, even comic and slightly despicable.
>
> For he understood nothing of that voracious love which throws itself upon things at random to assuage its hunger, that passion empty of pride, without human respect or conscience, plunging entire into the being which is loved, taking possession of his sentiments, palpitating with them and almost reaching the proportions of a pure idea through generosity and impersonality. (quoted in Pommier & Leleu, 1949/1965, p. 279)

In subjecting the draft to a rigorous reduction—a different kind of "vertigo," that of "an infinite correction" (Barthes, 1967/1982, p. 301)—did Flaubert throw out this *view* of his character, or merely the *description* of it? Are we to figure out so much from Charles's sobs and shouts of "mad distress" as he reads the love letters sent to his wife, or the look of "somber fury" that so startles Rodolphe at Argueil (3.11; Flaubert, 1857/1965, p. 254)? McCarthy's generous reading of Charles requires such an understanding: a sense that his utterances are more unique than the mere sentences he repeats and that they create new contexts of meaningfulness for even those phrases grown "soiled and grubby, like library books, as they pass from hand to hand" (p. xv).

What first appealed to me about McCarthy's essay, then, seems less true of Flaubert's novel the longer I live with it. Repetition of sentences (received ideas, hackneyed phrases we use to describe our feelings) does not doom us to repetition of utterances (which are unrepeatable). The "pursuit of originality" is neither pathetic nor futile, although our originality must always make use of available material. At a moment of uncharacteristic expansiveness, Flaubert's narrator holds forth on the sheer extralinguistic size of the utterance that inarticulate feeling cobbles together from whatever sentences are at hand:

> Emma was like all [Rodolphe's] mistresses; and the charm of novelty, gradually falling away like a garment, laid bare the eternal monotony of passion, that has always the same shape and the same language. He was unable to see, this man so full of experience [*pratique*], the variety of feelings hidden within

the same expressions. Since libertine or venal lips had murmured similar phrases, he only faintly believed in the candor of Emma's; he thought one should beware of exaggerated declarations which only serve to cloak a tepid love; as though the abundance [*plénitude*] of one's soul did not sometimes overflow with empty metaphors, since no one ever has been able to give the exact measure of his needs, his concepts, or his sorrows, and since the human tongue [*la parole humaine*] is like a cracked cauldron on which we beat out tunes to set a bear dancing when we would make the stars weep with our melodies. (2.12; Flaubert, 1857/1965, p. 138; cf. Flaubert, 1857/1972, p. 254)

There is difference at the heart of repetition, as McCarthy's version of Charles seems to suggest. Even Rodolphe, in his cynical repetition of "a word that always helps" (as it has in his seduction speeches), creates a true utterance in writing and sending his letter.

Our reaccentuations of received material—*idées reçues* as well as authoritative texts—have something in common with Charles's reaccentuations of cliché and *bêtise*. Performance theory encourages readers to imagine themselves as active handlers rather than passive receivers of texts (see, e.g., Barthes 1971/1986). If Bakhtin (1986) in one of his most visionary pronouncements is correct, we enrich "great works" of the past "with new meanings, new significance," as we read and interpret them over "*great time.*" We need not "modernize and distort" an old text to understand it in a genuinely "creative" way (pp. 4–5, 7). McCarthy's wide-ranging essay of 1964—part traditional close reading, part assessment of two distinct "epochs" in which a "great work" has lived—continues to impress me as a demonstration of Bakhtinian "outsideness." Her utterance does not merely repeat Flaubert's authoritative discourse (although it quotes the novel extensively): By performing the specificity of its own "epoch," the Populuxe era of McLuhan's "mechanical bride," the utterance shows the importance

> for the person who understands to be *located outside* the object of his or her creative understanding—in time, in space, in culture. . . . [O]ur real exterior can be seen and understood only by other people, because they are located outside us in space and because they are *others*. (Bakhtin, 1986, p. 7)

In this important respect the tourist venues of Ry, self-consciously responding to an authoritative discourse by highlighting similarity and difference, seem to me utterances of the same kind. Simply to stare down the *Grand-Rue* filled with automobiles on a morning in 1998, toward a hill atop which an equestrian might have taken in her first view of the entire town a century and a half earlier, is to enjoy a creative understanding of something (about distance, movement, speed, constraint) that the book did not yet understand in its own epoch.

As I correct my draft and my list of references, I wonder how long it will be before I visit France again. My snapshots and videotapes are melancholy reminders (like the cigar case, like Emma's yellowed satin shoes) of touristic eventfulness—something *truly* done, six years ago, four years ago—set off against the chronotope of repetition and circularity that is professional life in the American suburbs.

> How far off the ball seemed already! . . . Whenever Wednesday came round she said to herself as she awoke, "Ah! I was there a week—a fortnight—three weeks ago." And little by little the faces grew confused in her remembrance . . . but the wistful feeling remained with her. (1.8; Flaubert, 1857/1965, p. 40)

I am happy to see from the Web pages that, since my visit in 1998, the town of Ry, the Galerie Bovary, and the day trip "au pays d'Emma Bovary" are still in business and that the diorama room still looks the same.[16]

Like Vargas Llosa (1986) I am a "literary fetishist." But unlike him, I have a delightful time on my first "visit to Flaubert country" (pp. 34–35). The remedy for every petty tyrant you meet in a foreign country (usually these are waiters) is that kind, patient person who loves to talk and who shows up at the right moment in an unexpected place. I find myself talking to one, in Ry's tourist information office just across the *Grande-Rue* from Galerie Bovary. In our exchange of pleasantries, I have reached the point where one apologizes for how poorly one speaks French.

"No, I can understand you," she reassures me. "Your French is better than my English. I don't speak English at all." She tells me a funny story of leading a Bovary tour for Germans, Dutch, Italians, and English, all of whom arrived in the parking lot at more or less the same moment. "We couldn't understand each other. But we got along fine." She is making an elaborate gesture that signifies, "When you don't understand each other, you make an elaborate gesture."

I talk to her about the diorama room. "It's a little . . . strange."

She looks at me as if I've used the wrong word.

"The animated puppets," I tell her.

"Yes, it is a bit bizarre," she says thoughtfully. "But I think he intended it for children."

My mind races to the image of Emma ripping open her corset—two dots of red paint, signifying "nipple," atop two exposed doll breasts—and Léon's nonstop "take," a kind of no-exit leer.

"But the book is not for children," I suggest to her.

"Oh *no*." This takes her by surprise. Her head turns to the window, above the postcards of Ry and the paperback copies of *Madame Bovary*. I scan among the racks for a boxed, motorized Emma, batteries not included, but no such luck. All the while I am thinking of George Sand's comment about how Flaubert's sensational new novel was family reading, "good for the countless Madame Bovarys in flower" all over Europe (quoted in Lottman, 1989, p. 141). As my host's head turns back, I try to change the subject, to Madame Delamare.

"She has quite a reputation," I hazard.

"Yes."

"She was a . . . personage . . ." and here I pause, casting about for the adjectives. But my host thinks I have finished my thought.

"Yes, *personage*," she tells me, "a *great* personage."

"No, no," I protest. "A personage . . . scandalous . . . shocking." From my skimpy lexicon of conversational French, I have pulled up two words that betray an underlying bias, compounded of too many male myths—that the Delphine Delamare who once walked the streets of this town was nothing more than the terrain of Flaubert's map. A masculinist comment: I am a little embarrassed as soon as I make it. My thinking about Mme Delamare has not yet been reconstructed.

My host is thoughtful again. She turns her head once more toward the window—which, "in the provinces, . . . takes the place of the theatre" (2.7; Flaubert, 1857/1965, p. 91)—and looks straight down the *Grand-Rue,* in the direction of the overcrowded churchyard from which Delphine's headstone had been stolen. Meanwhile, I stare through the open door toward the parking lot. The rental car is still there. A mapkin lollops into view. I stand poised between Monsieur Homais's two epitaphs: "Traveler, stay," which suggests that I should hang around and give Ry a more alert reading, and "Your feet trample the lovely spouse," which suggests that I should make a timid exit (see Chambers, 1993, p. 197; Flaubert, 1857/1965, p. 252).

But my host's head swings back, and she is smiling graciously. "Well," she says, and pauses. "She's certainly done a lot for the town."

"Heritage," Barbara Kirshenblatt-Gimblett (1998) maintains, is not a timeless truth, much less an inheritance from ancestors. It is "a 'value-added' industry," "a new mode of cultural production in the present that has no recourse to the past" (p. 149). Commerce (as Kirshenblatt-Gimblett and Mary McCarthy have understood so much better than I have) drives the production of "facts," and the narration of what is "true." It takes money to build a monument. And monuments, not "truths" (as any professor of performance theory lost in Skokie, Illinois, can tell you) are what show up on street maps.

Notes

The author wishes to thank Mary Agnes Doyle, Ruth Laurion Bowman, and Michael Bowman (fellow-travelers to Ry) for numerous conversations about performance theory, tourism, and teaching literature and Judith Hamera, for editorial insight that helped the present essay find its form.

1. Throughout the present essay, the use of terms like *metalinguistics, utterance,* and *great time* reflects not only primary Bakhtin sources but the explication of "prosaics" by Morson and Emerson (1990). Utterances, these scholars observe, are "constituted by elements that are, from the point of view of traditional and Saussurean linguistics, extralinguistic":

> The sentence is a unit of language (in the traditional sense); the utterance is a unit of "speech communication" *(rechevoe obshchenie).* Utterances may be as short as a grunt and as long as *War and Peace,* and the distinction between them and sentences is not one of length. . . . One can respond to an utterance, but one cannot respond to a sentence. A sentence that is assertive in form asserts nothing unless it is framed as an utterance; and according to Bakhtin, it is the nature of this framing that is crucial. . . . [E]ach utterance is by its very nature unrepeatable. . . . The reasons we speak, the very reasons texts are made, lie in what is *un*repeatable about them. (pp. 125–126)

Wood views maps as utterances in this sense. To discuss a map as a text composed of various "languages" and sign systems, of course, is to move beyond the kinds of language that Bakhtin typically considers in his discussions of novels (see Bakhtin, 1975/1981). Map texts, like film texts, require critics to stretch the range of Bakhtin's examples and apply his theories by analogy. "An 'utterance,'" in the writings of a Bakhtin-influenced film theorist like Robert Stam, "can refer to any 'complex of signs,' from a spoken phrase to a poem, or song, or play or film" (Stam, Burgoyne, & Flitterman-Lewis, 1992, p. 203; see Stam, 1989).

2. In *Troilus and Cressida,* moreover, Shakespeare appears to give the language "mappery," a bookish or pedantic concern with representations and theories by a roomful of men who ought to be out doing things: "They call this bed-work, mapp'ry, closet-war" (1.3.205). All Shakespeare quotations are taken from *The Riverside Shakespeare* (Evans, 1974).

3. The similarity between Wood's observation and the substance of Flaubert's much-cited comments is striking enough to make us forget that Wood's map (whatever its distortions) aspires to be received as a "nonfictional" text, not a "fictional" one. Flaubert seems equally concerned that the representational act be as transparent as possible and that the represented object—not merely a character's speech and actions but the language that constitutes the character's interior life—reach the reader without the appearance of narrative mediation. Access to the character's interior

life, however, is one of narratologist Dorrit Cohn's signposts for distinguishing fiction from nonfiction. In *The Distinction of Fiction* (1999), Cohn revisits the impulse to use the term *transparency* in her earlier *Transparent Minds* (1978), an influential study of narrative techniques that arose from the "vogue" of free indirect discourse "launched by Flaubert in the 1850s" (p. 170; see, e.g., Cohn, 1978, pp. 134–136). The term "imagistically foregrounds the medium itself: the set of devices that allows a fictional text [employing a heterodiegetic or 'third-person omniscient' narrator] to penetrate to the silent thoughts and feelings of its characters, artifactually traversing a visual barrier that remains forever closed to real eyes in real life (and narratives concerned with real life)" (Cohn, 1999, p. 174). She thereby challenges recent critics of narrative power who conflate such metaphoric transparency with the literal powers of surveillance associated "with Bentham's glass-celled panopticon—or, by extension, with Foucault's panopticism" (Cohn, 1999, p. 174). The heterodiegetic narrator of realist fiction, she answers, has "transparent" access merely to the consciousness of hypothetical or invented persons—"purely inner experiences that no biographer can know about a real person's" experiences. This explains, in part, "why biographies that regale us with inside views of their subjects strike us as somehow illegitimate" or "'illicit' (fictionlike)." Her examination of borderline cases—in which the priority of biographers "is less to impress their public by their scrupulousness and more to attract it by their readability"—focuses on devices like free indirect discourse, which become "insidious" in the hands of biographers when employed to achieve the "voyeuristic illusion" of access to interior consciousness (Cohn, 1999, pp. 21, 26, 28). In this concern she echoes Roy Pascal (1977), who advises historians "to prefer the actual words of their historical characters or a narrative form that clearly demarcates the sphere of the narrator from that of the character" (p. 136; see LaCapra, 1982, p. 141). The use of free indirect discourse to achieve a Godlike narrative invisibility, characteristic of much modernist fiction, grows suspect when Cohn's biographer or Pascal's historian fails to attribute externally verifiable sources to the thoughts and feelings of historical lives. The demands of verification would put similar constraints on the rhetoric of Wood's cartographer.

    4. Wherever possible I have used existing translations of texts in French. Translations of passages from the two short books by Vérard (1959; 1983), Flaubert letters not translated by Steegmuller or others (Flaubert, 1974), and *Documents iconographiques* by Dumesnil (1948) are my own. I am grateful to my Northwestern colleague William D. Paden for checking a half-dozen passages and pointing out my blunders.

    5. "J'ai peur que la fin (qui dans la réalité a été la plus remplie) ne soit, dans mon livre, étriquée, comme dimension matérielle du moins, ce qui est beaucoup" (Flaubert, 1974, p. 497; see Vérard, 1959, pp. 9–11; Vérard, 1983, pp. 13–14). One of Flaubert's other fears expressed in this letter is that his leering admiration for his niece's new governess, Juliet Herbert, is becoming a little too obvious. Herbert and Flaubert would later collaborate on what would have been the first English translation of *Madame Bovary,* but it was never published and the manuscript has been

lost; the Eleanor Marx Aveling translation, later revised by de Man (Flaubert, 1857/1965), would be the first (see Lottman, 1989, pp. 128, 148).

6. Vérard (1959, pp. 41–42; 1983, pp. 68–71) reaches the shaky conclusion that fiction comes to the aid of a hidden truth: In showing us why and how Homais might have covered up a suicide, Flaubert provides the "evidence" that citizens in Ry actually did cover one up. Any explanation must overcome the obstacles that Delphine's death seems not to have stirred up much "suicide" talk at the time; that her death did not provoke a judicial inquest; and that she was buried in consecrated ground. Of the several Flaubert biographies in English or English translation that I have read, only Starkie's (1967) raises the objection, "There is no proof whatsoever that Delphine Delamare committed suicide, though all accounts now state that she did"—chiefly by passing along a version of Maxime du Camp's unreliable anecdote (pp. 293–294).

7. Vérard notes with excitement the appearance of *Grand-Rue* on the Ry cadaster of 1852, and later in the club-foot scene of the novel (see Vérard, 1959, p. 56; Flaubert, 1857/1972, p. 244).

8. In the novel Eugène's two houses have been condensed into one, although the "real" move from house to house might be reflected in Charles and Emma's move from Tostes to Yonville.

9. Chambers (1993) observes: "[I]n a place like Yonville, where people have names like Tuvache, Leboeuf, and Bovary, and where the lowing of cattle and the bleating of sheep are practically indistinguishable from human speech, the vapor emanating from the animals clearly figures a stupid, animalized society with a noxious discourse" (p. 190).

10. In June 1990, the Fédération Nationale des Écrivains de France, Académie des Provinces Françaises, installed a replacement marker at the gravesite: "To the memory of / Delphine Delamare / née Couturier / Madame Bovary / 1822–1848."

11. I am grateful for Professor Paden's phrase, in a personal communication, that Emma had entered a "negative condition of no-longer-existing."

12. Maraini (1998) attempts to demonstrate that the novelist callously appropriated details from his love affair with Louise Colet, from Colet's journals, even from her childhood memories; and more than this, that he proceeded with deliberate intent, "plotting his 'betrayal' all along" (p. 42). Her evidence that Emma represents Colet takes the form of a double-mapping: of the novel itself (her "interested" summary, like my hypothetical *Cliffs Notes* pamphlet, has a ratio scale of about 1:7) and of the voluminous correspondence. (Maraini's *Searching for Emma* oddly resembles a multipanel data map, in which equally sized areal templates of a "real" phenomenon are mapped with representations of different statistics.) While readers will be persuaded to different degrees by her conclusions, the now-familiar allegation of Flaubert's thefts from Colet seems hard to deny.

13. Biographers are quick to point out McCarthy's identification with Flaubert concerning the difficulty of discouraging readers from treating novels "as guessing games or treasure hunts for the real-life models" (Gelderman, 1988, p. 187). "Identifying the bodies in the 'blood-stained alley' behind *The Group* quickly became

a favorite pastime for McCarthy's acquaintances," writes Carol Brightman (1992). "Speculations . . . were rarely silenced by denials, any more than gossip about the originals of *Madame Bovary* were silenced a century before, as Mary McCarthy noted ruefully" in the 1964 essay published only a year after *The Group* (p. 482).

14. Compare de Man's translation (Flaubert, 1857/1965): "Fate willed it this way" (p. 255) perhaps makes the phrase sound a little grander.

15. "Il l'ouvrit et ne trouva rien" (3.11; Flaubert, 1857/1972, p. 446). Many translations blunt the joke, it seems to me: "He performed an autopsy, but found nothing" (Flaubert, 1857/1965, p. 255).

16. A brief, suggestive essay by Jean-Marie Privat (2004), accompanied by several snapshots and an audio clip of a tour guide's narration, gives readers of the online journal *ethnographiques.org* a glimpse of the Galerie Bovary Musée des Automates as it repeats itself into the 21st century. For reasonably current information about Ry tourism, see, e.g., www.terresdecrivains.com/article.php3?id_article =152;www.tourisme.fr/office-de-tourisme/ry.htm and www.cg76.fr/e102a15.htm

References

Aristotle. (1954). *Rhetoric* (W. R. Roberts, Trans.) and *Poetics* (I. Bywater, Trans.). New York: Modern Library.

Bakhtin, M. M. (1981). *The dialogic imagination: Four essays* (M. Holquist, Ed.; C. Emerson, Trans.). Austin: University of Texas Press. (Original work published 1975)

Bakhtin, M. M. (1986). *Speech genres and other late essays* (V. W. McGee, Trans.). Austin: University of Texas Press.

Barnes, J. (1984). *Flaubert's parrot*. New York: McGraw-Hill.

Barthes, R. (1972). *Mythologies* (Rev. ed., A. Lavers, Trans.). London: Granada. (Original work published 1957)

Barthes, R. (1982). Flaubert and the sentence (S. Heath, Trans.). In S. Sontag (Ed.), *A Barthes reader* (pp. 296–304). New York: Hill and & Wang. (Original work published 1967)

Barthes, R. (1986). From work to text. In *The rustle of language* (R. Howard, Trans., pp. 56–64). New York: Hill & Wang. (Original work published 1971)

Barthes, R. (1986). The reality effect. In *The rustle of language* (R. Howard, Trans., pp. 141–148). New York: Hill & Wang. (Original work published 1968)

Brightman, C. (1992). *Writing dangerously: Mary McCarthy and her world*. New York: Clarkson Potter.

Cammarano, S. (Librettist). (1986). *Lucia di Lammermoor, opera in three acts after Walter Scott* (N. Trans.). Booklet for sound recording [LP]. EMI Germany AVB-34066. (Original work completed 1835)

Chambers, R. (1993). *The writing of melancholy: Modes of opposition in early French modernism* (M. S. Trouille, Trans.). Chicago: University of Chicago Press.

Clarke, R. (2001). Reigning territorial plains—Blast Theory's "Desert Rain." *Performance Research, 6*(2), 43–50.

Cohn, D. (1978). *Transparent minds: Narrative modes for presenting consciousness in fiction.* Princeton, NJ: Princeton University Press.

Cohn, D. (1999). *The distinction of fiction.* Baltimore: Johns Hopkins University Press.

Culley, M. (Ed.). (1976). *The awakening,* by K. Chopin. New York: Norton.

Daguerre, L. J. M. (1969). *An historical and descriptive account of the various processes of the daguerréotype and the diorama, by Daguerre* (W. E. A. Aiken, Trans.). New York: Kraus Reprint. (Original work published 1839)

Derrida, J. (1994). *Specters of Marx: The state of the debt, the work of mourning, and the new international* (P. Kamuf, Trans.). London: Routledge.

Dumesnil, R. (1948). *Flaubert: Documents iconographiques.* Geneva: Pierre Cailler.

Dumesnil, R. (1965). The real source of *Madame Bovary* (P. de Man, Trans.). In *Madame Bovary,* by G. Flaubert (P. de Man, Ed., pp. 298–301). New York: Norton. (Original work published 1961)

Evans, G. B. (Ed.). (1974). *The Riverside Shakespeare.* Boston: Houghton Mifflin.

Finkelstein, J., & Lynch, R. (2001). The hotel room. *Performance Research, 6*(2), 61–66.

Flaubert, G. (1965). *Madame Bovary* (P. de Man, Ed.; P. de Man & E. M. Aveling, Trans.). New York: Norton. (Original work published 1857)

Flaubert, G. (1972). *Madame Bovary: Moeurs de province.* Paris: Gallimard. (Original work published 1857)

Flaubert, G. (1974). *Oeuvres complètes: Vol. 13. Correspondance, 1850–1859.* Paris: Club de l'honnête homme.

Gelderman, C. (1988). *Mary McCarthy: A life.* New York: St. Martin's.

Gough, R. (Ed.). (2001). On maps and mapping [Special issue]. *Performance Research, 6*(2).

Hine, T. (1987). *Populuxe.* New York: Alfred A. Knopf.

Jarvis, B. (1998). *Postmodern cartographies: The geographical imagination in contemporary American culture.* New York: St. Martin's.

Kamps, T. (2000). Small world: Dioramas in contemporary art. In T. Kamps & R. Rugoff (Eds.), *Small world: Dioramas in contemporary art* (pp. 6–11). San Diego, CA: Museum of Contemporary Art, San Diego.

Kelleher, J. (2001). Theatre PUR on ice. *Performance Research, 6*(2), 79–87.

Kirshenblatt-Gimblett, B. (1998). *Destination culture: Tourism, museums, and heritage.* Berkeley: University of California Press.

Kleist, H. von. (1997). The puppet theatre. In D. Constantine (Ed.), *Selected writings* (D. Constantine, Trans., pp. 411–416). London: J. M. Dent. (Original work published 1810)

LaCapra, D. (1982). *Madame Bovary on trial.* Ithaca, NY: Cornell University Press.

Lott, E. (1993). *Love and theft: Blackface minstrelsy and the American working class.* Oxford, UK: Oxford University Press.

Lottman, H. (1989). *Flaubert: A biography*. Boston: Little, Brown.

Maraini, D. (1998). *Searching for Emma: Gustave Flaubert and Madame Bovary* (V. J. Bertolini, Trans.). Chicago: University of Chicago Press. (Original work published 1993)

Margolies, E. (2001). Vagueness gridlocked: A map of the smells of New York (December 1999 to January 2000). *Performance Research, 6*(2), 88–97.

McCarthy, M. (1964). Foreword. In *Madame Bovary*, by G. Flaubert (M. Marmur, Trans.), pp. vii–xxiii. New York: Signet.

McLuhan, M. (1951). *The mechanical bride: Folklore of industrial man*. Boston: Beacon Press.

Melrose, S. (2001). (Re)marking the overlooked or Stanislavski's napkin. *Performance Research, 6*(2), 4–19.

Meyer, M. (2001). Mapping the body politic. *Performance Research, 6*(2), 67–74.

Monmonier, M. (1991). *How to lie with maps*. Chicago: University of Chicago Press.

Morson, G. S., & Emerson, C. (1990). *Mikhail Bakhtin: Creation of a prosaics*. Stanford, CA: Stanford University Press.

Nelson, R. (2001). Set map slip = palimpsest (working title). *Performance Research, 6*(2), 20-29.

Nelson, V. (2001). *The secret life of puppets*. Cambridge, MA: Harvard University Press.

Pascal, R. (1977). *The dual voice: Free indirect speech and its functioning in the nineteenth-century European novel*. Manchester, UK: Manchester University Press.

Pearson, M. (2001). "You can't tell by looking . . ." *Performance Research, 6*(2), 31–38.

Pommier, J., & Leleu, G. (Eds.). (1965). Gustave Flaubert: Scenarios and scenes (P. de Man, Trans.). In *Madame Bovary*, by G. Flaubert (P. de Man, Ed., pp. 259–279). New York: Norton. (Original work published 1949)

Privat, J. M. (2004, April). Emma à Ry: Notes de recherche. *ethnographiques.org, 5*, n. p. Retrieved September 16, 2004, from www.ethnographiques.org/documents/ article/ArPrivat.html#som3.

Roadside America. (1963). Shartlesville, PA: Roadside America.

Rosenbaum, S. (2001). The map: Shifts, overwrites, overlays. *Performance Research, 6*(2), 54–59.

Rugoff, R. (2000). Bubble worlds. In T. Kamps & R. Rugoff (Eds.), *Small world: Dioramas in contemporary art* (pp. 12–16). San Diego, CA: Museum of Contemporary Art, San Diego.

Segel, H. B. (1995). *Pinocchio's progeny: Puppets, marionettes, automatons, and robots in modernist and avant-garde drama*. Baltimore: Johns Hopkins University Press.

Sonenberg, M. (1989). Cartographies. In *Cartographies* (pp. 3–21). Pittsburgh, PA: University of Pittsburgh Press.

Stam, R. (1989). *Subversive pleasures: Bakhtin, cultural criticism, and film*. Baltimore: Johns Hopkins University Press.

238   Synthesizing Scholarship

Stam, R., Burgoyne, R., & Flitterman-Lewis, S. (1992). *New vocabularies in film semiotics: Structuralism, post-structuralism, and beyond.* New York: Routledge.

Starkie, E. (1967). *Flaubert: The making of the master.* London: Weidenfeld & Nicolson.

Steegmuller, F. (1950). *Flaubert and Madame Bovary: A double portrait* (Rev. ed.). New York: Vintage.

Steegmuller, F. (Ed.). (1980). *The letters of Gustave Flaubert 1830–1857* (F. Steegmuller, Trans.). Cambridge, MA: Harvard University Press.

Troyat, H. (1992). *Flaubert* (J. Pinkham, Trans.). New York: Viking. (Original work published 1988)

Vargas Llosa, M. (1986). *The perpetual orgy: Flaubert and Madame Bovary* (H. Lane, Trans.). New York: Farrar Straus Giroux. (Original work published 1975)

Vérard, R. (1959). *Épilogue de "L'affaire Bovary": La victoire de Ry.* Rouen: Éditions Maugard.

Vérard, R. (1983). *Ry, pays de Madame Bovary.* Ry: Galerie Bovary Musée des Automates.

Wood, D. (1992). *The power of maps.* New York: Guilford.

White, H. (1978). *Tropics of discourse: Essays in cultural criticism.* Baltimore: Johns Hopkins University Press.

White, H. (1987). *The content of the form: Narrative discourse and historical representation.* Baltimore: Johns Hopkins University Press.

V

Embracing Performances

Introduction

Judith Hamera

S cholars choose performance-based approaches to critical analysis for many reasons, among them:

- The challenges of engaging culture as an embodied process, not a thing, text, or a set of variables.
- The rigors of working across, betwixt and between conceptual categories like space and place, here/now and there/then, archive and repertoire, production and consumption.
- The metatheoretical and methodological opportunities to reflect on and change how dimensions of difference, location, history, and daily practice are represented in academic discourse.

But, truth be told, they also do so for another reason, one they might confess to a colleague over a meal at a conference, or offer in a bracing moment of self-disclosure to a special student or an extraordinary class. They might share this with the shame of an apostate or the zeal of a convert. They choose performance because they've been bowled over, or knocked flat, or knocked out by it. The particular performance may have involved presentation of an everyday conversation or family story. It may have reframed a classic artifact, opening it up for new possibilities, or it may have involved a new voice that irrevocably ruptured a seemingly univocal telling of history. It may have contained innovations undertaken by individuals and societies traumatized by civil war, or it could have consisted of a partnership between these survivors and artists that represented those experiences. Whatever the particular inspiring event, performance scholars were changed. Performance could never again be dismissed as "faking"; the material and affective evidence of the power of these acts of poiesis was simply too compelling, too inviting, too paradigm shifting to dismiss or ignore. Scholars who turn to performance do so because they have been hailed by other performers in the present, or by the residues of hands or echoes of voices from the past. These do not beckon or admonish from behind distant prosceniums, across the expansive moats of orchestra pits. Rather, the manifold potentials of performance offer a firm, generous embrace, too welcoming and, finally, too potentially productive to refuse.

That's why scholars really embrace performance. That's probably why you will too.

When you do, you will learn that Plato was right: Performance is contagious. And you will learn that he was profoundly wrong. To see communication and culture as made things, not "givens" or degraded violations of an ideal, to be astonished, angered, and engaged by their affective, social, and political power, is to be inspired to account for how and why this is so in the most rigorous and principled ways. It is to ask ever more finely honed questions, to forge new models and put your body on the line to find and share a clearer, more precise sense of what expression is and does in—and as— world making. It is to reach out in solidarity to other theorists, historians, and geographers, to artists and novelists, to informant-partners in research to create communities of/in knowing—as Conquergood says, knowing how and knowing who, even, I would add, trying to know why. Finally, to embrace performance is to see scholarship itself as poiesis, as a creative thing, a relational, aesthetic, political and affective labor and not simply a cognitive one.

Experience is not scholarship. Joan Scott (1991) tells us this. Performance links experience, theory, and the work of close critique in ways that make precise analytical claims about cultural production and consumption, and expose how both culture and our claims are themselves constructed things, products of hearts and souls, minds and hands.

Soyini Madison's essay has the final word in *Opening Acts*. Here, she ludically and lovingly performs her version of how and why so many of us have embraced this approach to communication and culture. Her evocative theoretical poetics and her heartfelt characterizations of performance itself recall the politicized playfulness that Maria Lugones (1994) characterizes as a preeminently ethical stance: " . . . [T]he playful attitude involves openness to surprise, openness to being a fool, openness to self-construction or reconstruction and to construction or reconstruction of the 'worlds' we inhabit playfully" (p. 636).

References

Lugones, M. (1994). Playfulness, "world"-travelling, and loving perception. In D. S. Madison (Ed.)., *The woman that I am: The literature and culture of contemporary women of color* (pp. 626–638). New York: St. Martin's.

Scott, J. W. (1991). The evidence of experience. *Critical Inquiry 17*(4), 773–797.

8

Performing Theory/Embodied Writing

D. Soyini Madison

Prologue: Embodied Writing

*(The performer sits under a spotlight surrounded by books on performance.
She touches, smells, and tastes some of the books. She holds one of the books up to
her ear. She notices you are there. She looks up to speak.)*

I

Performance has become too popular. It seems that everyone I know and
don't know is thinking, speaking, and writing in the language of performance, or trying to. Performance is everywhere these days. Perhaps I should
celebrate: Intellectuals far and wide are considering the sexy and stately implications of performance. While I have found the insights of thinkers beyond
the spheres of theater and performance studies to be helpful and inspiring—
their work frequently guiding my own—recently, I have experienced momentary pangs, uneasy feelings of wanting to claim turf, of unhappily wincing
when I hear the word *performance* slip so easily through the lips of "progres-
sives" who still, deep down, primarily regard performance as "pretending."
Mimesis rules! The others, a substantial few, who know and do more of

performance, are more helpful. But too many of them see performance as all of everyday life or *only* everyday life. So I worry (Coco Fusco worries too),[1] and I wonder about their singleness of vision for quotidian locations and for art. Can we see the stage in the dark?

II

Provoked by suppressed resentment and my own silent turf war, I imagine an oblique metaphor—a personification—where Performance becomes a subject and an object, both a perpetrator and a victim, where performance *performs* like a promiscuous lover, enticing this one and that one, wanting everyone to love her and wanting to love everyone in return. She seeks and she is sought. Performance *is* everything, yet she becomes the *one* thing. Indiscriminate in the pleasure she gets and gives, there is a natural striving for her, and through all her encounters and travels, there are those who speak of her very well and there are others who live cautiously inside her presence. I know some who do both. Now I will admit, within my own metaphor, I am guilty of gluttony. I have taken Performance for myself. Sometimes she was given to me with more love than I deserved. Like a possessive devotee or lover I want to hold on to her, not wanting her to be with anyone but me and my kind because we've known her for a longer time— who she is and how to treat her. I've begun to feel protective of her. Lately, more than ever, I've found myself bristling at those who are not ready or willing to put in the time with Performance: to honor properly, to learn sufficiently, to work skillfully, and to believe heartily in her possibilities.

III

What I want to say is: I love performance most when I enter into it, when it calls me forward shamelessly, across those hard-edged maps into spaces where I must go, terrains that are foreign, scary, uninhabitable, but necessary. I must go to them to know myself more, to know you more. I enter performance as a witness and a doer. Performance is hard work. We see the familiar for the very first time, and after that we can no longer speak or reason about what we thought we knew in the exact same way, lest we forget the performance. Yes, I claim performance romanticism; it is overblown and embarrassing. But it is true. I am a performance essentialist: vulgar peformancism.

Performance helps me see. It illumines like good theory. It orders the world, and it lets the world loose. It is a top spun out of control that spins its way back to its beginning. Like good theory, performance is a blur of meaning, language, and a bit of pain. Whirling past, faster than I can catch up. Testing me, often refuting me, pulling away and moving toward me. I'm almost there with it. I hold on. I keep my hands on the performance and my eyes on the theory. I am playful, but I am not playing. I do not appreciate carelessness. I pay attention. I do not let go or look away, because I have learned that all the meanings, languages, and bits of pain will come into clarity and utility like a liberation song. I need this clarity for the ones I love. Now I enter a truth, a piece of the world, discovered. What is here is not an answer or a resolve but something more, it is a "realizing."[2] Whether settled or unsettled, finished or just beginning, this realizing is a truth. Performance helps me live a truth while theory helps me name it—or maybe it is the other way around. My mind and body are locked together in a nice little divine kind of unity: The theory knows and feels, and the performance feels and unlearns. I know I am a(n) un/learning body in the process of feeling. You too.

The theory that gets in my head and sticks—the good parts or the parts relevant to what I must become and do in my life—performs. That *this* theory performs me is an existential fact. That I choose to perform it is my craft. I perform theory through time, through (un)consciousness, nervousness,[3] and effort. This theory/performance coupling is not an easy assignment. Performance thrills me, theory does not. I would surely lose myself without performance, but I cannot live well without theory.

IV

Theory endures an ancient schizophrenia. Somewhere—for Theory—between being loved and hated, revered and scorned, there is the splitting up of various intrigues and struggles, pretensions, and honest pleasures. You've known Theory to be both a mean-spirited gatekeeper and a warm welcome call to those on another side of the wall. Inside the wall, where language is seldom free, where words rarely match your first intuition, and where voices hardly speak your name or your old neighborhood, you know that once you are inside, you must choose. Theory? How much theory? Why? Okay! You keep trying on the language, again and again, listening, until some parts of it begin to fit your tongue. Some words need more practice. Practice. Check the spelling. The word isn't in the *American Heritage Dictionary*. Practice. Certain voices, in time, begin to feel familiar. It's late, after 1 a.m. You won't sleep tonight.

In the morning seminar, on this day, finally, the voice that grows familiar is reaching toward your name, your old neighborhood. It is a long stretch, but there is motion, and you hear something you can use and carry with you, back home.

You sense that theory is more than adoration or disdain. It is more than language, gatekeepers, belonging, respect, or isolation. It is all and nothing more than *recognition*. You think you know something, but theory leads you to *know* it *again*. You were always aware of power, beauty, pain, language, race, and yourself. But theory circles you back to all of them, including yourself. Breaking the parts open, piece by piece, theory demands that you take notice—pay closer attention. You see again and greet anew. Things are more complicated, because things *are more*. Whether you agree with theory or not, even if you argue with it, it makes you feel and see differently. You speak differently and more. The recognition is not unrecognized.

Tired and sleepy, now, you go outside and sit against another side of the wall. You hear the voices and sounds from your old neighborhood. It is at this moment that you remember where theories come from.

Is inside the wall high? Is outside the wall low? [4] You cannot sleep. You *recognize* that theory is contingent on location. There is flesh[5] and bone here on this side of the wall that speaks for its own life, not by breaking parts open, piece by piece, but by sealing them together with fire and blood. Here, the words live under your tongue. Theory in this terrain is yours; it is all yours, because now you remember how it was given to you, sometimes with affection and sometimes forced down your throat with shouts or a switch. This theory makes body contact. Bodies that most often look like yours. You realize you are part of two locations and more: both sides of the wall and the in-betweens. Theories come from everywhere, and you decide to go back across, inside the wall, to the seminar . . . to the books . . . to *recognize* again and more.

V

You are not alone. I cross inside and outside and to the in-betweens of the wall too. But when I think back on the very first moments of my theoretical realizing, on the inside, those moments of recognition that have enlarged me to see further out, four men in particular—theoretical "fathers"[6]—come to mind. It seems so long ago when I first met them. Yet meeting them is a continuous occurrence, even when they are literally absent. These fathers are long on insight, but they have also troubled me. They have come to occupy the inside, the outside, and the in-between. I recognize them: Karl Marx, Ferdinand de Saussure, Jacques Derrida, and Frantz Fanon. I will recognize them again in playfulness and dialogue, but I can do this with integrity and freedom only through performance. Performance will relocate them in time and space: to know again and meet anew. This relocation is a second meeting or perhaps a third or a fourth. I meet them as the not-not-me.[7] For the sake of performing theory and embodied writing, I beg here for a space of imagination, for joy and purpose.

Performing Theory

(Three areas of a performance space are lit: up center, down right, and center left. At center stage is a large ladder; next to it is a flip chart. Down right is an old black rotary telephone sitting on a stool; center left is a small desk with an antique lamp, books, pens, and a writing pad. There is a screen hanging upstage of the desk.)

Scene 1

Karl Marx: "The Telephone Conversation"
(The time is between time and timelessness)

(The performer enters the space. The performer "performs" an elderly woman in manner, voice, and gesture. She walks to the telephone, picks it up, sits on the stool, and carefully balances the phone on her lap. Before she picks up the receiver, she looks down at the phone and becomes amused. She laughs quietly with her hand down on the receiver. She picks up the receiver and dials all 18 digits of the long distance number and the saving code. In good humor and precision, she mumbles inaudibly each number as she dials.)
One, zero, one, zero, eight, one, one, eight, zero, four, three, four, nine, six, two, two, zero, one. *(a pause, she enjoys humming a tune until the other party picks up the telephone)* Hello Karl, Karl, is that you? How are you? Yeah, yeah, it's me! I'm so happy to hear your voice too. It's been so long. I miss you, my friend! I miss you so very, very much. *(a pause)* Oh, yes I really do. I saw something today that reminded me of you, and I rushed home right away to call you. I do miss our times together. We've got to do better with keeping up! It's been too long, too long. *(a pause)* Oh my, has it been that long? *(pause, hesitation, and concern)* How is Mr. Engels? I read his letter to Joe in the newspaper.[9] *(laughs)* He's still trying to convince those vulgar Marxists that you aren't an economic determinist! *(a pause)* Yes, yes, you're right, Karl. I tell those people that even YOU don't recognize what some of

them are calling Marxism these days! 1848,[10] those were the days . . . what
promise, what hope, what tragedy. And then there was 1968, those were the
days . . . what promise, what hope, what tragedy.

 Oh, Karl, guess what I did? *(pause)* No, no, I'm still smoking. I know, I
know. My friend, *(amused)* with your bad habits, you should not lecture
me.[11] Yes, yes, let me tell you what I did . . . I took a trip to Philadelphia! Yes,
I finally went to Philly! *(pause)* I know I said I'd never step foot in that
city . . . Constitution, William Penn, brotherly love . . . too many dreams
turned sour, too many visions made into a mockery! The ghosts of that city
should be weeping! Weeping, I tell you! *(pause)* Uh huh. Uh huh, I know,
Karl, you've always said my boycott didn't make sense. I remember how
you'd say with a smirk: "What does it matter that one woman refuses to go
within one hundred miles of Independence Hall?" But I knew you found it
charming. I knew you understood on principle. I will not remind you of your
unique and various contradictions. I even promised myself before I picked up
the phone that we would not end up fussing with each other. *(pauses and
shakes her head)* I shall stay on the subject of Philadelphia—the city of *brotherly* love. *(Changes, her mood, excited.)* Well, I tell you, when I got there the
city was all lit up with Christmas lights. Huh? What? *(bewildered)* Christmas?
(pause) What is Christmas?! Karl, you remember Christmas! Christmas . . .
That holiday for Christians and most everybody else. *(pause)* Christians?!
Opium for the masses! Remember?! Oh Karl, you've got to get out into the
world more. You've been cooped up too long with those books. *(pause)* Your
magnum opus? But you completed *Capital* over a hundred years ago. One
magnum opus in a lifetime is enough! Give it a rest and get out more; mingle
with the masses. Have a worker over for dinner! *(pause)* Sorry, I know you
don't like for me to joke like that . . . Hmm . . . where was I? Christmas season in Philadelphia! Karl, you remember Christmas, the season where capitalism is not just an economy but a culture! Hah, that would make a nice
bumper sticker: "Capitalism, a culture where everything is subordinated to
consumption, by Karl Marx." *(amused)* All right! All right! When I was in
Philly, I walked along the river bank every day. Oh, the art! There were statues—sculptures placed along the bank—bigger than life and more real. Each
sculpture told a story, Karl, of revolution, of alienation, of consciousness.
You would have loved it. I will take you there when you are feeling better.
What? *(pause)* No, I don't think the artists were leftists. *(pause)* Why?
Because I could actually understand the art and it truly moved me. Remem-
ber that Dadaist poet? Oh, what is his name? Tzara![12] Yes, that's it! He said,
"The odd thing about revolution is that the further left people go politically,
the more bourgeois they like their art!" Oh, but the art, Karl, there in
Philadelphia . . . that art was socialist realism at its very best! No, no, no, not

simply pragmatic but imaginary and beautiful. Yeah, yeah. One statue was of a man lying on a woman's lap. A woman, Karl, a woman. Her lap so small, holding the body of a man three times her size; but, it was her lap, the strength of her knees, her legs, her arms, holding him close that kept him from falling. Her lap kept his work-weary, sick body from falling to the ground. He was a dying man, but in her lap there was hope. *(pause)* How do I know? What do you mean how do I know? It was all there in his eyes. In his eyes . . . *you* were there. Karl, you were there in his eyes. *(Pause)* I know, because in his eyes was history, the struggles and yearnings of human beings to own their own labor and their own bodies. The man lying in the woman's lap had your eyes telling us that history is neither straight progressions nor random acts, but it is always, always a dialectic among dialectics. It is always the work, the hope, for Change! Do you remember our mantra in the old days? *(nods into telephone)* Yes, we used to say it all comes down to the material interests of the dominant classes? Hah! A lot has changed in almost two centuries. Has that changed too? They say the world is more complicated now. They say there is no such thing as the State anymore and that we live in a global economy. You know what I tell 'em, Karl? I tell 'em they need a good dose of Marxism 101! *(grumbles)* No such thing as the State, rubbish!

Remember what you told me? It was about 1881, I believe. After all these years, I can still remember . . . *(Recites the words as if reading from a book)* "Economic relations and modes of production shape, but do not purely deter-mine existence or else every struggle would be the same."[13] I've got a memory like an elephant! Karl, it is art that gives us hope and possibility. Even today, at noon, in the city, when the children play the music loud enough to make my eyebrows hurt, and every time I go to Philly and see that man lying in the woman's tiny lap, at first, I get a little mad, but then, I think about why we make art. "The ideas of the ruling class are, in every age, the ruling ideas."[14] "The class that is the dominant material force is, at the same time, the domi-nant intellectual force."[15] Your words, my friend, are more true to me now than ever, but there is something about the way the beat of that music makes me tap, tap, tap my feet, hah! And something about that man's eyes being your eyes: All of it keeps me believing. It reminds me and keeps me believing. I don't get mad so much, because I remember to believe in the miracle of consciousness.

All right, all right, I'm getting a little optimistic, a little sentimental. I've seen you stop breathing at such a combination! Shall I be more severe? Will that make you happy? No, I will not, because I know you too well. Human consciousness,[16] in thought and in memory, is making you smile. Still, with these many miles between us, I can feel your smile. Today, I saw a painting, *(pause)* no, no, it was not in Philadelphia. It was here in Chicago. *(pause)* Of course! Chicago will always be my home. It is the lake, the parks, and the neighborhoods. No other city in the world has this lake front! *(a pause)* Today, walking home from the university, I saw a painting on the side of a building. It was a painting of a group of workers: men, women, and children. They were all standing together, each of them reaching out with one hand from the wall. They were in a field or a factory, I couldn't tell which. Maybe they were on a farm, or, uh . . . in a diamond mine. No, they were in a large house with bars and no doors. I'm just not sure. They all had their arms outstretched as though they were reaching out from the flat surface of the wall. They were reaching for us to come into the painting. No, they were reaching for us to carry them away from the painting. No, they were reaching for . . . I'm just not sure. They all had the same longing. Their faces were familiar to me. Just beneath the mural, the artist wrote down these words. *(She takes a piece of paper from her pocket.)* He must have read all your stuff on alienation. I wrote it down so I could read it to you just the way he wrote it. *(She begins reading slowly from the paper.)* "The *alienation* of the worker from the product he makes means not only that his labor becomes an object— taking on its own existence—but that it exists outside of him—alien to him— and that it stands opposed to him. The life which he has given to the object is now against him as an alien and hostile force."[17] How's that for depressing, but you must admit that's a pretty smart kid! What? No! No! Those are YOUR words?! That little plagiarist! Karl, I must be slipping because that one sure got past me. Well, old boy, you're a pretty smart kid yourself. You rest well, and power to the people. *(hesitates)* Karl, not so much arsenic. They tell me that green tea with a little bit of honey is better for the pain. Take care. I will see you soon, I promise. *(pause)* Good-bye, my friend. *(The performer puts down the phone and moves down center stage.)*

Scene 2

Ferdinand de Saussure and Jacques Derrida: "The Audition"
(The time is now)

(The performer stands downstage of the ladder and speaks to the audience. She is now a woman in her early 50s.)
I just got over my midlife crises, and I was finally happy. I no longer dyed my gray, and I stopped changing my hair style every hour. I gained weight and I didn't panic, at least not too much. So, in celebration of my new freedom, I decided I would do something I always wanted to do but never dared to try—audition for a chorus line! My friend Linda told me about a

community theater company on the north side that was auditioning that day. I was in luck! I felt confident, even though I never danced on stage before, and the last dance class I took ... mmm ... I was about seven years old. It didn't matter, because I was in charge of my life and ready for new adventures. When I walked in the audition hall, I was told by the stage manager that I would be auditioning for two acts: a backup dancer for Act 1 and 2. To my surprise, the acts were to be choreographed by different directors. For Act 1 the director was Ferdinand de Saussure, the famous structuralist, and for Act 2 the director was Jacques Derrida, the famous poststructuralist. What an interesting audition this would be. *(The performer moves further down stage and peers out into the audience to listen for instructions from the director. She spots him and listens intently for a brief moment before she speaks.)* May I just say, Mr. Saussure, I am so pleased to meet you. I am a great admirer of your work ... my, my, I didn't know you were into dancing too. I must say before we begin that I think your concept of *la langue* and *la parole* is just fascinating, just brilliant and ... *(Interrupted by "Saussure," she abruptly stops to listen to his instructions. She assumes a more serious demeanor.)* Yes, I'm ready to dance. *(She listens and moves awkwardly, but without exaggeration, around the space as she tries to mark and make sense of Saussure's directions.)* Yes, stay within this line? Here, right here? This line connects to the opposite angle there? This angle links back to that curve that is conjoined in the opposite direction to this line? This is the dance pattern. Yes, I absolutely will stay within the lines. Yes, I will make every effort to accentuate the connections. Mr. Saussure, I can do this ... I teach performance studies. I can do this ... yes, I can ... I think ... *(Mocks a warm-up exercise. She stops and looks up at Mr. Saussure. She is delighted by his presence.)*

The script? *(Very excited, she picks up the script from a step on the ladder.)* You mean this is actually a speaking part! *(As she silently reads the script, her excitement turns to disappointment.)* This is what you want me to say? You want me to dance to this? *(She pauses and takes a deep breath. Determined to repress her frustration, in earnest she performs the script in a semimechanical voice and movement. She is conscious of staying within the lines and kicking each leg on all the "kick, kicks.")* "We are to be analytical, not evaluative. KICK, KICK." Yes, Mr. Saussure, I will make it faster. How fast? All right. *(She is more expressive and faster, but goes over the "line.")* "We are to be analytical, not evaluative. KICK, KICK." *(She stops and addresses Saussure.)* No, I didn't realize I had gone over the line. Yes, I will do better. One foot directly in front of the other. I understand. *(She performs with more determination.)* "We are to be analytical, not evaluative. KICK,

KICK." *(looks up)* Was that okay? Not so good? Oh, I see. Mr. Saussure, I feel compelled to say something. *(The performer stands and looks directly out and over toward the audience section to speak to Saussure. She is speaking honestly and admiringly, but because she is overwhelmed by his presence, in her respect and idolization of Saussure, her manner and speech are awkward and pedantic.)* I have studied your work for many years. Your conceptualization of the signifier and the signified is the foundation of meaning and language. Signifier as inscription and signified as concept—no relation, arbitrary—but together they make the sign: That is brilliant, pure brilliance! Signifier is the symbol; signified is the thing. WOW! You said it all with your idea of signification! You are the man! Look how far we've come! *(teasing)* And I'm not signifying. *(under her breath)* Oh, it's a black thing; you wouldn't understand . . . Not amused? *(embarrassed)* Back to work. *(With precision, she walks the "lines" like a robot. She tries to contain her discomfort as she continues to read the script moving within the imaginary lines and kicking each leg on the kick, kick.)* "It is the underlying rules of cultural texts and practices which interest structuralists. KICK, KICK. It is structure which makes meaning possible. KICK, KICK. The task of structuralism, therefore, is to make explicit the rules and conventions—the structure—which govern the production of meaning. KICK KICK." *(She stops abruptly.)* Mr. Saussure, I am sorry, but this is not what I had in mind. I don't think I can . . . Yes, of course. I will continue. *(Ordered by Saussure to continue, she begins again, determined to do better. With more energy and verve, she walks proudly, speaks assertively, and kicks confidently.)* "Language is a system—KICK, KICK—a pattern of binary oppositions—KICK, KICK—structuralists try to uncover the grammar, syntax, or patterns of particular human systems of meaning—KICK, KICK—whether they be kinship, narratives, totems, images, or myths—KICK, KICK." *(She stops again and turns to the other audience members.)* Maybe this isn't quite so bad. I think I'm beginning to enjoy it. *(turning to Saussure)* When do we get to the *parole* and *langue*? What? Oh, yes, sorry, I will just stay within the lines, within the lines! *(She discovers she is now at the section of the script on langue and parole. She is overjoyed and lets out a joyful cheer.)* Oh yes! Here we go! There is *langue* and *parole*, structure and performance. It is the homogeneity of the structure—KICK, KICK—which makes the heterogeneity of the performance possible—KICK, KICK—YEAH!" *(She is very happy and pleased with herself. She bows several times with great histrionics.)* THANK YOU EVERYONE, AND THANK YOU CLAUDE LEVI-STRAUSS![18] (She feels grand and continues to bow to the audience. She turns to Saussure.) So, I got the part! *(She is stunned and upset. She stops to focus on Saussure.)* NO! What do you mean NO?! Wait a minute, wait just a minute. I stayed within your structure, paying attention only to the lines, the combinations, the attachments, and the opposites! I know this stuff! In the beginning was the word and the word created the text—BINARIES, BINARIES, BINARIES! And furthermore, I never, never, never, NEVER got D-O-G *(spelling the letters)* confused with the four-legged animal that wags its tail and goes ruff, ruff—ARBITRARY, ARBITRARY, ARBITRARY. Not only that. *(She is getting more upset.)* I not once, not once, paid any attention to history or the author's intent, or my own need to break out of this frigging STRUCTURE, STRUCTURE, STRUCTURE! I know the mantra of structuralism: "the scientific enterprise to unveil the rules, codes, systems of cultural practices!" I can play that part! I am sufficiently repressed! So, I ask you, Mr. Saussure, why didn't I get the part? What?! Roland Barthes![19] What does he have to do with this! You didn't tell me HE was here! *(She takes a deep breath and pauses. She then gains her composure. She speaks to Saussure with direction and self-possession.)* Mr. Saussure, not to worry, not to worry at all, I am ready with great PLEA-SURE to meet Mr. Derrida. *(The performer walks to the ladder. She stands downstage of a large childlike drawing on the stage floor. She picks up the drawing and tapes it to the ladder. The ladder is now in full view of the audience. It is a crayon drawing of the Tower of Babel, and written across the image is the misspelling: "towr of bable." The performer stands downstage of the ladder. Speaking out and above the audience, she addresses Jacques Derrida.)*

Hello, Mr. Derrida. I am here to audition for Act 2 in the chorus line. *(startled)* Excuse me? There is no Act 2? But, the stage manager and Mr. Saussure said that . . . Oh, I see. Uhmm. *(gently)* If there is no Act 2, then what am I auditioning for? You want me to *erupt the* essence of the dance? *(gently)* You mean "disrupt," don't you? *(nods slowly)* You mean "erupt." Ooooh-Kaaaeeee . . . But . . . *(with caution)* can you give me a little help here? *(looks around in the space)* Who am I? What is my motivation? Which dance? *(At the bottom of the Tower of Babel is a scroll; the performer moves toward it.)* This is for me? *(The performer picks up the scroll and moves downstage.)* Open it and read it? *(The performer unwraps the scroll and a huge sheet of paper rolls out. She reads the words that are written in bold disjointed letters. The performer stops and starts, struggling to read and make sense of what it says.)* Signifiers do not produce *(pause)* signifieds. They produce more *(pause)* signifiers. But Mr. Derrida, aren't I suppose to dance? *(Suddenly music comes up. It sounds like jazz. It is faintly heard, then it gets louder. It is Miles Davis's "Bitches' Brew." The music plays.)* . . . But, Mr. Derrida, this is not dance music . . . well, I can't get an identifiable beat. . . . *(She quickly apologizes sensing she may have offended Mr. Derrida.)* Oh, I didn't mean . . . Yes, I know . . . Miles is brilliant . . . no offense. But what about the dance? I need the steps! I need a script! I need a character! I need a beat! *(annoyed, but trying very hard to conceal it)* No, Mr. Saussure did not give me the part. I wasn't able to stay within the lines. *(pacing back and forth in frustration)* Look, I really do want to work with you, Mr. Derrida. I am one of your strongest defenders. All the attacks on deconstruction and postmodernism, do you know what I tell your critics? I tell them to actually READ you! *(pauses briefly to listen to Derrida's response. She hesitates.)* Well . . . ummm . . . many of them say that they *have* read you. But as for ME . . . listen, I believe in citation[20] AND the order of the supplement![21] *(starts to get excited)* I KNOW you are trying to open more voices, more alternatives, and more experiences beyond those of master narratives! I KNOW you want us to break open exclusive hierarchies! I am with you on all that! Prisoner of language[22] doesn't bother me in the least! I GET it! I FEEL you! *(calms down and asks the question sincerely)* But, Mr. Derrida, I really would appreciate a little more direction here? *(A member of the audience comes forward; across his back in large bold letters is a sign: "Deus ex Machina." He gives the performer an oversized book, almost too heavy to handle; the performer looks at Deus ex Machina in bewilderment. Deus Ex leaves the stage.)* What do I do with this? *(A bellowing voice with a French accent booms over the stage. In a tone that is a combination of camp and authority, the voice speaks loudly.)*

"   D   i   f   f   é   r   a   n   c   e   "

(The performer looks at the book and realizes it is a grotesquely oversized dictionary.) I know what *Différence* means; I don't have to look it up in a dictionary. Is *Différance* even IN a dictionary?! *(exasperated)* Mr. Derrida, I came here to fulfill a dream. All I wanted to do was audition for a chorus line and have a little fun for a change . . . Can't we be critics and have fun too? I want to be relevant, AND I want to play! *(She slowly puts down the book. She straightens up and arches her back.)* You want ERUPT! Hah! I'll dance it. . . . I'll dance erupt for you! *(With abandon, determination, and joy the performer dances her ideas of Différance to the music of Miles Davis. Through improvisational movement, which is neither comic nor burlesque, and without regard for technique, beat, or appearances, the performer "dances" her version of Différance with honest pleasure. When the dance ends, the performer moves to a flip chart or chalk board and writes "Différance" in bold letters. She draws two arrows pointing out from the word: one pointing to the word* differ, *the other pointing to the word* defer. *After the performer has written all three words in bold on the board or chart, with good humor and playfulness, she "teaches" the meaning of Différance by performing in "Sesame Street" fashion. The Sesame Street theme music is now heard in the background.)* "Différance," meaning to

differ and defer *(pointing to the written words). Differ* means DIFFERENT. We understand language because words are different from one another. A language, boys and girls, is not one word or two words, for example *(her voice takes on a variety of ranges, accents, and expressions):* be me, be me, be me, be me, be me, be me. Now, can we understand that? Of course we cannot! A language is not a few different words like: knock/clock/rock/flock/boom/boy/beast/me/you/no/yes. You see, boys and girls, the more DIFFERENT words there are in a language, then the more rich and wondrous and exciting and perfect that language is. In other words, my little friends, the bigger our language, the bigger our meanings. And, the bigger our meanings, the bigger and truer our experiences and realities become. *(moving closer to the audience)* Now, so that I know you understand, repeat after me: The more different words . . . *(audience repeats)* in a language . . . *(audience repeats)* the bigger . . . *(audience repeats)* and more true. . . . *(audience repeats)* our world becomes *(audience repeats).* Very good! Very good! But we have not completed our lesson yet! Differ or different is just the first part of Différance. Now we are ready to learn the second part. Are we all ready to learn more? Very good! The second part, boys and girls, is *(pause)* DEFER. When we say *defer,* we are saying that meanings are never static and that they must always defer to other meanings. *Defer* means to yield to, submit to, to succumb to, or refer to another. *Defer* is the indefinite referral of signifier to signifier, or word to word, for example, let's take this dictionary so kindly provided by Deus Ex. *(The performer opens the large book and pulls out a small card attached to a red ribbon. She begins to read it.)* Black—the color of coal *(Attached to the first card is a series of cards all strung, one after the other, on a bright red string. The performer reads from each card. She is no longer performing "Sesame Street," and the theme song has stopped. The performer is reading each card, without parody or melodrama, in a straightforward manner.)* Black—opposite of white. Black—without light. Black—dirty. Black—angry. Black—threatening. Black—deadly. Black—Negro. Black—to boycott. Black—to exclude. Black—television reception. Black—showing no loss and usually a profit. *(The performer has come to the last card. She sees that, at the end of the string, are numerous other strings, countless strings. They are cumbersome yet spectacular. She drops the cards and strings to the floor as she notices another card between the pages of the book. She takes the card from the pages of the book and reads it.)* Black body—a theoretical surface or body capable of completely absorbing all the radiation falling on it. The energy radiated per second by each unit area of a perfect black body is proportional solely to the fourth power of its absolute temperature. *(performer looks out at Mr. Derrida)*

Différance—to defer and to differ. Do I get the part?

Scene 3

Frantz Fanon: "An Angry Love Letter to Frantz Fanon"
(The time is April 1998)

(The performer moves to the table downstage. She sits down and turns on the lamp at the table, music begins playing. The music is Awadagin Pratt, "Live From South Africa: Preludes, Fugues and Intermezzi." She picks up a letter, and briefly reads it silently. She ponders a moment and then signs the letter.) "Love and Strength," _____ . *(The performer picks up the letter and begins reading it aloud.)* Dear Frantz, I write to you now, 30 years after I first met you, because I finally hear the voices of patience, and I think I finally hear you too, at least parts of you. It has been a long time, but I couldn't write to you a moment sooner. It has taken this long for me to understand my feelings of love and my feelings of anger. I remember that day so clearly when I first met you. It was the summer of 1968 on the 1C train. I was leaving South Shore and going to the Loop.[23] I remember the dress I wore—it was green, a micro-miniskirt, with small white polka dots—but I can't remember why I was going downtown. There was hardly anyone on the train that morning, it was quiet and peaceful, and I sat alone. I opened the book; I started reading; and I fell in love. *Wretched of the Earth,* my god, something deeply wanting in me had finally found a place to be clear and to be understood. A black man writing about colonialism and race with such brave eloquence and fury—not harangues of honkey vengeance or Negro victimization or black romanticism—but an intellectual and a theorist—like Che, Nkruma, Lumumba, and Fidel—whose words cast revolution and made it happen. It was 1968, and the last vestiges of the colonial world were crumbling. The East was now battling what seemed to be a far greater challenge: the end of colonialism and the dawn of a troubled freedom. For me, you were the carrier of the word and logic. Every revolutionary worth their salt carried Fanon in their back pocket. That summer, I read your books like they were my lifeline, not once, but again and again, devouring them like a starving child. You were my fantasy. We moved between Algeria and Paris together, holding hands and whispering under the moon. You were my armor against loneliness, and my refuge against men who could never be as smart or as revolutionary as you. It was the summer of 1968, and I craved for your life. How did I love thee? Let me count each revolutionary way:

(On the screen is a projection of a white woman holding a young boy. Their eyes are looking out, and the boy is pointing. An Algerian woman peers behind them from her veil. We see her silhouetted.) I loved you because

I could no longer believe the simple act of seeing was *(pause)* simple. The dialectic of the Look: "Mama, see the Negro! I'm frightened!"[24] The colonizer Looks at the dark body. The Look is intractable, alive, in motion. The Look is hate, is fear, and is desire. The Look penetrates dark skin and enters the bloodstream and flows through the dark body. It feeds every cell. The dark body becomes host for the Look. It is now contained inside that body like a cancer. The body absorbs the Look in an uneasy, unrelenting hardness. It is trained that way from so many Looks in its lifetime. The dark body sees itself by the Look—to be hated, to be feared, to be desired. The dark body sees itself through the Look of the colonizer, but then you said stop. You told us that Looking is so much more than seeing a distortion of yourself. Looking is seeing an Other—the scopic drive—the dark body must also look at/into the Colonizer. The dark body sees the Colonizer and Looks: I love the Colonizer; I desire the Colonizer; I want the Colonizer to love and desire me; I fear the Colonizer; I want to be the Colonizer; I hate the Colonizer; I want to kill the Colonizer. The blood flowing through dark bodies contains, absorbs, yet fights in motions that are infinite and detailed.

I loved you because you believed in armed struggle. A theorist for the revolution who believed in taking freedom, not in protest but in battle: an eye for an eye, because all levels of listening had failed, and words were mute from accusatory screams. You made it so—the psychic leap—the mind that dictates killing as noble for a cause worthy of no compromise. You sat with the tortured and the torturers, spoon-feeding fragments of their shattered madness in the clinics of fragile refuge. You tried to heal them. The progressive, innovative doctor from Martinique transgressing the practice of psychiatry and the idea of madness and medicine. The clinic is a social world. Decolonize the mind—for both the colonized and the colonizer—but you could not heal them and then send them out into the same sick world; you quit the clinic to confront a nation whose only antidote was violence. "By any means necessary."[25] Death was necessary and you didn't back down. "Take back your life," you said. "Take back your mind," you said. "Take back your manhood; take back your nation." It was 1968, I was riding the 1C train, and you had theorized "black power" before Stokely[26] walked through Richmond. Why did you have to leave us so soon?

I loved you in the summer of 1968 because you made me think, like no one before, about rootedness and loss, about the sameness between fear and desire, about what an emancipated black masculinity might be, and about the decolonization of the mind. But now, decades later, I am mad as hell with you. My anger is testing my love, a love that is clearly a mixture of nostalgia and appreciation but is nonetheless very precarious these days. How dost thou anger me? Let me count every feminist way. I am angry with you for theoretical matricide.[27] Neither black women nor white women in your theory of race can THINK. Women are bodies without brains. They covet, they lust, they betray, but they do not reason. While you are contemplative of the dark male body, marking him as complexly emasculated as a consequence of white power, you are then disdainful of the dark female body, marking her as wantonly sexual at the service of white power. Dark men are the victims, some with the will to resist. Dark women are the betrayers, all with the desire to comply. For you, black women bear children—a particular race loyalty is required. A particularity that absolves black men. You married a white woman and made children with her. Are your mulatto children more authentically black than the mulatto children of a black mother married to a white man? When we look into the eyes of mixed-race children, do we judge their blackness on the basis of whether their mother was white or black? White mother okay, black mother not okay? You cast the black woman as betrayer—as desiring the white man, desiring him to desire her, desiring to be white. While we are to believe that black male sexual acts with white women are an initiation, a black male rite and right of passage into manhood?! You want us to believe that white women suffer from neurotic negrophobia and sexual frustration and that they indulge in fantasies of rape by black men. Do I take you out of context? No, I don't think so! Is your thinking on gender more complicated? No, I don't think so. Who is the mother of your children? Why don't you know her better? Why don't you know me better? I'm very upset with you, Frantz. You did not know Mayotte Capecia.[28] You did not know the life surrounding her, her remembrances, her history, her dreams, because for you, Frantz, memory, history, and dream were encumbrances in a revolution, in what you called "the knowledge of the practice of action." Frantz, did you ever come to realize that we live inside history for the seminal purpose of remembering it?! Don't we dream for the seminal purpose of making the possibilities of history more universally wonderful?! I am very angry with you, Frantz, but, fool that I am . . . after all these years . . . I still love you. Your plea, "O my body, make me always a man who questions!"[29] how can I stay angry with you? Your words are written across my heart: "In the world through which I travel, I am endlessly creating myself."[30] So young, you left before time and experience could grip you with harder questions about Mayotte and black mothers. You left before you could create yourself again under the light of women's bodies where mind and matter did matter so much more than the gaze of a young Martiniquan psychiatrist could discover before death. Time is more sublime than the blessed, and you did not have time enough to decipher the nuances replete in the culture of women and, perhaps, your own.

Angry at you and at death coming too soon, *(A male performer, quietly and without notice, sits upstage in semidarkness.)* I still remain forever in love with you. You gave me—us—more than you took away. You gave us the day-to-day standing in the face of torture. *(The performer stops reading the letter. She sits at the desk. A man seated upstage barely visible in the light is heard reading the words of Fanon.)* "You must therefore weigh as heavily as you can upon the body of your torturer in order that his soul, lost in some byway, may find itself once more . . . And then there is that overwhelming silence—but of course, the body cries out—that silence that overwhelms the torturer."[31]

Epilogue: Embodied Writing

(The performer has returned to the first space of the prologue. She sits under the spotlight, again, surrounded by books on performance. She looks up and speaks to you.)

I

Each one of them helped me see my way to the edge of many rivers of knowing and not knowing. They go back and forth, so do I. And in their guidance, I laugh and think and I realize. These fathers helped me see the river in the darkness, and they have helped lead me to it. But, they cannot make me get in the water. I cannot enter the river. I cannot get my feet wet. I dare not swim in the river. Can I bear to hear the sounds when water crashes against rock? To swim and to hear I need the mothers: mothers who pounded bone and chain for their breath and mine. I need the Other fathers who are more ancient and more My own.

II

The women sit by the river with the men, dark wet skin shining like broken crystals under moonlight and ancient hopes. They are old black men and women, as old as the door of no return.[32] They are my *being.* I fight to remember them and to love them decently. They are always reminding me, commanding me, always, to get IN the water and swim: "Woman," they say, "You must go beyond realization, deeper, into the currents of action." They say, "Seeing is not enough. You must hear." I Know that I cannot hear the sounds below the rivers at a distance. I know I must get in the water and swim. I must remember the swimming lessons they taught me. I learned how to swim upstream, against enormous currents, with my muscles and my grit long before I even learned how to see the river with open eyes.

III

The stories the old folks told us—the stories we tell each other—press against hard surfaces for us to touch and hold. When the storms come in numbers so great that we cannot grasp breath and there is nowhere safe just to lay our heads—the inside peace of an untroubled life—we must remember that strength will come after the storm and the story. The generations of stories they told us—to heal and to teach—make order of worlds too messy and too endless for our own recent paths to name: remnants of life, yet whole and completely lived, given to us for safekeeping. We keep the circle moving. We must, because our lives depend on it. My parents and theirs and theirs were a sword and an armor. They inherited a killing field of love and protection for their children. How can we simply remain on the edge of rivers, pondering? The old Africans have told us, again and again, that they wait, below water, with their progeny; they hope for us to listen and walk into the depths of water.

In their memory, we imagine ourselves past the everyday fog of uncertain histories. We invent ourselves upon their laboring lives, but then we must seek. The histories of our collective mothers and fathers are a tightrope path to our collective present. We balance and keep ourselves from falling.

IV

Too much work to be done, too many distractions. My knees and arms get weak. I am in the river feeling tired and forgetful, but I made it in and I am still here. I am not on the edge anymore. I hear voices rising up from beneath. They say: "Reach for the stories, remember them, or make them up, but don't fall and keep swimming." My mothers and sisters chronicle the substance: the lessons of mothering and daughtering and good work and loneliness and how they loved their men and how they saved them. My fathers and brothers carved protection in their flesh and held their women with freedom and chants of a new day. I am now swimming at top speed, but the water thickens just as the elders foretold, and I slow down.

The accusations come echoing from ivory walls:

Scholar, hah! She is nothing but a thoughtless romantic!

She is an essentialist in the reverie of a false past!

She is a foundationalist, a biological determinist!

I thought she was a critic! Where is the ambiguity? Where is the theory?

Ugh! Identity politics! Nostalgia!

She is an absolutist! Shoot her!

All this time, we thought she was a poststructuralist!

Impostor! Impostor!

Shoot her! Now!

My head splits. I repress rage. My screams are muffled in deep unruly whispers. Then it happens—memory—I remember I am in the river and I can swim. I remember I can walk the tightrope and not fall. I make a new story for this occasion. I repeat the old ones—not in my head but in my heart. The stories save me from myself and from them. I recreate the screams. I revision the blindness. *(The performer begins to stack the books, very carefully, on top of one another. She makes three stacks and places them right next to each other. All three stacks are exactly the same height. The spines of the books face the audience and each stack is level with the next. The performer gets the telephone from the Karl Marx scene and places it in front of the first stack. She gets the script from Ferdinand de Saussure and places it in front of the second stack. She places the dictionary from Jacques Derrida on top of the Saussure script. She goes to the desk and folds the letter to Frantz Fanon and puts it in an envelope. She then places the letter in front of the third stack. She then goes back to the desk and gets a candle out of the drawer. She places the candle on top of the letter and lights it. She sits on the stack of books. Looking up from the "props" she has laid before the books, she then looks up for a moment at you. She speaks.)*
I remember I can walk the tightrope and not fall. I make a new story for this occasion. I repeat the old ones—not in my head but in my heart. The stories save me from myself and from the tower. I recreate the screams. I revision the blindness. Now, sit close and listen to the story.

I remembered the story in the river while I was swimming.

Shh! What I say is True. All of it is true. I have imagined it.

The names most of all are true.

I learned the names in the tower without sleep.

Listen and know the names, and remember the story. Here are the beginnings.

Beginnings are important.

Each word makes the story older and more new.

Some of us have forgotten the beginnings and how to change them, and now there is craziness in our people.

They see the tower from the river.

The river points in all directions.

The story will save us, but we must make more beginnings.

Here it is. Another beginning.

I will perform it for you.

(Slow fade to black. The only light is from the candle.)

I will perform it for you

It goes like this . . .

(Performer blows out candle.)

Notes

1. In the spring of 1998, the performance artist Coco Fusco spoke at Duke University. Her presentation brilliantly described the significance of performance as an art form and communicative model for change. Fusco also shared a provocative video of spectator responses to *The Cage,* a performance in collaboration with Guillermo Gomez-Peña. Fusco was concerned that so many performance studies scholars are focused on the performances in everyday life that too few are paying attention to the works of performance artists, particularly artists of color. In *Let's Get It On,* edited by Catherine Ugwu (1995), Fusco states: "Although no thorough survey of performance art of the past decade can reasonably overlook the contributions of artists of color, there is no consensus as to the significance of our increased visibility. Our presence has been read as a sign of the milieu's 'new' cultural diversity, but our entry and the postmodern debates that encircle us have also been associated with the dismantling of hierarchical categories that set 'high art' performances apart from other performative practices of vernacular cultures which—for some—signals the end of performance as an art form" (p. 158).

2. Don Geiger's essay "Poetic Realizing as Knowing" (1973) informs my conceptualization of "realizing." "An experience requires not only consciousness or

awareness but also 'awareness of awareness.' . . . [F]or a person to have an experience he [sic] must also be aware that he is having it . . . . An experience is our realization of it" (p. 312).

3. In Delia Pollock's (1998) important essay "Performing Writing," she introduces "six excursions into performing writing"; one of them is nervousness. Pollock states: "[P]erformative writing is nervous. It anxiously crossed various stories, theories, texts, intertexts, and spheres of practice, unable to settle into a clear, linear course, neither willing nor able to stop moving, restless, transient and transitive, traversing special and temporal borders, linked as it is in what Michael Taussig calls 'a chain of narratives sensuously feeding back into the reality thus (dis)enchanted'" (p. 90).

4. In "The Highs and Lows of Black Feminist Thought," Barbara Christian (1994) discusses the characteristics of what she calls "high thought language" and "low thought language." Christian states: "I'd grown up with a sharp division between the "high" thought, language, behavior expected in school and in church and the "low" thought, language, behavior that persisted at home and in the yards and the streets . . . It is often in the poem, the story, the play, rather than in Western philosophical theorizing, that feminist thought/feeling evolves, challenges and renews itself" (p. 576).

5. Theories of the flesh privilege agency and interrogate notions of the "lethargic masses" or "voiceless victims." The question "Where do theories come from?" is answered by honoring the extraordinary in the ordinary indigenous analysis, expressions and meditations of what bell hooks refers to as "homeplace." See Madison (1993, p. 214).

6. I use this term to mark my first theoretical thinking, in the language of the academy, represented by four men. Also I juxtapose the idea of "theoretical fathers" with those of indigenous *mothers* at the end of this essay.

7. Richard Schechner's (1985) notion of "not-not-me" argues that, in performance, we are doubly not ourselves, and in that doubling we are positively more of who we are (p. 112).

8. Karl Marx was born in 1818 and died in 1883. He was plagued much of his life with skin sores called carbuncles that would break out over his entire body. He was in poor health and agonized over these skin eruptions.

9. The reference here is to a famous letter Friedrich Engels wrote to Joseph Bloch in defense of Karl Marx to the young Marxist enthusiast who reduced Marx's more complex ideas to economic determinism. In the letter Engels writes: "Therefore if somebody twists this into saying that the economic factor is the only determining one, he is transforming that proposition into a meaningless, abstract, absurd phrase." See Marx and Engels (1977, pp. 75–76).

10. In 1848 Marx and Engels wrote *The Communist Manifesto,* and students and workers united in a revolution that spread through Europe.

11. Marx smoked also, had an affair, and took arsenic for his painful skin disease.

12. Tristan Tzara was the famous Dadaist poet and performer. On July 23, 1918, Tzara read the first Dada manifesto: "Let us destroy let us be good let us create a new

force of gravity NO = YES Dada means nothing. . . . The bourgeois salad in the eternal basin is insipid and I hate good sense" (quoted in Goldberg, 1988, p. 73).

13. Marx and Engels (1977, pp. 75–76).

14. Marx (1964, p. 78).

15. Ibid.

16. *Consciousness* here is not referring, in the Freudian sense, to a smaller realm that is in contrast to the vast realm of the unconscious. Here I refer to the "mutual self-awareness of a group" as defined by Raymond Williams (1983), as in class consciousness and the awareness of alienation as opposed to false consciousness (p. 321).

17. Marx (1964, pp. 169–170).

18. Here I allude to Claude Levi-Strauss's idea that *langue* is culture, its general rules and law, and *parole* is the specific idiosyncrasies of each culture. Individual cultural myths are *parole,* while all encompassing—a universal underlying structure—is *langue.*

19. Roland Barthes is more interested in connotation and popular culture; he posits that all signs constitute endless and multiple signification.

20. This is an allusion to Derrida's (1976) concept of citation as repetition, that which is always already said and done before, yet each time governed by specific participants, time and space.

21. Derrida (1976) discusses the "strange economy of the supplement," meaning the unstable and slippery interplay and tensions between opposites and binary oppositions. Derrida states: "[T]he indefinite process of the supplementary has always already infiltrated presence, always already inscribed there the space of repetition and the splitting of the self from pure self-presence" (p. 163).

22. "Prisoner of language" refers to criticisms that language is overdetermined in poststructuralist theories and that, for Derrida, life and experience are all constituted by language as language presupposes existence.

23. Downtown Chicago, south of Randolph Street, is traditionally referred to as the Loop because it is shaped like a loop.

24. This is an allusion to the famous quote in *Black Skin, White Masks* (Fanon, 1967): A little white boy pointing to a black man in horror says: "Mama, see the Negro! I'm frightened!" (pp. 112–114).

25. "By any means necessary" was a 1960s appropriation from Malcolm X that has resurfaced again in hip hop. The performer uses the Malcolm X allusion as a trope in conjoining her history and coming to consciousness with Fanon's ideology.

26. Fanon was theorizing "Black Power" in terms of colonial revolution and the liberation of the black body before the phrase was born out of civil rights protest and later defined more fully by Stokely Carmichael and Charles Hamilton.

27. bell hooks (1996) writes of Fanon: "In retrospect I see in his work a profound lack of recognition of the presence of the mothering body, of the female body that thinks. It is the symbolic matricide enacted in his work that necessarily severed the connection the moment I embarked on a critical journey with feminism that began with the recovery of the mother's body" (p. 81).

28. Mayotte Capecia's autobiography *Je suis martiniquaise* is condemned by Fanon as committing "racial suicide." Lola Young's (1996) important essay

"Missing Persons: Fantasizing Black Women in *Black Skin, White Masks*" describes Fanon's harsh condemnation of Capecia: "Fanon is keen to develop a sense of Capecia's unconscious, even without access to her dreams. . . . Fanon only refers to black women's experiences in terms which mark her as the betrayer" (p. 92).

29. From Fanon (1967).
30. Ibid.
31. From Fanon (1963).
32. I am referring here to Elmira Castle, the slave castle in Cape Coast, Ghana, West Africa, where the slaves were captured and held in the dungeon until they were led out from the door of no return, overlooking the ocean and directly routed onto the ships where they would cross the Atlantic to North and South America.

References

Christian, B. (1994). The highs and lows of black feminist thought. In D. S. Madison (Ed.), *The woman that I am: The literature and culture of contemporary women of color* (pp. 573–578). New York: St. Martin's.

Derrida, J. (1976). *Of grammatology.* Baltimore: John Hopkins University Press.

Fanon, F. (1963). *Wretched of the earth.* New York: Grove.

Fanon, F. (1967). *Black skin, white masks.* New York: Grove.

Fusco, C. (1995). Performing and the power of the popular. In C. Ugwu (Ed.), *Let's get it on: The politics of black performance* (pp. 158–175). Seattle, WA: Bay.

Geiger, D. (1973). Poetic realizing as knowing. *Quarterly Journal of Speech 59*(3), 311–318.

Goldberg, R. (1988). *Performance art: From futurism to the present.* New York: Abrams.

hooks, b. (1996). Feminism as a persistent critique of history: What's love got to do with it? In A. Read (Ed.), *The fact of blackness: Frantz Fanon and visual representation* (pp. 76–85). Seattle, WA: Bay.

Madison, D. S. (1993). That was my occupation: Oral narrative, performance, and black feminist thought. *Text and Performance Quarterly, 13*(3), 213–232.

Marx, K. (1964). *Selected writings in sociology and social philosophy* (T. B. Bottomore & M. Rubel, Eds.; T. B. Bottomore, Trans.). New York: McGraw-Hill.

Marx, K., & Engels, F. (1977). *Selected letters.* Peking: Foreign Languages Press.

Pollock, D. (1998). Performing writing. In P. Phelan & J. Lane (Eds.), *The ends of performance.* New York: New York University Press.

Schechner, R. (1985). *Between theater and anthropology.* Philadelphia: University of Pennsylvania Press.

Williams, R. (1983). *Keywords: A vocabulary of culture and society.* New York: Oxford University Press.

Young, L. (1996). Missing persons: Fantasizing black women in *Black skin, white masks.* In A. Read (Ed.), *The fact of blackness: Frantz Fanon and visual representation* (pp. 86–97). Seattle, WA: Bay.

Index

poetic transcriptions and, 138
poststructuralist overdetermination
of, n264
Sebald's use of literary, 175–176, 187
Serbo-Croatian, n100
symbolic, 24
"The Highs and Lows of Black
Feminist Thought" (Christian)
and, n263
utterance of conversational turn
taking and, 34–35
Lee, Robert E., 108–109
Lefebvre, Henri, 85–86
Let's Get It On, n262
Libeskind, Daniel, 84
Lincoln, Abraham, 120–121
Lionnet, Franoise, n71
Literacy. *See* Books as performance
*London Labour and the London
Poor*, 146
Longstreet, James, 108
Louisiana. *See* Burden Research
Foundation of Louisiana State
University
LSU Rural Life Museum and Windrush
Gardens, 165–166, 177–178

MacCannell, Dean, 114
MacIntyre, Alasdair, 32
Madame Bovary, 201–202, 204,
208–212
graveside marker and, n234
and map in Flaubert's hand, 212–218
mapping of, 222–224
repetition of reality in, 219–220
resistance of, 225–231
Madison, D. Soyini, 241
critical social theory and, 7
poetic transcriptions and, 138
"Making History Go", 136
*The Making of the English Working
Class*, 146
"On Maps and Mapping", 200
Maps/mapping
books as, 207–212
as discourse, 202–206
Madame Bovary and, 222–224
"On Maps and Mapping", 200
Martin, Sella, 151–154
Marx, Karl, 247–250, n263
Marxism, 39

Mayhew, Henry, 146
McCarthy, Mary, 225–229, n234
McClellan, George, 108
McElvany,, 91, 93
McGreevy, Patrick, 63
McLuhan, Marshall, 225–226, 229
Melrose, Susan, 200–201
Membership and experiential space, 54–55
Memory. *See also* Genealogy of
performance
as chance aggregations (LSU), 189–190
everyday life and, 36–37
genealogical history and, 173–174, 176
hauntologie and, 87–89
and representation in history, 136–138
Roach on, n191
Merrill, Lisa, 138–139
Messy texts, n71
Metalinguistics, 203, n232
Metaphors and tourism, 104
Metonyms, 92–93, n100, 175–176
Milosevic, Slobodan, n99
Mimesis, 3–4
Mimesis, 32
Minstrel shows, 150
"Missing Persons: Fantasizing Black
Women in *Black Skin, White
Masks*" (Young), n264–265
Mladi Most, 90–91
Modus operandi. *See Habitus*
Monmonier, Mark, 208
Morality and conversational
turn taking, 34
Mostar
conceptual map of, 88–89
documentary production and, 96–99
production of, 86–90
reproduction of, 90–96
symbolism of Stari Most in, 82–86
Movement. *See* Kinesthetics
Mulvey, L., 125
Museum dioramas, 204–205
Muslim-Croat Federation, n100
My Bondage and My Freedom, 153
Myerhoff, Barbara, 19

*A Narrative of the Most Remarkable
Particulars in the Life of James
Albert Ukawsaw Gronniosaw,
an African Prince, as Related
by Himself*, 148–149

About the Editor

Judith Hamera received her BA (1980) in mass communication from Wayne State University and her MA (1982) and PhD (1987) in interpretation and performance studies respectively from Northwestern University. She is currently the Acting Associate Dean of the College of Arts and Letters and Professor of Communication Studies and Theatre Arts and Dance at California State University, Los Angeles. She has served as editor of *Text and Performance Quarterly*, the journal of the National Communication Association Division of Performance Studies. Her publications have appeared in *Cultural Studies, TDR: The Drama Review, Modern Drama, Text and Performance Quarterly, Theatre Topics,* and *Women and Language.* She is the recipient of the National Communication Association's Lilla Heston Award for Outstanding Scholarship in Interpretation and Performance Studies and was named President's Distinguished Professor at California State University in 2004. She is coeditor, with D. Soyini Madison, of the *Sage Handbook of Performance Studies.*

About the Contributors

Leonard Clyde Hawes is Professor of Communication at the University of Utah. His first book, *The Pragmatics of Analoguing,* was a refiguration of social science methodology, and he is currently completing a book manuscript—*Contingent Conflicts and Immanent Detours*—that traces the intersections of communication studies, conflict studies, cultural studies, and performance studies. He is the author of a series of articles on dialogue, power, conversation, and politics in such journals as *Text and Performance Quarterly, Communication Theory,* and *Communication Yearbook.* For the past several years, he has divided his time between the University of Utah, the University of Aalborg, and the University of Copenhagen, where he works with the Danish Human Rights Commission on the cultural divisions between the diasporic Muslim community in Copenhagen and the various communities of Danish nationals.

Bryant Keith Alexander is Professor of Performance and Pedagogical Studies in the Department of Communication Studies at California State University, Los Angeles, and currently serves as the Acting Chair of the Department of Liberal Studies. His essays have appeared in *Qualitative Inquiry, Communication Quarterly, Theatre Annual, Theatre Topics, Text and Performance Quarterly,* and *Cultural Studies Critical Methodologies,* among others. He is the coeditor of *Performing Education: Pedagogy, Identity and Reform.*

Sonja Arsham Kuftinec is Associate Professor of Theater Arts and Dance at the University of Minnesota. She also works as a director and facilitator with Seeds of Peace, creating theater with youth in former Yugoslavia, South Asia, the Middle East, and Minnesota. Her book *Staging America: Cornerstone and Community-Based Theater* (2003) was recently cited as one of the three best books in theater history for 2003.

Michael S. Bowman teaches performance studies at Louisiana State University, where he is Associate Professor and Director of Graduate Studies in the Department of Communication Studies. He currently serves as editor of the National Communication Association journal of performance studies, *Text and Performance Quarterly.*

Dwight Conquergood was Associate Professor of Performance Studies at Northwestern University and chaired the department for six years. His many publications include *I am a Shaman: A Hmong Life Story with Ethnographic Commentary* and numerous articles in *TDR: The Drama Review, Text and Performance Quarterly, Communication Monographs,* and the *Quarterly Journal of Speech.* He co-produced two award-winning documentaries based on his research: *Between Two Worlds: The Hmong Shaman in America* and *The Heart Broken in Half.*

Ruth Laurion Bowman is Associate Professor of Communication Studies at Louisiana State University, where she teaches courses in performance studies and is the producing director of the HopKins Black Box, an experimental lab theater. Her essays have appeared in *Text and Performance Quarterly, Theatre Topics,* and various collections.

Paul Edwards, Associate Professor of Performance Studies at Northwestern University, received his PhD in 1980 from the University of Texas at Austin. His published essays and monographs have appeared in *Text and Performance Quarterly, Theatre Annual, Shakespeare Quarterly,* and several edited books. He has directed over 40 stage productions, including many original adaptations of novels and short stories; professional awards include the Joseph Jefferson Award (1996) and Citation (1993) and the After Dark Award (1996). Career achievement awards include the National Communication Association's Lilla Heston Award for Distinguished Research (2001) and the Leslie Irene Coger Award for Distinguished Performance (1997), as well as the Northwestern University Alumni Association's Excellence in Teaching Award (2001).

D. Soyini Madison is an internationally known scholar in performance studies and critical ethnography. Her published works focus on performance ethnography and the intersections between gender and critical race theory. Her teaching centers on myth and popular culture, performance ethnography, performance of literature for social change, and the political economy of performance. Madison is a Fulbright Scholar and recently completed a visiting lectureship at the University of Ghana. She also recently returned from the Rockefeller Foundation fellowship in Belagio, Italy, where she was writing her current project focusing on staging/performing local debates surrounding human rights and traditional religious practices as these debates are influenced by the global market and national development. She has taught a graduate course in performance ethnography for 14 years.